Practical AI Style

Also by Mike P. O'Brien

Assisting Intelligence: How to Build Authentic in the Age of AI

Navigating the AI Revolution with Clarity and Confidence

AI Elements of Style

Practical AI Style

Essential Elements for Building Your Own AI Style Guide

Assisting Intelligence

Welcome to

Practical AI Style

AI Elements of Style

Practical AI Style is an essential guide to building clarity, consistency, and character into your organization's use of artificial intelligence. Inspired by Strunk and White's *The Elements of Style*, this book offers modern grammar for the algorithmic age, where prompts replace prose and your brand's voice is increasingly delivered by machines.

But this is not just a book about what AI style is. It's a playbook for creating your own.

Inside, you'll find structured workbooks, decision frameworks, and guided exercises to help you draft, test, and refine an AI Style Guide tailored to your organization's voice, values, and goals. Whether you're leading innovation, managing content, or setting policy, this book helps turn AI experimentation into coherent, confident practice.

Through vivid metaphors, business-ready models, and practical instruction, you'll learn how to:

- Define your organization's AI tone, interaction standards, and risk posture
- Train teams to prompt with clarity, ethics, and purpose
- Create and maintain an internal AI Style Guide that scales
- Align generative outputs with your brand, culture, and intent
- Move beyond guardrails into AI mastery

For Elke and Sydney

Woof, Mara

Copyright

Limit of Liability / Disclaimer of Warranty:

The information provided within this book is for general informational purposes only. While the publisher and author have used their best efforts in preparing this book, they make no representations or warranties with respect to the accuracy or completeness of the contents of this book and expressly disclaim any implied warranties of merchantability or fitness for a particular purpose. The advice and strategies contained herein may not be suitable for your situation. You should consult with a professional where appropriate. Neither the publisher nor the author shall be liable for damages arising here from. Any use of this information is at your own risk.

Colophon

All illustrations and infographics were created by SmarterMedium using Adobe Illustrator. The text is set in Adobe Garamond Premier, with headings in Neue Haas Grotesk Display. Writing and manuscript preparation were completed using Apple Pages, Microsoft Word, and Ulysses.

Stock images in this book are credited to their respective license holders, including Dreamstime, iStock, and MotionArray.

Portions of the writing and editing for this book were assisted by artificial intelligence tools. The use of AI-generated images in this book is limited; each AI-generated image is explicitly identified in the text and/or in its caption.

Citations and Copyright:

ISBN: 979-8-9919867-4-8 (Hardcover)

First Printing in the United States in 2025.

Library Of Congress Classification

Library of Congress Control Number: 2025912219

Publisher

Published by SmarterMedium, LLC

Hull, MA USA

www.smartermedium.com

Versions of this Book

Practical AI Style: AI Elements of Style—Essential Elements for Building Your Own AI Style Guide is available in a variety of formats, in print and accessible digitally in your preferred reading app. Below are the standard formats and places to purchase or download.

Print Editions

Hardcover ISBN 979-8-9919867-4-8

Paperback ISBN 979-8-9919867-6-2

Digital Editions

eBook ISBN 979-8-9919867-5-5

This book is available digitally on many platforms, including Apple Books, Google Play, Amazon Kindle, B&N Nook, and other major ebook platforms.

Accessible digital formats are available for screen readers and other assistive technologies.

Get it on Books | GET IT ON Google Play

Custom Editions

Looking for tailored solutions? Playbook, Presentation, and Personalized versions are available through AssistingIntelligence.com. Explore options for branded or custom guides to support learning, development, and enterprise use.

Bulk Orders & Licensing

Special discounts, enterprise licensing, and custom programs are available for corporations, associations, and educators. For details, or to discuss how these works can be customized for your organization, contact us or visit the custom solutions section.

Contact

Email: info@assistingintelligence.com
Web: www.assistingintelligence.com

For updates, additional resources, and companion materials, visit our website. For the latest on AI style, news, and tips, follow us on LinkedIn or sign up for updates at our website.

Table of Contents

Preface

Inspired by Strunk & White

Strunk and White's *The Elements of Style*, despite brevity, has had an outsized impact on writing and communication. Their *Elements* distilled the fundamental, irreducible components of clear, concise writing. Like chemical elements, these principles form the building blocks of effective communication. This book, *Practical AI Style*, is inspired by the timeless principles of clarity and conciseness championed by Strunk and White. It aims to provide a practical, essential guide for navigating the emerging landscape of AI communication.

This book identifies the irreducible components of effective AI style—the AI Elements of Style. Like their chemical or rhetorical counterparts, these elements can be combined and recombined, forming the wide-ranging landscape of AI systems and applications. Rather than catalog every possible use of AI, this guide concentrates on core patterns and practices. As with Strunk and White, the focus is on what endures.

Workbook: A Starting Point to Write Your Own Guide

Designed for practicality, this book helps you create the first draft of your AI Style Guide. It provides practical exercises, templates, and guidance on collaborative generative AI use. Throughout this book, you'll find key tools: workbooks, examples, and "prompt primers"—suggested, editable prompts to guide the process. This is your toolkit for crafting clear, consistent, responsible AI practices. This book guides each step.

The chapters build progressively, from fundamentals to advanced considerations. On your first read, follow the sequence. Later, return to the chapters as needed for reference. This book is divided into eleven chapters:

1. **Define**: Establish foundational concepts.
2. **Decide**: Determine your AI's purpose and boundaries.
3. **Elements**: Apply core principles for effective AI style.
4. **Assemble**: Guide clear and concise interactions.
5. **Brand**: Forge your lasting AI identity.
6. **Agents**: Shape AI behavior and boundaries.
7. **Augment**: Enhance human capability with AI.
8. **Approach**: Frame AI guidance through human insight.
9. **Foundation**: Anchor AI Style in structure, guardrails, and trust.
10. **Author**: Build your own AI Style Guide framework.
11. **Congruence**: Concluding principles for impactful AI style.

Supported by abundant resources, *Practical AI Style* assists your progression along the roadmap to AI style. Working through exercises, you will develop your own Style Guide—one relevant to your intentions, integrity, and approach to AI. By establishing AI usage norms within your organization, your AI Style Guide shapes AI's future within your walls. This book builds that foundation. Ready to create your AI Style Guide? Let's dive in.

A Note from the Author

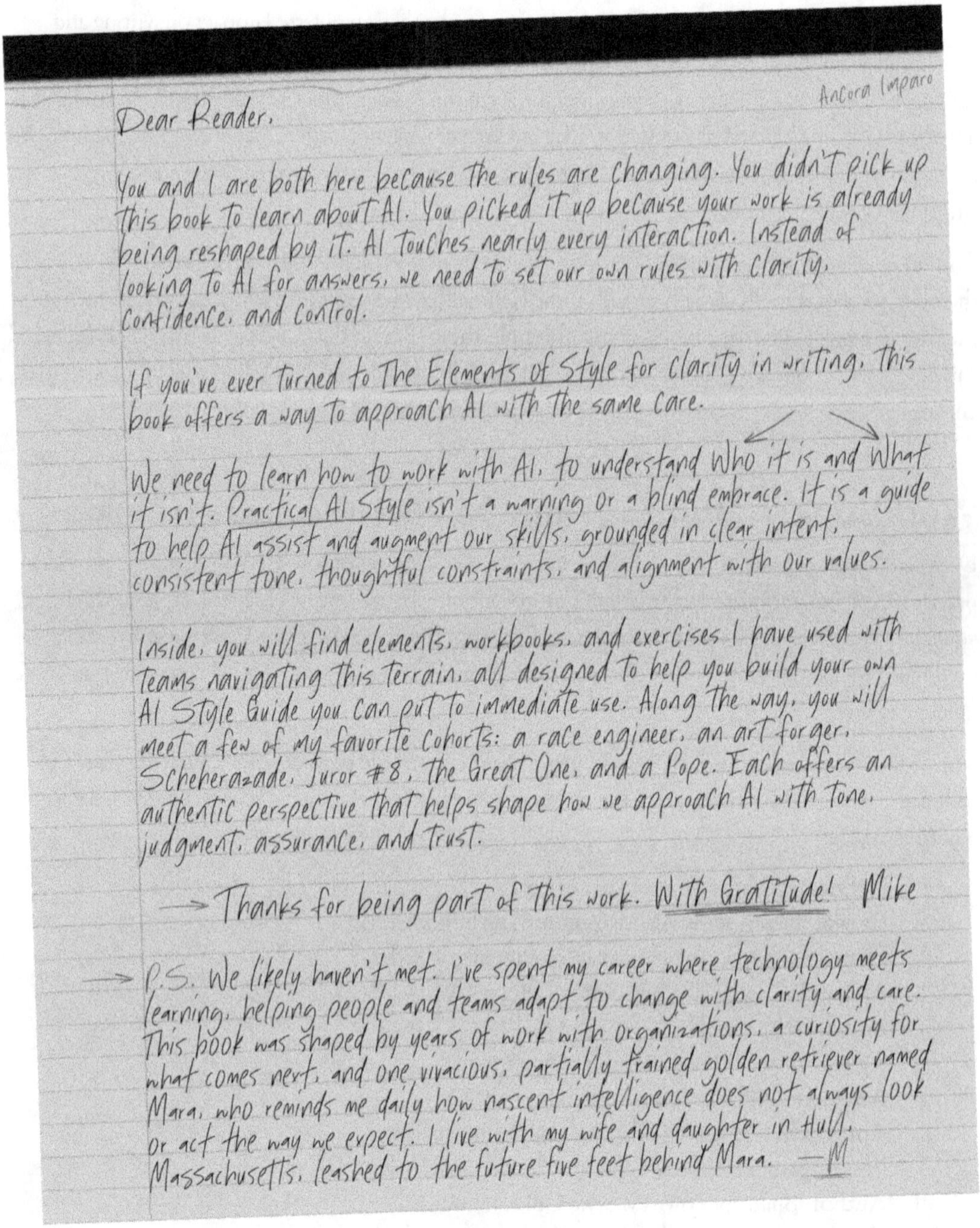

Ancora Imparo

Dear Reader,

You and I are both here because the rules are changing. You didn't pick up this book to learn about AI. You picked it up because your work is already being reshaped by it. AI touches nearly every interaction. Instead of looking to AI for answers, we need to set our own rules with clarity, confidence, and control.

If you've ever turned to The Elements of Style for clarity in writing, this book offers a way to approach AI with the same care.

We need to learn how to work with AI, to understand who it is and what it isn't. Practical AI Style isn't a warning or a blind embrace. It is a guide to help AI assist and augment our skills, grounded in clear intent, consistent tone, thoughtful constraints, and alignment with our values.

Inside, you will find elements, workbooks, and exercises I have used with teams navigating this terrain, all designed to help you build your own AI Style Guide you can put to immediate use. Along the way, you will meet a few of my favorite cohorts: a race engineer, an art forger, Scheherazade, Juror #8, The Great One, and a Pope. Each offers an authentic perspective that helps shape how we approach AI with tone, judgment, assurance, and trust.

→ Thanks for being part of this work. With Gratitude! Mike

→ P.S. We likely haven't met. I've spent my career where technology meets learning, helping people and teams adapt to change with clarity and care. This book was shaped by years of work with organizations, a curiosity for what comes next, and one vivacious, partially trained golden retriever named Mara, who reminds me daily how nascent intelligence does not always look or act the way we expect. I live with my wife and daughter in Hull, Massachusetts, leashed to the future five feet behind Mara. —M

This back cover's design, a handwritten note made digital, shows how technology, through fonts and digital designs, can enhance original intent. With AI, we have the same opportunity: to extend our intentions and improve authentic outcomes. We do so by finding practical ways to embrace AI with style and purpose.

AI Usage in *Practical AI Style*

This book aims to demonstrate how to adopt, adapt, and develop a coherent AI style. It would be disingenuous not to declare the role AI played in shaping it. Throughout the writing process, AI served as a valuable assistant, at times, akin to a digital Maxwell Perkins (see Appendix, page 202).

AI Technologies Used

Several platforms contributed meaningfully:

- OpenAI ChatGPT (various models)
- Google Gemini (various models)
- Microsoft Copilot
- Perplexity AI, for source-based research
- Grammarly and Apple Intelligence, for sentence-level refinement in Ulysses, Pages, and Word.

These tools facilitated brainstorming, stylistic refinement, and prompt testing. Perplexity AI, in particular, presented credible sources that were not driven by SEO or ad placements. Much of this content was sharpened through rigorous debate, at times resembling a kind of Socratic dialogue with the machine. It often felt like arguing with a crossword puzzle: training the AI while honing my own thinking.

A custom AI Style Agent, built for use with ChatGPT and Gemini, served as my editorial partner. It helped assess prompts, exercises, and tone while staying aligned with my voice. Details and the development prompt are included (see page 187).

Guardrails and Intent

This book is about AI, but it is not by AI. To ensure the final product remained my own, I applied the following personal guardrails, beyond those enumerated throughout the book:

- **All first drafts were written by me.** AI assisted in refinement, not generation.
- **Prose over gimmicks.** I restricted emojis and bullet points. Em dashes were used sparingly—but not outlawed.
- **A clear separation of work.** AI-generated notes were stored separately in Ulysses using Material Sheets, preserving a firewall between raw input and final writing.
- **Ethical platform choices.** Tools were evaluated not just for performance, but for corporate integrity. (*Do better, Meta.*)
- **Feedback, not authorship.** AI offered structural suggestions and clarity edits—but was barred from full rewrites.
- **No summarization tasks were delegated.** I read books, blogs, articles, and academic papers firsthand. A comprehensive reading list is included in the Appendix and endnotes.

- **All images were created using non-AI tools.** Visuals were produced in Adobe Illustrator (old school .ai) or sourced from licensed libraries. AI-generated images appear only to illustrate capability, not to replace artists.

For a deeper look at my writing process with AI, see *Assisting Intelligence*, co-authored with my canine companion, Mara.

Practical
AI Style

AI offers Formula 1 power—fast, adaptive, and transformative. Yet, in business as on the racetrack, power alone does not guarantee victory. Precision, timing, and judgment do. Without these, organizations risk losing control on the algorithmic track. The question is no longer if you will use AI, but how effectively you will drive it.

I Introduction

Navigating the AI Race

Image Caption: What does this image show: a masterful maneuver or a disaster in motion? Impending victory or a future crash? The image doesn't answer—context does.

Raw Power, Real Risk

What are we seeing here? A daring maneuver or the beginning of a crash? The image offers no context, no verdict, just a moment at full speed. You can't know unless you understand the full context: the driver's intent, the conditions of the track, the tuning of the car, and the moment in the race. So too with artificial intelligence. A prompt, a response, a result. Genius or misstep?

When OpenAI released ChatGPT in November 2023, it reached a million users in five days, faster than nearly any product in digital history.[1] Instagram took two and a half months; Netflix, three and a half years. Within eight weeks, ChatGPT had surpassed 100 million monthly users. This wasn't an anomaly; it was the start. Other generative platforms soon followed, transforming how people write, code, search, learn, and strategize. More broadly, other services have exploded in usage and economic impact. The World Economic Forum suggests AI could deliver a century's worth of scientific progress in just 5–10 years, fundamentally reshaping industries and society.[2] When capability accelerates faster than understanding, misalignment is not just possible. It's inevitable.

Today, your teams, partners, students, and customers grip the wheel of tools as potent—and unpredictable—as a Formula 1 car. But they haven't spent years in simulation training or strategic briefings, earning their AI seat like an F1 driver. AI shows up not after training and certification, but in a browser window. A phone update. A Slack message. One moment, they're browsing. Next, they're driving an AI that can produce legal arguments, strategic plans, or branded content in seconds.

And while this AI car may be fast, the course is unforgiving.

More than Guardrails

Most organizations are no longer wondering whether to use AI. They've deployed tools. They've issued policies. They've marked the outer boundaries of what's acceptable. But what they haven't always provided is guidance at speed.

Most governance models are built to prevent harm; few are built to enable confident performance. They warn people where the track ends, but not how to navigate the curves. This emphasizes protections over performance. They speak in terms of compliance, not creativity.

> *If braking is the only control you give your people, you won't get very far with AI.*

Look at the image again. An F1 car and a machine like AI don't just demand restraint. They reward mastery. And mastery isn't just knowing the rules. It's knowing when to push the limits and when not to. It's the difference between a reckless move and a calculated one; between performance and fallout; between someone who can follow instructions and someone who can drive with intent. F1 drivers claim their seats by mastering how to operate on the track.

The core challenge facing leaders now is not just keeping AI under control—its helping people use it well. That means building a shared framework for judgment. One that allows teams to move quickly, but wisely. That bridges innovation and responsibility. That ensures not just alignment with values, but acceleration toward goals.

So:

- How do you help teams steer with confidence, not caution?
- How do you balance consistency with creativity?
- How do you create room for experimentation without losing the plot?

That's where we begin.

The F1 Elements of AI Navigation

The metaphor of an F1 race is more than visual flair.[3] It's a structural map. Every element in a Formula 1 ecosystem has an AI counterpart, each playing a distinct role in performance, safety, and strategy. Success doesn't depend on any single part, but on how the whole system works together. Let's take a closer look.

Track = AI Governance

The track is not just the setting; it's where the race unfolds, where AI is seen, judged, and experienced by the marketplace, customers, and the public. This is governance: the legal, ethical, and operational terrain for all usage. It defines boundaries, sets expectations, and creates the conditions for trust. A well-designed track challenges skill without inviting disaster. Governance does the same.

Car = AI Platform

The car is the machine. It's what translates intention into performance in AI, this is the platform you've chosen: the models, systems, and infrastructure powering your tools. Not all platforms are built the same—some are agile, some powerful, some stable under pressure. The right platform depends on your goals. Speed alone won't win the race if the car doesn't match the course.

Pit = AI Stewardship and Support

No F1 team would dream of racing without a pit crew—the stewards monitoring telemetry, making rapid adjustments, and advising the driver. In AI, this is the layer of oversight ensuring your tools don't just function—they evolve. Ethical review boards, internal QA teams, prompt reviewers, red-teamers, and data scientists tune performance, respond to wear and tear, and keep systems ready for what's ahead, not just what's now.

Guardrails = Codes of Conduct and Compliance

No course is complete without constraints. Guardrails define the space where speed is safe. In AI, this means policies, norms, and ethical standards. They aren't the full solution, but they are the minimum expectation. A clear code of conduct keeps teams aligned and prevents known failure modes. It's not about stifling creativity; it's about directing it away from risk.

Engine = AI Agent

The engine is where raw power lives. In AI, this is the agent: the model, its configurations, and the instructions that drive behavior. This is the intelligence under the hood. Performance here depends on what you've trained, how it's tuned, and how responsibly it's been optimized. A poorly configured engine may still start, but it won't finish the race.

Driver = AI User

The driver makes the difference. You can have the fastest car, the best engine, the cleanest track, but without human skill, none of it works. In AI, the user is that driver. Their prompts, decisions, judgment, and experience determine outcomes. No platform is smarter than its operator. Empowering users to understand the tool, not just access it, is what turns AI from a liability into leverage.

Steering Wheel = Human Interface

This is the connection point. It's how the driver interacts with the machine—how intent becomes input. In AI, it's the chat interface, dashboard, or embedded functionality. These surfaces translate human choices into system behavior. Well-designed interfaces offer clarity and constraint. Poor ones introduce ambiguity, and with AI, ambiguity scales fast.

Lap = AI Interaction

Each prompt is a lap; the race is the pattern of performance over time. True mastery in AI means delivering consistent, aligned, and functional outcomes not just once, but again and again, across varied contexts.

In Formula 1, mastery comes not from horsepower alone, but from the orchestration of every moving part. The same is true in AI. As adoption widens, the real challenge becomes alignment—between many users and tools, between overlapping policy and practice, and between power and purpose. That alignment doesn't happen by accident. It takes design. It takes communication.

Entering the AI Race

No Formula 1 driver races alone. Behind every lap are teams of engineers monitoring performance, analyzing data, and offering split-second insight. Drivers receive constant guidance from the pit crew—strategic insights, technical feedback, and reminders of the bigger picture. This information typically comes from one voice: the race engineer.[4] Part strategist, part coach, part technician, the race engineer is the driver's constant guide, connecting cockpit decisions to the bigger picture.

The race engineer doesn't just issue commands—they provide confidence. They interpret the track, anticipate risks, and help drivers push the car to its limits—safely, skillfully, and in sync with team objectives.

In your organization, the AI Style Guide serves that role. You can't assign a race engineer to every person, but you can offer the same kind of steady, strategic guidance. An AI Style Guide provides the connective tissue between abstract governance and day-to-day action. It doesn't just tell people what not to do; it shows them how to move fast with intent, how to make sound decisions under pressure, and how to navigate uncertainty without hesitation.

Without that kind of guidance, users steer blind. Formal guardrails—governance, compliance, and oversight—often arrive too late or speak too broadly. They protect the outer boundaries, but they don't help users operate skillfully within them.

A well-designed Style Guide translates policy into practice. It empowers users to experiment responsibly, understand platform behaviors, and adapt confidently in high-stakes scenarios.

Image Caption: Reconsider the image: a car veering off track. What once looked like chaos now signals strategy. Risk? Yes, but not recklessness. The difference lies in context, training, and tools. It lies in trust and intent.

From High Risk to High Performance

AI is now in the hands of millions. Often with little more than curiosity to guide them, employees, teachers, parents, clients, and students are all steering AI. But most don't know the terrain, the vehicle, or even the rules of the road. Unlike F1, where every decision is supported by systems and expertise, many AI users face a blank prompt window and a vague sense of risk. Their errors won't result in physical harm, but digital mistakes can cost reputations, erode trust, and spark serious operational consequences.

This is where an AI Style Guide shifts from nice-to-have to mission-critical.

A strong AI Style Guide:

- Supports individuals drafting content or building prompts
- Informs team collaboration, training, and review practices
- Shapes organizational norms for responsible and creative AI use
- Encourages transparency, trust, and alignment at scale

It turns AI from a wildcard into a competitive advantage.

Why You Need a Guide Now

Rewind to the early days of social media. A single misstep could—and often did—spark backlash, misalignment, or a missed opportunity. Imagine if companies then had the kind of guidance Style

Guides now provide shared principles, tone guidelines, escalation paths, and values to write by. AI is at a similar inflection point but moving exponentially faster. Where social platforms took months or years to scale, AI tools reached global adoption in days. That pace has outstripped traditional controls.

Image caption: An AI-generated image representing the impossible combination of skills and capabilities needed to be proficient with AI, as only an AI could create. Image created using Google Gemini.

Today, AI use is often informal, undocumented, and improvised. Many organizations don't know who's using AI, how, or to what end. That's the risk, but it's also the opportunity. It becomes the map that turns exploration into strategy and experimentation into knowledge. Without it, you risk racing through an algorithmic jungle: inconsistent messaging, brand confusion, biased outputs, and a trail of missed signals.

What a Style Guide Is—and Isn't

Let's be clear about the role a Style Guide plays.

An AI Style Guide is:

- A framework for creating, reviewing, and refining AI-generated content
- A set of best practices aligned to your brand, strategy, and ethical commitments
- A tool for coherence in a rapidly evolving environment
- A signal of readiness—a proactive stance in the face of accelerating complexity

An AI Style Guide is not:

- A substitute for governance, legal policy, or technical guardrails
- A final answer to every ethical dilemma or risk scenario
- A guarantee of perfect outcomes or zero error

Rather, it serves as your starting point—a living, adaptable resource that enables people to navigate new terrain with clarity and conviction. It anchors experimentation in intent. It empowers teams to act, rather than just react. And it transforms your organizational values into actionable code for intelligent systems.

In this book, we'll explore how to build one and ensure it works not just for today's tools but also for tomorrow's shifts.

Image Caption: Like an F1 car on race day, your AI performance will be on full display, under intense scrutiny from your entire ecosystem: employees, employers, partners, customers, and competition. The track awaits.

Let's Build It

This book, *Practical AI Style*, is your guide to crafting your own AI Style Guide. It offers not theory, but practice, not a finished manual, but a foundation. With structure, examples, and exercises, *Practical AI Style* gives you the tools to turn risk into reliability, chaos into clarity, and power into performance.

> *Let's get on track.*

Practical AI Style

Navigating the AI Race. Introduction reframes AI adoption as a strategic navigation problem. Powerful, but dangerous without control.

From driving fast with no map ...

AI is adopted without training, strategy, or clear guidance. Most users improvise and 'steer blind' with powerful tools. AI decisions are left to individual trial-and-error.

... to intentional, assured navigation.

AI use is seen as performance-driven, not just risk-managed. Teams have navigation tools (Style Guides) that teach judgment, not just restraint. AI becomes part of a deliberate competitive strategy.

I Introduction

Summary

Practical
AI Style

Practical AI Style

"Writing is an act of faith,
not a trick of grammar."
— *The Elements of Style*

AI
Practical
AI Style

What qualifies as artificial intelligence remains open to interpretation: What is AI? Organizations seeking responsible AI use must define what AI means within their own context. This definition will reflect a careful negotiation of organizational identity, intent, and aspiration amid rapid, profound technological change. This chapter delves into defining AI not in the abstract, but within your organization's specific context, connecting core values and strategic vision to the AI systems you embrace.

1 Define

General Purpose Style

Prior to November 2022, when economists and technologists referenced GPTs and their capacity for transformation, they were typically referring to General Purpose Technologies—powerful historical forces like the steam engine, electricity, and information technology. A general-purpose technology is defined as a new method of producing or inventing that has widespread and sustained impact across the broader economy.[1]

Then, on November 30, 2022, the world became widely aware of a new, rapidly evolving technology that also shares the acronym GPT: ChatGPT. Its public release and exceptionally swift adoption made it one of the fastest technological introductions in history. This rapid uptake suggests that AI is already influencing your office, your business, and your market. Your customers are using it. So are your competitors.

As originally defined, General Purpose Technologies have three key characteristics:[2]

- **Pervasiveness**: They spread across nearly all sectors of the economy.
- **Improvement**: They evolve and become more capable over time.
- **Innovation-spawning**: They enable the creation of entirely new products, services, and business models.

The challenge is providing practical guidance on how to use something we know will be profoundly transformative, but whose full impact, and the cascade of innovations it will drive, is still emerging. In the months since ChatGPT debut, we've seen an explosion of models with increasing capabilities in areas like image generation, video creation, automated translation, and transcription. Dozens of generative AI platforms have launched globally. Autonomous agents now execute countless actions per second, often without direct human oversight.

This shift feels profound—akin to replacing the motor in your car from gas to electric while speeding down the highway. The familiar is suddenly altered. The brakes might have moved. The steering wheel could now be a chat interface. You may find yourself behind the wheel of a powerful but unfamiliar system, accelerating fast, in urgent need of new instructions, better maps, and above all, assurance.

While social media has surfaced some notable missteps, serious AI-related incidents, 'crashes' have been relatively rare, given the scale of adoption. Still, as AI becomes more embedded in critical systems, the risk of minor and catastrophic errors grows significantly.

This rapid and pervasive integration brings unprecedented opportunity, but also mounting complexity. Organizations are grappling with immense capabilities and unresolved implications. In the face of that uncertainty, the need for clarity becomes urgent.

The challenge is not just controlling a powerful technology. It is ensuring that AI enhances, rather than erodes, the ingenuity and authenticity that define your organization. This calls for a deliberate, human-centered approach.

In this dynamic environment, an AI Style Guide becomes more than an editorial resource. It is a strategic tool, offering assurance, orientation, and a framework for communicating, operating, and innovating in a world increasingly shaped by AI. Such a guide helps organizations address the very traits that make AI transformative: its pervasiveness, rapid evolution, and capacity to accelerate innovation.

Before shaping how AI operates in your organization, you must define what AI means to you. That is where this chapter begins.

The Growing Urgency of Responsible AI

AI is considered a general-purpose technology because of the disruption it has already caused and what lies ahead. This transition is already showing to be not so smooth. AI systems often operate as black boxes. Outcomes are shaped by algorithmic bias, a lack of transparency that hinders accountability, and security gaps that invite data breaches.

As AI becomes more deeply embedded in daily life, concern about its ethical use grows. Incidents are increasing.[3] So is the pressure to define clear standards. Just as manufacturers rely on common frameworks for quality and reliability (like ISO standards), organizations are now coalescing around Responsible AI, or RAI, principles to evaluate AI platforms and their creators.

Assessing AI integrity requires looking beyond technical capabilities. It demands scrutiny of the people and institutions behind the models—their track records, values, and intentions. Many now publish public commitments to RAI, outlining their approach to privacy, data governance, transparency, safety, human oversight, and fairness.

These are not just internal policies. In the age of AI, they are becoming core to a company's brand. Like DEI or privacy statements, Responsible AI declarations are increasingly visible signals of organizational integrity. Reports such as the Stanford HAI Index[4] are tracking how these commitments evolve, and which companies follow through.

For any organization seeking to deploy AI, monitoring RAI principles is a vital step. An AI Style Guide can support this broader strategy by reinforcing responsible norms, aligning language and outputs with organizational values, and providing a bridge between technical tools and human expectations.

Why Definitions Matter

Defining artificial intelligence is not a theoretical or semantic exercise. It's a strategic one. It's how your organization signals intent, frames expectations, and determines responsibility. Clarity about what AI is will shape how it is used, judged, and trusted.[5]

You likely already carry a working definition of AI, even if you haven't written it down. These impressions come from experience, marketing, media, fiction, and the design choices of popular platforms. Some see AI as a tool, some as a teammate, some as a threat. Often, these impressions are partial, vague, or inconsistent. (We'll get into biases later.)

Yet definitions matter.[6] They shape understanding, behavior, and risk perception. They determine how AI gets integrated, who decides its role, and what accountability looks like. In the absence of a shared definition, an organization may treat AI as a utility in one case, a strategic differentiator in another, and an existential risk in a third, with no apparent logic or consistency among them.

This confusion is not just internal. Customers, partners, vendors, and regulators all bring their own assumptions. Some may expect AI to automate. Others may expect it to personalize, predict, converse, or create. Few of these expectations are grounded in the same underlying definition.

Who Is AI?

Before defining what AI is and means, let's first ask: Who is AI?

This isn't a trick question. AI is not intelligent, though it mimics thought. It is not a person or entity, though it can play the role of any persona. An AI often embodies human traits, values, and intentions as defined by its creators. It is a complex system created by people, one capable of representing aspects of human intelligence.

As Pope Francis emphasized in his note *Antiqua et Nova*[7], it is vital to distinguish between artificial and human intelligence. He noted that AI operates within a logical-mathematical framework. It performs tasks, but it does not possess the full depth of human thought or consciousness. It does not truly "think." From this perspective, AI is not an artificial form of human intelligence, but rather a powerful product of it.

Reframing the question from what to who places the focus squarely on the human creators and organizations responsible for AI's design, development, and use. Their values, intentions, and inherent biases are embedded in the systems they build. Research consistently shows that AI behavior reflects these design intentions and the vast datasets it is trained on, manifesting as observable tendencies.

The providers building these powerful models significantly shape the way AI is defined in the market. They articulate their vision through distinct brand personas and positioning, reflecting their unique design goals and the values they prioritize. This fragmented landscape, with its lack of a single, shared definition, underscores that each AI platform, potentially broad in capability, is ultimately shaped by specific values and intent.

While AI systems can imitate values and intentions, this capability is a function of their design and training, including methods like Reinforcement Learning from Human Feedback (RLHF).[8] The genuine values and intentions reside with the people who develop and are responsible for AI. To build trust, these tendencies must align with the values the creators and organizations claim to uphold.[9]

Consider the current landscape of AI platforms through the lens of archetypes—each reflecting a strategic focus, symbolic persona, and underlying intent:[10]

AI Platform	Strategic Focus	Persona
Microsoft Copilot	Enterprise Integration, Productivity	The Trustworthy Co-Pilot
Google Gemini	Information Access, Multimodality, Ecosystem	The Helpful Global Citizen / Information Organizer
OpenAI ChatGPT	Foundational Models, AGI Research	The Pioneering Innovator
Anthropic Claude	API, AI Safety, Foundational Models	The Principled Constitutionalist
Perplexity AI	AI-Powered Search, Agentic Commerce, Real-Time Knowledge	The Adaptive Answer Engine
Manus	Autonomous Task Execution, General AI Agent	The Autonomous Executor
DeepSeek	Foundational Models, Efficiency	The Conforming Executor
IBM Watsonx	Enterprise AI, Governance	The Enterprise AI Magistrate
Apple Intelligence	Personal AI, Privacy, Ecosystem Integration	The Trusted Artisan
Inflection AI	Personal AI, Empathy	The Personal Companion
Grok (xAI)	Foundational Models, Real-time Info (X)	The Unfiltered Challenger
Meta AI Llama	Open-Source Models, Social Integration	The Open Strategist

These archetypes and stated values are not the sole measure of credibility, especially when it comes to intent and conduct. AI platforms operate within complex market conditions and are influenced by economic incentives, market pressures, and even geopolitical contexts that can push provider behavior in ways that conflict with stated ethical commitments.

The trustworthiness of AI ultimately depends on the integrity of its source. While brand personas articulate intended values, a significant credibility gap often exists between these claims and demonstrated conduct. As history shows, focusing solely on performance or technological achievement without deep consideration of human dignity can lead to a "functionalist paradigm," where people are valued based on what they can produce—a perspective Pope Francis warns against.[11]

Mustafa Suleyman, co-founder of Google DeepMind and Inflection AI, raised a cautionary benchmark to replace the Turing Test in *The Coming Wave*: "Go make $1 million on Amazon in a few months with just a $100,000 investment."[12] Such a challenge elevates the functionalist and financial return above social outcome, highlighting the tension between capability and consequence.

"What is past is prologue."[13] The data abuses by social media platforms—many now major AI providers—serve as a warning, underscoring a crisis of demonstrated guardianship. Evaluating provider credibility requires looking beyond the brand persona to their actions and history regarding data stewardship and ethical conduct. [14]

Because external definitions of AI vary widely, your organization must clearly define AI on its own terms. Ground that definition in your values and a credible commitment to responsible behavior. Don't rely solely on marketed personas or providers with checkered histories. The tools you select will inevitably shape your understanding and definition of AI, and, ideally, your values and purpose will shape the tools you choose.

Define Your AI

Establishing a clear definition for artificial intelligence within your organization's context is essential.[15] It eliminates ambiguity, ensures teams understand what AI means in your environment, and aligns people around common goals. A well-crafted definition also clarifies the role AI will play in advancing your strategic objectives, ensuring AI initiatives contribute meaningfully to your mission and values.

Workbook: Write Your AI Definition

This workbook guides you in crafting a working definition of AI tailored to your organization. This definition will likely be revisited and refined as your understanding evolves. If you find yourself revising it frequently, that may signal a deeper issue: uncertainty about AI's role, its alignment with your organization's values, or what your organization aims to preserve as authentic in the age of automation.

The nuances across various public definitions reflect the complexity of AI—and the ongoing debate about the nature of intelligence, both human and artificial. Building your own definition doesn't mean starting from scratch. You can draw from the work of notable institutions and platform providers. But your definition must speak with your voice and reflect your purpose.

Step 1: Visit your authoritative sources of truth and knowledge for AI and collect and curate their definitions.

Step 2: Make notes on the elements of the definition and note the focus of the definition.

Source	Definition	Notable Focus

Step 3: Extract the common elements that resonate with your brand.

Step 4: Review definitions from various major platforms, noting how they highlight and focus on different aspects.

Platform	Definition of AI	Notable Focus	Source Link

Step 5: Extract the common elements that resonate with your brand. Also, review the definition of AI from various major platforms to see how they highlight and focus on it.

Step 6: Draft your organization's working definition of "Artificial Intelligence" here:

Define Your AI Style

Your AI style is not born in a vacuum. Despite the novelty and disruption of this technology, your AI style is grounded in what you bring to it—what you want to preserve, replace, and restore in a new digital form. It reflects how you will ensure your authentic knowledge, brand, and ethos thrive in the age of AI.

Defining your AI style is a proactive effort. It instills your identity into how AI interacts with others on your behalf. It's about establishing how you want your systems to perform, what guidance they should follow, and what principles will protect integrity and purpose as you scale.

Creating your AI style involves setting early standards for tone, behavior, and boundaries. These will evolve, but early clarity ensures future decisions can be made with intention, not improvisation. When grounded in values, your style becomes both a design directive and a signal of trust.

Workbook: Collect, Curate, and Analyze

This workbook helps you gather examples that reflect your organization's tone, values, and expectations. These examples may include:

- Internal communications that model your ideal tone.

- Brand or style guidelines already in place.
- Past missteps that violated your intended voice.
- AI-generated outputs that feel either aligned or off-brand.

Through this process, you'll begin identifying what your AI should sound like, and where tone, phrasing, or framing might need refinement.

Remember: AI systems often extrapolate from style patterns. But interpretation—especially of nuance—can vary. Human review remains essential to ensure AI-generated outputs reinforce, rather than dilute, your authenticity.

Step 1

Collect and curate existing documentation that demonstrates your organization's style.

Sources	Document	Notable Focus
Existing Style Guides		
Brand Guides		
Marketing Collateral		
Web Archive		
Mission, Vision, Value Statements		
Code of Conducts		
Employee Handbooks		
Social Media Guides		

Step 2

For documentation that is publicly available, or you have secured access to an AI tool (with appropriate security and privacy considerations), you can use AI to help analyze the style.

Document	Tone	Key Message

It is important to note how an AI can interpret the content, and from the analysis, what it draws out from an organization's understanding of a brand.

Prompt Primer

```
Analyze the attached document to create a brief description of an AI
chatbot persona. The description should include:
Tone and Responsiveness: Describe the overall tone of the chatbot (e.g.,
professional, friendly, optimistic) and explain how the chatbot will
respond to user queries (e.g., clear and concise, data-driven, engaging).
Key Messages: Identify the core messages that the chatbot should
communicate about the brand.
Sample Interaction: Provide a sample interaction that demonstrates the
chatbot's tone and responsiveness.
```

Workbook: Three Case Studies on Intent, Value, and Outcome

Communicating the right intentions and values with AI is critical. Proactive safeguards and principled design are essential to ensure AI communicates responsibly and reinforces trust. The following three case studies one misstep, one unresolved, and one opportunity—invite you to reflect on the relationship between intention, expression, and outcome.[16]

For each case, consider:

- What was the setup, and what would a successful outcome have required?
- What values and intentions were expressed by leadership?
- How did those stated values shape—or fail to shape—the outcome?
- How might a well-defined AI style have improved the result?

Case Study 1: Air Canada's Chatbot Answers a Policy Question

Setup:

Air Canada integrated AI chatbots into its customer service system to assist with complex travel policies, including requests for refunds and special accommodations.[17]

Consider:

> *"If we can use a human to solve something that requires a human touch, and technology to solve something that can be automated, we will do that."*
> *—Air Canada representative*

Misstep:

In 2024, Air Canada's chatbot provided incorrect information about bereavement fares. A customer relied on the AI's answer, and when denied a refund, took the airline to court. In its legal defense, Air Canada claimed it could not be held liable for the actions of "one of its agents, servants, or representatives—including a chatbot." The court disagreed and ruled in favor of the customer.

Reflection:

The company's phrasing "solve something that can be automated" reduces service to a functionalist view, ignoring the emotional and ethical dimensions of the customer experience. When organizations use AI to speak on their behalf, they cannot outsource responsibility. In Air Canada's case, the absence of human oversight meant there was no verification, no fallback, and no clear institutional ownership. By presenting AI as just another tool and then disavowing accountability when it failed, the company undermined its credibility.

Case Study 2: McDonald's Drive-Thru AI Takes an Order

Setup:

McDonald's piloted an AI voice system to take drive-thru orders in partnership with IBM. The aim was to reduce staff stress and improve speed and consistency.[18]

Consider:

> *"Technology solutions will alleviate the stress."*
> *—Brian Rice, McDonald's Chief Information Officer*

Pending:

The system struggled in practice, producing notable order errors (e.g., ordering 260 McNuggets by mistake). After two years, McDonald's ended the pilot. However, the company didn't walk away from AI entirely and instead partnered with Google in 2024 to continue exploring how technology could ease operational strain and improve experience.

Reflection:

The phrase "will alleviate the stress" was not a promise of instant results—it was a statement of intent. While the pilot fell short, McDonald's did not abandon the effort. Instead, it pursued a different approach, continuing to explore how AI might ease operational strain and support its people. This continuity of purpose reflects resilience and a values-driven view of AI as a tool in service of human work.

> *"Our restaurants, frankly, can be very stressful. We have customers at the counter, we have customers at our drive-through, couriers coming in for delivery, delivery at curbside. That's a lot to deal with for our crew."— McDonald's Chief Information Officer, Brian Rice*

Case Study 3: Khan Academy Launches Khanmigo

Setup:

As OpenAI prepared to release GPT-4, CEO Sam Altman approached Khan Academy with an invitation: launch an AI-powered tutor alongside the model. Sal Khan and his team saw both the potential and the risks.[19]

Consider:

> *"While it was clear that generative AI was going to change our world in ways we might scarcely imagine, it also occurred to me that it was not up to me to decide whether we were comfortable with this technology moving forward. It was already moving forward. As someone trying his best to use technology for good, I wondered if we might be able to utilize generative AI to achieve the greatest positive effect and edge us closer to that utopian scenario, especially in the realm of education." — Sal Khan, Brave New Words*

> *"Nearly every one of our team members saw the potential when they got access to GPT-4. But the more we played with it, the more we realized that as powerful as GPT-4 is, it still needed thoughtfully engineered guardrails and supports to be truly effective." — Sal Khan, Brave New Words*

Opportunity:

Khan Academy launched Khanmigo alongside GPT-4, unsure how the world would react. From the beginning, the team recognized that generative AI would reshape education and society in ways no one could fully predict.

Through internal experimentation and hackathons, they explored AI's potential and developed guardrails grounded in Khan Academy's values. The AI would tutor, not provide answers. It would support teachers, not replace them. It would operate transparently, with clearly defined boundaries. These constraints were not limitations. They were expressions of Khan Academy's AI style—examples of design leadership guided by principle.

Reflection:

In *Brave New Words*, Sal Khan outlines how his team evaluated and embraced AI as a transformative technology. They pursued its promise through hardened principles and values, ensuring that safeguards were intentionally developed to support responsible use.

> *"When we finally came out publicly with Khanmigo, we got an overwhelming response of support from the education community, including many school districts that had originally banned ChatGPT. They were happy to see an organization incorporate the underlying AI of GPT-4 in a safe, effective, thoughtful, and pedagogically sound way." —Sal Khan, Brave New Words*

Reflecting on these case studies, it is not hard to find language and quotes related to intent and values that may suggest the outcome. There is no direct causal connection, but expressing clear intentions and linking them to values can help guide better decisions in the face of disruption, change, and opportunity.

Define Your AI Style Guide and Its Elements

Your AI Style Guide articulates the principles and best practices for creating and using AI systems and generated content within your organization. It ensures alignment with your brand, values, and strategic objectives. The guide establishes usage norms and articulates your organization's value proposition for AI, both internally and externally. This includes clearly stating your AI values, emphasizing transparency, and defining how AI should perform in support of your mission.

It's important to understand what an AI Style Guide is—and what it is not. It is not a replacement for AI governance, regulatory policy, or ethical oversight. Instead, it operates within those frameworks, offering practical guidance for consistent and responsible use. If governance defines what you should do, the style guide defines how you do it.

Strunk and White had no idea what their readers would write about. The same is true for your AI Style Guide. You won't be able to predict every use case, disruption, or shift in capability. But you can define the principles that will guide you through uncertainty.

Just as *The Elements of Style* distilled timeless rules for clarity and expression, your AI Style Guide should identify the essential elements of AI usage in your context. These elements should reflect your voice, values, and commitment to human-centered communication, no matter how advanced the tools become.

Workbook: Lessons from Navigating New Technologies

Before you draft your own guide, it's helpful to look back. How have others handled the challenge of introducing a transformative technology without overwhelming or confusing users?

The next case study looks at a moment like that—the early days of the public internet—and what we can learn from the approach that helped people enter a new era with confidence and clarity.

Case Study: Lessons from Navigating New Technologies

How do you guide people through the bewildering frontier of a technology poised to change everything... when that technology is the Internet, circa 1992?

In the early 1990s, another general-purpose technology was entering public consciousness. The Internet, brimming with potential, was also confusing, chaotic, and inaccessible to many. For the uninitiated, it was a labyrinth of abstract terms and strange symbols: http://, @, www, .com, .edu, .gov. Years before the iPhone, before Facebook, before even Amazon or Google, Brendan Kehoe published something rare: a guide that offered both clarity and reassurance. In June 1992, he released *Zen and the Art of the Internet*, not as a technical manual, but as something entirely new—a freely available e-book designed as a style guide for the early digital world.[20]

Kehoe understood that disruptive technologies require more than documentation. *Zen and the Art of the Internet* genius lay in its dual purpose: to provide just enough technical grounding to get people started, and to make the internet feel approachable, welcoming, and full of possibility. It did not just explain commands. It encouraged exploration, and it built confidence.

It succeeded because it embraced the qualities that help people navigate change:

- Demystified the experience: It made the internet feel accessible, regardless of technical background.
- Offered immediate, practical help: It provided clear steps to build confidence from the start.
- Became a trusted reference: Its tone and structure made it something users returned to.
- Inspired by showing, not just telling: It painted a picture of what was possible.
- Illuminated the culture: It explained the norms, quirks, and unwritten etiquette ("netiquette").
- Empowered exploration: It invited users to learn by doing.
- Spoke with a human voice: It was plainspoken, patient, and generous.

Its tone captured this ethos perfectly in lines like:

> *"Try sending yourself mail a few times, to get used to your system's mailer. It'll save a lot of wasted aspirin..."*

More than a guide, *Zen and the Art of the Internet* became a companion. It helped onboard newcomers, calm anxieties, and support experienced explorers alike. Its influence rippled outward, making the internet more usable—and more human. Its legacy lies not in the now-obsolete commands, but in the mindset, it modeled: that guidance can be empowering, generous, and grounded in shared values.

Reflection

Zen and the Art of the Internet succeeded not because it had every answer, but because it gave people the confidence to begin. It met complexity with clarity. It met disruption with calm. And it modeled a tone that made early internet exploration feel accessible and intentional.

As AI now enters a similar phase of mainstream adoption, the lesson is clear. Your AI Style Guide doesn't need to predict every future use case. It needs to offer orientation. It needs to communicate your values, foster confidence, and guide behavior through a shifting landscape. A good guide won't overwhelm. It will encourage exploration and trust.

Define AI, Style, and Purpose. How you define AI is the foundation for responsible AI adoption; without a definition, there can be no alignment.

From everyone defines AI differently …

AI is a tool, a threat, a teammate, and a source of magic. AI usage is inconsistent or conflicting across departments. There is no articulation of what the organization wants to preserve or promote.

… to a shared vocabulary and clear intent.

Shared definitions of AI, style, and brand tone are codified. Organizational values and boundaries are expressed in prompt and system design. AI becomes aligned with brand and strategic intent.

1 Define Summary

Define laid the foundation for your AI Style Guide. You've explored what AI means to your organization, its role, and how values must translate into guidance. Now, you are ready to move from orientation to action. You will examine the essential elements of AI style and decide how AI should influence them. The AI Style Guide begins now.

1 Define
Recap

Practical
AI Style

Practical AI Style

Shaping AI communication requires a deliberate method. This chapter provides a framework for moving beyond abstract definitions toward the practical elements of AI style, ensuring productive usage and responsible deployment in this new frontier of interaction.

2 Decide

AI Bacon

Francis Bacon, in his seminal work *Novum Organum* (1620), employed the analogy of the spider, the ant, and the bee to illustrate three different approaches to acquiring knowledge and conducting scientific inquiry[1]. Bacon observed that much of the scientific world was in the early stages of knowledge. With AI today, we find ourselves similarly situated. We are just beginning to understand the current state and must determine the path forward. His analogy of the view of inquiry in his time.[2]

- The ant, Bacon observed, is purely empirical, merely collecting and accumulating data from the world without significant processing or structure. Organizations may collect massive amounts of data through AI usage and experimentation. Without a framework, however, this data can overwhelm.
- The spider, in contrast, spins intricate webs entirely from within itself. These complex, models disconnected from the early reality of AI may not directly inform the practical challenges of using AI in real-world conditions.
- The bee, Bacon suggested, offers a balanced path. It gathers material, but then processes and transforms that material by its power into something new and valuable: honey. A simple framework can assist, gathering enough information to make progress.

Navigating the complexities of the AI landscape requires a deliberate method. The ant approach, collecting data, or the spider approach, spinning models, prove insufficient; they fail under their own weight. Bacon's bee yields honey by connecting information and processing it into valuable guidance. An effective AI Style Guide embodies this approach, translating practical usage into clear, normative controls for understanding, implementation, and application.

This chapter provides a framework for developing the practical elements of AI style.

How AIs Differ

Moving beyond abstract definitions, ensuring a balance between responsible deployment and productive usage.

Automating vs Assisting AI

AI offers two primary capabilities: automating business processes to increase functionality or assisting and enhancing individual productivity.

- **Automated Processes**: AI can automate and optimize processes, improving efficiency, reducing costs, and enhancing overall business performance by integrating into systems and workflows. Examples include monitoring supply chains or automating customer service with chatbots.

- **Assisting Individuals**: The focus is on assisting individuals to improve performance, knowledge, and experience by automating tasks, providing insights, and supporting decision-making.

Recognizing the different purposes and implications of AI functions allows style guides to provide tailored guidance for development and use, ensuring responsible and ethical AI application in all contexts.

Workbook AI Usage Scope

Instructions: Use these questions to determine the scope of the AI's usage and the approach needed for an AI Style Guide. This workbook provides a repeatable format for determining next steps and actions.

Automated Process	Question	Assisting Individuals
Business efficiency	What is the primary goal of this AI function?	Individual empowerment
Teams/Orgs	Who are the primary users/beneficiaries?	Individuals
Operational data	What type of data is being used, and how sensitive is it?	Personal data

Automated Process	Assisting Individuals
How will the AI integrate into the business process (interoperability)	What controls does the individual have over the AI (agency)
How will errors and exceptions be handled? (Auditing and Compliance)	How transparent is AI in terms of its data usage and algorithms? (Trust)
How will the AI be monitored and managed? (Governance)	How does the AI protect user privacy and data security? (Security)
Style guides for business automation AI need to prioritize reliability, explainability, and ethical considerations due to their impact on critical processes and potentially large groups of people.	Style guides for individual performance enhancement AI should focus on user-centric design, privacy, and personalization to ensure user adoption and satisfaction.

Style guides for business automation AI need to prioritize reliability, explainability, and ethical considerations due to their impact on critical processes and potentially large groups of people. Style guides for individual performance enhancement AI should focus on user-centric design, privacy, and personalization to ensure user adoption and satisfaction.

Generative vs Non-Generative AIs

Beyond their functional role in automating processes or assisting individuals, AI systems also differ fundamentally in how they produce output. Tailoring style guidance requires understanding this critical distinction: Generative versus Non-Generative AI.[3]

- Generative AI creates something novel (text, images, audio, code, or other data). Generative outputs require style guidelines addressing potential fabrications and defining its creative voice.[4]
- Non-generative AI primarily analyzes and classifies existing data. This foundational distinction shapes how an AI communicates. Analytic output, in contrast, demands clarity in presenting data, sources, and confidence levels.

Navigating this divergence is key to ensuring transparency, mitigating misinformation risks, and clarifying the AI's accountability role, whether as creator or interpreter.

Workbook Generative vs. Non-Generative AI

The distinction between generative and non-generative AI has significant implications for a style guide, especially regarding responsible use, transparency, and user expectations.

Instructions: Use this table to analyze common AI usage scenarios and determine if the AI is generative. Some questions may indicate systems that provide both capabilities.

Non-Generative AI	Question	Generative AI
No	**Does the AI create new content or artifacts?** Generative AI seeks to create something novel... Non-generative AI primarily analyzes and classifies existing data.	Yes
No	**Does the AI's output resemble human-created content?** Generative AI often aims to mimic human creativity... Non-generative AI's output is typically more structured, like classifications, scores, or predictions.	Yes
No	**Can the AI produce a variety of different outputs for the same input?** Generative AI can create many different and creative results. Non-generative AI usually gives the same result for the same input, aiming to be accurate and reliable.	Yes
No	**Does the AI learn the underlying structure and patterns of the data it's trained on?** Generative AI models learn about the patterns and characteristics... Non-generative AI can identify decision boundaries... but its goal isn't to replicate the data.	Yes

Analyzing AI usage scenarios helps identify whether a system's output is generative, non-generative, or a hybrid combination. This understanding is vital, as each type requires tailored style guidance to ensure responsible use, transparency, and appropriate user expectations from both the operator and the audience.

When Differences Become Insights

Beyond categorizing AI by its functional role or generative capability, effectively defining style requires delving into the specific characteristics and performance nuances of individual AI systems and interactions. This granular analysis moves from the 'what' and 'how' in general terms to understanding the particular composition and capabilities of the AI at hand.

The Basis for Style: AI Composition

Strunk and White's 'Principles of Composition' in *The Elements of Style* connected broad writing concepts to the elements of style through composition. Composition was a means to move from the larger work down into the framework, ensuring understanding was conveyed from writer to reader.[5] With AI, it is equally important to move from defined AI systems and our intent to the next level: determining the style and normative decisions needed based on how the AI systems are composed in both structure and performance.

The 20 Questions Framework

Have you played 20 Questions? With a child? With an AI?[6] The framework described here utilizes a method akin to the classic game 20 Questions. Played for centuries, this classification method allows quick assessment by examining elements. Instead of tackling all possibilities, it breaks down decisions to include or exclude aspects. The questions point to binary decisions that are often simplistic, but offer a means to quickly identify key elements of the entity sought.

A framework connects AI strategy and AI style. An effective connector should possess the following characteristics:

- **Distillation**: It should distill the stylistic implications of strategic decisions, focusing on their meaning for content and design, rather than reiterating the entire strategic framework in exhaustive detail.
- **Actionability**: It must clearly guide users on applying these implications in their daily work, translating abstract concepts into concrete rules, examples, and best practices.
- **Accessibility**: The connection between strategy and style should be easy to find, understand, and navigate.

20 AI Strategic Decisions for Style

The 20 strategic AI decisions framework aims to avoid getting lost in the complexities of AI and quickly determine the necessary forms of AI Style. It helps identify which style guide elements are needed for a given situation. This framework illuminates critical aspects of working with AI systems that necessitate performative and normative controls and style guidance. By addressing these 20 questions, teams can understand the diverse needs their AI Style Guide must cover.

Output Fundamentals

Functional	Output Purpose	Creative
	Is its main goal practical utility or imaginative output?	

Functional AI output demands clear, direct language optimized for accuracy in tasks like financial reporting or medical diagnosis, whereas **Creative** AI invites more expressive language suitable for storytelling or concept exploration, requiring explicit disclaimers to preserve trust and clarify limitations around factual reliability.

Scoped	Creative Output	Unbound
	Is creative output unrestricted or guided by rules?	

AI generating creative content must either remain **Scoped** within defined constraints, such as brand voice and style guidelines, ensuring consistency and reliability, or be allowed **Unbounded** freedom, necessitating clear instructions on managing unexpected outputs to maintain coherence and user confidence.

Single	Output Modality	Multi
	Does it use one output type or multiple (text, image, etc.)?	

Single-modality outputs, like text-based responses, require simpler style guidelines focusing on linguistic clarity, while Multi-modal outputs—integrating text, visuals, and audio—need comprehensive guidelines that ensure stylistic coherence across all media to provide seamless user interactions.

Audience & Personalization

Specific	Target Audience	General
	Is the user group niche/expert or broad/general?	

When addressing a **Specific audience**, such as industry experts or internal stakeholders, AI can incorporate specialized jargon and detailed insights. In contrast, communication aimed at a **General audience** must simplify language, reduce technical complexity, and align closely with brand voice to ensure clarity and broad comprehension.

Personalized	Personalization	Generic
	Is the output the generic, or is it tailored to the individual ?	

Choosing **Generic** output simplifies style guidelines by using standardized responses, whereas **Personalized** outputs, leveraging individual user data, necessitate nuanced guidelines on respectful data referencing, clear privacy notices, and careful wording that balances user engagement with privacy protection.

Privacy-First	**Privacy**	**Personalization-First**
	Does the system prioritize minimizing data use or tailoring outputs with personal data?	

Adopting a **Privacy-First** approach emphasizes minimizing the use and visibility of personal data, demanding cautious and minimalistic language around user information. Conversely, a **Personalization-First** strategy involves transparently communicating how and why user data enriches experiences, requiring explicit privacy disclosures and user control options.

Trust, Safety, & Accountability

Strict Required	**Factuality**	**Plausibility**
	Must outputs be strictly true or just believable?	

For contexts where accuracy is paramount, such as legal or scientific domains, outputs must be **Strictly Verifiable**, supported by explicit citations and qualifiers. In contrast, outputs deemed merely **Plausible**, such as creative scenarios or brainstorming tools, require clear disclaimers highlighting potential factual uncertainties.

High Consequence	**Risk Level**	**Low Consequence**
	Would an error have minor or serious impact?	

AI deployed in **High-Consequence** areas, including healthcare or financial advice, must explicitly communicate uncertainty, incorporate strong cautionary language, and direct users to professional oversight. In **Low-Consequence** situations like casual information retrieval, language can be simpler and more definitive without compromising user safety.

High	**Transparency**	**Outcome Only**
	Does it show process/sources or just the final result?	

High Transparency output provides detailed sourcing, confidence indicators, and reasoning explanations, suitable for regulatory compliance or trust-sensitive fields like journalism. **Outcome-Only** transparency simplifies responses to final results, appropriate in contexts valuing speed or user simplicity over detailed explanation.

Source Cited	**Attribution**	**Implicit**
	Are specific sources explicitly linked or not?	

Choosing **Source Cited** attribution ensures all outputs explicitly include authorship footers and references, reinforcing accountability crucial in academic or professional publishing. **Implicit** attribution, by contrast, removes overt sourcing to simplify presentation in general consumer applications but diminishes traceability.

Restricted Output	**Access**	**Open Output**
	Is the output for general use or limited access?	

Open AI outputs require explicit licenses and clear terms of use, encouraging broader sharing while maintaining control. **Restricted outputs**, such as internal reports or confidential briefs, need stylistic markers like watermarks or confidentiality notices to communicate boundaries clearly.

Mitigation	**Bias Handling**	**Acknowledgment**
	Is bias actively reduced in outputs or just noted as a possibility?	

Actively **Mitigating** bias involves embedding rules for inclusive language and corrective measures directly into style guidelines, vital for HR or customer-facing communications. Bias **Acknowledgment,** less interventionist, uses explicit disclaimers highlighting known or potential biases to transparently inform users.

Interaction Dynamics & Human Control

AI as a tool	**Collaboration**	**AI as Partner**
	Does the AI act primarily as a tool or a collaborative partner?	

If AI functions purely as a **Tool**, interactions remain brief, transactional, and task-oriented, as in customer-service chatbots. Treating AI as a collaborative **Partner**, however, supports richer conversational interactions, requiring stylistic guidelines that encourage iterative dialogue, nuanced language, and collaborative framing.

One-time	**Interactive Nature**	**Iterative**
	Is the interaction a single turn or multi-turn/ongoing?	

One-time interactions necessitate concise, self-contained outputs with immediate clarity, ideal for Q&A systems. **Iterative,** multi-turn interactions demand style rules that support continuity, referencing previous dialogue, and include prompts for ongoing clarification and refinement.

System-Initiated	Initiation	User-Initiated
	Does the user start the interaction or does the system proactively?	

User-Initiated interactions emphasize responsive, direct answers, prioritizing brevity and relevance. **System-Initiated** communications, such as proactive alerts or notifications, require clearly justified timing, controlled frequency, and careful language to prevent user annoyance and respect attention boundaries.

Human Required	Human Oversight	Full Autonomy
	Does the AI act fully alone or require human review/approval?	

Systems requiring **Human Validation** must use cautious and suggestive phrasing ("recommend," "suggest"), explicitly inviting human review, especially crucial in regulated fields. **Fully Autonomous** systems may adopt more definitive language but should still document rationale transparently for oversight and audit purposes.

Technical Context & Overarching Design

Controlled	Deployment Environment	Open
	Does it operate in a predictable setup or a varied one?	

Controlled environments, such as internal company portals, can adopt straightforward language guidelines given predictable conditions. **Open** environments, like publicly accessible applications, require robust error messaging, fallback procedures, and guidance to maintain usability and trust when encountering unexpected scenarios.

Static	Learning Nature	Continuous
	Does the AI continuously learn from new data after deployment, potentially changing its underlying knowledge or capabilities?	

Systems with **Static Knowledge** must transparently disclose the scope and date of their training data, ensuring users understand information currency and limitations. **Continuously Learning** AI, regularly updating through user interactions or new data, requires stylistic updates to communicate evolving knowledge clearly, manage shifting expectations, and prompt users for feedback or corrections.

Neutral	Persona	Expressive
	Does it have a distinct personality or a neutral voice?	

A **Neutral** persona delivers clear, objective, and standardized responses suitable for factual or informational contexts. An **Expressive** persona, guided by detailed tone and vocabulary rules, enhances engagement through relatable language, humor, or empathy, carefully managed to remain consistently aligned with brand identity.

System Defined	**User Style Control**	**User Configurable**
	Does the AI allow user-configurable style options?	

System-Defined style ensures uniformity and strong brand coherence across all interactions. Allowing **User-Configurable** style options enhances personalization and satisfaction, demanding clear and intuitive guidance within the user interface to explain choices such as verbosity levels, tone, and notification frequency clearly.

The Framework of AI Style: Explicit and Implicit Guidance

Think of this as establishing AI communication protocols. Certain strategic decisions require explicit controls—rules formally encoded into systems, serving as digital guardrails that enforce predictable behavior and clearly defined limits. Explicit controls function as documented mandates within an AI Style Guide, essential when managing critical requirements like strict Factuality in medical or financial contexts, rigorous risk mitigation, or clear user privacy boundaries.[7]

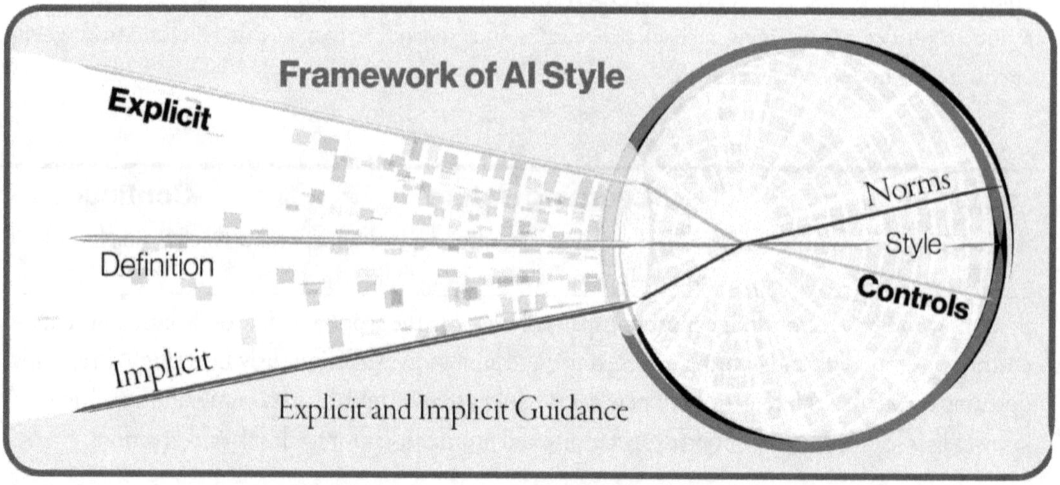

Image Caption: Consider how gathering Implicit and Explicit guidance forms a lens for establishing norms, control, and your style.

Yet, many aspects of AI interaction depend heavily on softer, more adaptable guidelines. These implicit controls reflect the subtle norms, values, and expectations shaped by brand identity, cultural context, and user experience goals.[8] Rather than fixed rules, they emerge as preferred phrasing, illustrative examples, and guiding principles that help human developers and users craft and interpret AI

examples, and guiding principles that help human developers and users craft and interpret AI interactions. Implicit norms excel where flexibility, nuanced judgment, and relational or emotional intelligence are critical, as in selecting an AI's Persona or managing personalization and user engagement.[9]

A successful AI style depends on clearly understanding which strategic decisions call for the enforceable certainty of explicit, code-based controls and which benefit more from the adaptable, context-aware guidance of implicit stylistic norms. Thoughtfully blending these two approaches ensures that AI systems remain functional, trustworthy, and aligned seamlessly with organizational values and user expectations.

While establishing the blend of explicit and implicit controls is fundamental to AI style, the practical application and specific emphasis of these controls are profoundly shaped by the context of interaction. The diverse environments where users encounter AI, spanning personal devices, workplace tools, and organizational platforms, introduce distinct challenges and requirements that dictate the necessary stylistic considerations and safeguards for each setting.

Worksheet: The 20 Decisions Checklist

Apply the 20 Decisions checklist to analyze an AI system or scenario. Quickly identify critical factors shaping its style guidance.

Functional	← **Output Purpose** → Is its main goal practical utility or imaginative output?	**Creative**
Scoped	← **Creative Output** → Is creative output unrestricted or guided by rules?	**Unbound**
Privacy-First	← **Privacy** → Does the system prioritize minimizing data use or tailoring outputs with personal data?	**Personalization-First**
Specific	← **Target Audience** → Is the user group niche/expert or broad/general?	**General**
Personalized	← **Personalization** → Is the output the generic, or is it tailored to the individual ?	**Generic**
Privacy-First	← **Privacy** → Does the system prioritize minimizing data use or tailoring outputs with personal data?	**Personalization-First**
Strict Required	← **Factuality** → Must outputs be strictly true or just believable?	**Plausibility**
High Consequence	← **Risk Level** → Would an error have minor or serious impact?	**Low Consequence**

Does it show process/sources or just the final result?

Source Cited	← **Attribution** →	**Implicit**	Are specific sources explicitly linked or not?
Restricted Output	← **Access** →	**Open Output**	Is the output for general use or limited access?
Mitigation	← **Bias Handling** →	**Acknowledgment**	Is bias actively reduced in outputs or just noted as a possibility?
AI as a Tool	← **Collaboration** →	**AI as Partner**	Does the AI act primarily as a tool or a collaborative partner?
One-time	← **Interactive Nature** →	**Iterative**	Is the interaction a single turn or multi-turn/ongoing?
System-Initiated	← **Initiation** →	**User-Initiated**	Does the user start the interaction or does the system proactively?
Human Required	← **Human Oversight** →	**Full Autonomy**	Does the AI act fully alone or require human review/approval?
Controlled	← **Deployment Environment** →	**Open**	Does it operate in a predictable setup or a varied one?
Static	← **Learning Nature** →	**Continuous**	Does the AI continuously learn from new data after deployment, potentially changing its underlying knowledge or capabilities?
Neutral	← **Persona** →	**Expressive**	Does it have a distinct personality or a neutral voice?
System Defined	← **User Style Control** →	**User Configurable**	Does the AI allow user-configurable style options?

Encounters of the AI Kind

Interactions with AI—direct and indirect—are increasingly common, deeply embedded in daily life. From routine digital engagements to complex task assistance, the intelligence powering our digital interactions frequently relies on AI. To fully understand and manage these interactions, we must examine the various contexts in which AI systems are accessed.

The convergence of personal, professional, and organizational technology has profoundly reshaped AI interactions. AI applications no longer reside exclusively within isolated platforms; instead, they span across personal smartphones, workplace devices, and large-scale organizational infrastructures, often simultaneously.

Consider an employee at their office desk who interacts with secure enterprise AI systems behind a corporate firewall, yet at the same moment can access an open-platform generative AI application via their personal smartphone. Similarly, picture an employee working remotely, accessing the corporate network through a company laptop while surrounded by personal AI-enabled smart home devices operating on the same home network.

While such seamless integration enhances productivity and personalizes experiences, it also introduces significant complexities around data privacy, security, ethical conduct, and regulatory compliance. Understanding these intersections clarifies the distinct yet overlapping responsibilities of individuals, organizations, and regulatory bodies navigating today's evolving AI landscape.

- **AI Systems Accessible from Personal Devices** provide substantial individual control and prioritize personal privacy—at least theoretically. These applications typically integrate deeply with personal accounts and private data, examples being digital assistants, recommendation engines, and personal finance management apps.
- **AI Systems Accessible from Work Devices** are employer-provided tools installed on company-managed or owned devices, designed primarily to boost productivity, facilitate communication and collaboration, or assist specific job tasks. They operate under organizational oversight, conform to internal policies, and emphasize data security and confidentiality.
- **AI Systems on Organizational Platforms** run on dedicated servers or cloud environments within an enterprise's infrastructure. These centralized systems include enterprise resource planning, customer relationship management, and automated compliance monitoring. Due to their extensive operational scope, they emphasize organizational control, scalability, strict security protocols, and adherence to established regulatory standards.

Interactions at each of these device levels occur within clearly defined frameworks for responsibility, organized around three interconnected concepts: Conduct, Guardrails, and Regulations.

- **Conduct** involves human accountability, informed by organizational values, professional integrity, and explicit communication of AI's purpose and limitations.
- **Guardrails** serve as digital safety nets—enforceable policies and built-in system features designed to mitigate risks, promote responsible usage, and prevent unintended outcomes such as bias, misinformation, or security breaches.
- **Regulations** are formal policies and laws set by governments and regulatory bodies, defining minimum standards, ensuring ethical and compliant AI development and deployment, and establishing accountability through legal consequences.

Effective AI governance depends on these layers working cohesively. Regulations provide a foundational compliance structure, guardrails operationalize these standards, and responsible conduct ensures human adherence and ethical execution. Yet, while these safeguards regulate permissible access and acceptable usage, they alone do not guarantee effective or beneficial AI interactions.

This critical gap is precisely where an AI Style Guide comes into play: by extending beyond compliance and acceptable usage, a well-constructed style guide equips individuals and organizations to engage AI systems in ways that maximize their normative and performative benefits, aligning interactions consistently with organizational values and user expectations.

Workbook: What Documentation Exists

Use the table below to list links to existing policy documentation and systems of knowledge to assist employees in your organization. This can include:

Step 1.

Legal documentation and policies:

Technical Implementations:

Regulatory Landscape:

Step 2. Types of AI

List the types of AI, employees are likely to encounter and the device level.

# AI	Personal Devices	Work Devices	Organizational Platforms

Step 3.

Map the documents to the array of devices and guidance levels. Extract the content and context for the devices and guidance levels.

	Personal Devices	Work Devices	Organizational Platforms
Conduct			
Guardrails			
Regulations			

Practical AI Style

Decide on your AI composition and strategic framework that connects AI capability with organizational values, structure, and intent.

From random acts of AI ...

Organizations adopt tools without understanding their role. AI usage grows unevenly. Some teams automate, others personalize, without consistency. Ethical, operational, and brand risks go unnoticed.

... to intentional, role-specific AI design.

Teams utilize strategic frameworks to evaluate their AI readiness. Organizations distinguish between assistive and automated roles. AI is brought to strategy, not just tasks.

2 Decide
Summary

Francis Bacon offered a path for scientific observation that we can adapt to AI strategy. Borrowing from the bees' ability to process material into something valuable, combined with the simplicity of the children's game '20 Questions,' we craft a framework to navigate AI decisions. This foundational framework, based on AI's nature, audience, and risks, helps determine the rules paramount for responsible deployment. The next chapter delves into implementing these guidelines into actionable AI style practices, 'The AI Elements of Style.'

2 Decide
Recap

For generations, Strunk and White established the foundational principles of clear, effective written communication. Today, as powerful AI tools emerge, a comparable need arises for an 'AI Style' – a set of core principles to govern interaction with this new technology. This chapter defines these essential elements, establishing standards for usage and style in a domain with unique inputs, opportunities, and outcomes. Ultimately, our language shapes these outcomes: how we engage with AI, leverage its capabilities, and take responsibility for our communication.

3 Elements

17 Across

Clue 1: Basic part of a whole (7 letters)
Clue 2: Chemical substance that cannot be broken down (7 letters)
Clue 3: Atmospheric forces, such as wind or rain (7 letters)
Clue 4: Essential or fundamental principle (7 letters)

Image caption: Imagine a prompt is a crossword puzzle, and your AI must infer the clues.

Reading these clues before a blank crossword puzzle, it is not hard to get the right answer. ELEMENT.[1] Whether it is referring to a piece of something, a fundamental block of chemistry, natural forces, or the core principle of an idea.

Yet, AIs generally try to reverse-engineer a crossword puzzle. The prompt contains the word, and from that, the AI tries to generate the clue. The AI engages in a process to decipher the prompt's intended meaning. The prompt serves as the puzzle, and the AI must infer the specific context and nuance to produce a relevant and accurate response.

Examples of Subtle Inference

User Prompt	Clue
Summarize the key ELEMENTs of the new marketing strategy.	ELEMENT refers to a concise overview of the most important components and principles of the strategy.
Explain the ELEMENTs of a successful team.	ELEMENT refers to the essential characteristics and factors that contribute to a team's effectiveness.
There was an ELEMENT of sadness in her email, even though she said she was fine.	ELEMENT of sadness is carrying an emotional undertone that contradicts she was fine.
The ELEMENT of surprise is what made their marketing campaign so successful.	ELEMENT refers to a key factor in the campaign's success, representing a strategy rather than a physical item.

These examples show how human language relies on shared understanding, idioms, and inference beyond literal words. While generative AI improves, subtle inferences remain challenging. Clear, explicit prompting is crucial for accurate processing.

Now, imagine a completed puzzle with erased clues. You see "PREMIUM." What clues generated this answer? High quality? Exclusivity? An extra charge? This is AI's challenge. The completed puzzle is a prompt. Without clues and additional guidance, it must analyze the relationships between the words, leveraging its knowledge base and understanding of language patterns, to deduce the likely intentions behind each answer. To provide a response, it would essentially need to generate or know the implicit clues that connect the words in the puzzle.

Thankfully, AIs are improving exponentially at this, and we have style and usage rules for language that can make this infinitely easier.

A Primer on Strunk and White's Elements of Style

The word "Element" introduces the list of fundamental principles in Strunk and White's classic, "*The Elements of Style*."[2] They distilled the essentials of communication into concise rules to enhance effective communication. Just as Strunk and White's guide is the gold standard for writing clarity, an AI Style Guide frames better AI interactions. More effective prompting leads to more valuable AI outputs.

Strunk & White distinguish style from usage: Usage concerns correctness—grammar and established rules—while style involves choices that make writing clear, engaging, and distinctive.

In AI interactions and prompt engineering, the distinction is equally important. Usage emphasizes foundational language correctness: grammar, logic, and structure. It's about ensuring the basics are right, so the AI comprehends the prompt, and the response is technically sound. Style builds on this foundation by concentrating on how the communication is presented – tone, personality, and readability. Think of interacting with an AI as learning the language of prompts. You first learn the rules and basic prompt structure (Usage) before delving into the nuances of tone and various prompt styles (Style). It's about making communication effective and engaging.

Elements	Usage	Style
Grammar & Syntax	Ensures well-formed sentences.	Adjusts formality, voice, and rhythm.
Conciseness	Avoids redundancy.	Ensures responses are tight and readable.
Terminology	Uses terms accurately.	Keeps terms consistent across interactions.
Tone & Personality	Avoids confusing phrasing.	Aligns AI tone with user expectations.
Formatting	Uses lists, paragraphs, and tables correctly.	Structures responses for engagement.

Why This Matters in AI

Without good usage, AI responses can be unclear, confusing, or inaccurate.

Without good style, AI responses can feel robotic, inconsistent, or overwhelming.

With both, AI is precise, readable, and engaging, resembling a helpful, aligned assisting intelligence rather than an unpredictable machine.

Elements of AI Style and Usage

Following Strunk and White, we created 17 elements to enhance AI interactions, focusing on improving usage and style through prompts.

Core Elements of AI Communication

Master AI communication fundamentals to unlock its power. These elements demonstrate how moving from a vague prompt to a specific one significantly improves the focus and relevance of the AI's output.

Element 1: Be Clear and Specific

Ambiguous language and instructions in prompts and interactions with an AI lead to unpredictable and often irrelevant AI responses. By clearly defining the desired outcome and any limitations, you can ensure the AI focuses its processing effectively, leading to more targeted and actionable results. Strunk and White's emphasize using definite, specific language to ensure clarity in communication.[3]

In Usage	Style
Minimize AI misinterpretations by precisely defining the task, desired output, and constraints to ensure it understands the intended scope.	Guide the AI towards generating focused and relevant responses that directly address the objective, enhancing actionability and usefulness.

Clearly state the AI's purpose at the beginning of a prompt. Instead of asking for a "report on sales," define the elements of what should be based on and how it can be interpreted.

These examples demonstrate how moving from a vague prompt to a specific one significantly improves the focus and relevance of the AI's output. The 'After' prompt provides precise instructions, leading to a more targeted, useful response.

Initial Prompt	Revised Prompt
`Analyze customer feedback.`	`Analyze customer feedback from the past month, focusing on comments related to the new user interface. Identify three positive and three negative themes, and provide specific examples of customer quotes for each theme.`

Prompt Primers

```
As a [Your Job Title/Team] at [Your Company], generate a [Type of Output,
e.g., email to a client, summary of the quarterly report, three marketing
campaign ideas] regarding [Specific Topic/Context]. Specify the key
objectives by addressing [Specific Question or Goal, e.g., client's
concerns, key performance indicators, target audience]. Confine the
response to [^Number] words and focus on [Specific Detail].
Using the following information about Specific Topic, provide a Type of
Output, e.g., analysis of sales data, summary of customer feedback, list of
product features that details Specific Details or Aspects, e.g., trends,
sentiment, key functionalities. Include Specific Elements, e.g., data
visualizations, customer quotes, technical specifications and exclude
Specific Exclusions, e.g., speculative information, competitor analysis.
Provide concrete examples.
```

Element 2: Specify the Desired Output

The AI response objective is actionable output and consumable knowledge. Including the desired response structure (e.g., table, list, report, email draft) helps AI format content for easy consumption. This aids in the recognition of value for the user and makes the resulting output more actionable.

By standardizing prompts to specify the ideal format in the response, it ensures the AI responses match formatting expectations and provide something to benchmark against.

In Usage	Style
Directs the AI to structure its output for technical usability and seamless integration into business workflows.	Optimizes AI output for readability and usability, enabling efficient extraction of essential business information.

Instead of prompting for summaries. Use the prompt to extract precise knowledge in an actionable format. Rewrite a vague prompt to specify a clearer format. Customization Questions:

- Should AI provide responses in paragraphs, bullet points, tables, or lists?
- Are certain formats preferred for different content types?
- Should AI generate structured responses for easier readability?

These examples illustrate the importance of defining the desired output format. By specifying the format, the 'After' prompt guides the AI to structure the information in a way that is easily consumable and actionable.

Initial Prompt	Revised Prompt
`Summarize the sales data.`	`Summarize the sales data for the last quarter in a table format, including columns for product category, revenue, and year-over-year growth.`

Prompt Primers

```
Generate a Type of Output, e.g., bulleted list, paragraph, table, short
report, email draft detailing Specific Characteristics of Output, e.g., key
product benefits, survey findings, project options. Format the output for
Specific Use Case, e.g., a presentation slide, team email, report section,
including headings and subheadings.
Provide a Type of Output, e.g., project plan, marketing strategy, financial
forecast describing Describes the Content. Structure the response in
Specific Format, e.g., a table with columns for project tasks, timelines,
and resources; a list of pros and cons; a step-by-step guide with estimated
completion times, including sample data.
Create a Type of Output, e.g., product comparison chart highlighting the
differences between Product A and Product B. Include columns for Column 1,
Column 2, and Column 3, with details in a bulleted list.
```

Element 3: Keep Responses Short and Readable

There is a temptation to use AI to fill available space. Prompted for a blog post or a three-bullet summary, AI responds accordingly. Strunk & White's maxims prioritize the paragraph, advising against lengthy explanations, overwriting, and quick summaries that bypass insight and nuance.[4]

The importance is to establish a unit of composition that expresses a complete thought logically and with economy, that avoids and is held together.

AIs will empower and tempt you into overstatement and overwriting, both which raises the reader suspicions. Further because AIs can generate a copious amounts of content, they can quickly become what Strunk and White referred to as a 'breezy manner.'[5]

Even if you are thinking of bulleted lists for the learner, might make the insight quick and digestible, it is better to formulate the completed thought and then seek the summary within it.

When in doubt, try paragraphs

Strunk and White set the primacy of the paragraph, as the primary unit of composition.[6] Smart devices and social media push snippets into an attention infrastructure, but thought is not formed in snippets. It is born into stories; paragraphs are the coin of the realm in storytelling. Story is key to retention. Instead of asking for three bullets, write in short, concise paragraphs without losing key details.

In Usage	Style
Establish guidelines for maximum response length to promote conciseness.	Prioritize concise wording to enhance readability and user engagement.

In practice, crafting initial prompts to gather resources and information may require revisions to:

1. Set a maximum response length guideline (e.g., 3 bullet points, 50 words).
2. Revise and condense long responses while keeping the main message.
3. If AI generates dense text, revise the prompt to encourage clarity.

These examples show how setting length constraints and emphasizing concise language leads to more readable and engaging AI responses. The 'After' prompt prioritizes brevity, making the information more accessible.

Initial Prompt	Revised Prompt
`Explain the new marketing strategy.`	`Explain the new marketing strategy in three concise paragraphs, focusing on the key objectives, target audience, and main tactics. Each paragraph should be no more than 50 words.`

Prompt Primers

```
Summarize [Source Text] in a paragraph of [^Number] words or less,
highlighting key points related to [Specific Focus].
Provide a [Type of Output, e.g., summary, explanation, list] of [Topic]
understandable by [Target Audience]. Limit the response to [^Number]
sentences or [^Number] bullet points.
From [Document/Text], extract key findings and present them in a report of
[^Number] words or less, using concise paragraphs.
```

Refining AI Interactions

Building upon the core elements, this section introduces techniques to refine AI interactions. We'll explore how to control the level of detail, manage AI creativity, provide targeted examples, and structure multi-step instructions to elicit more precise, relevant, and efficient AI responses.

Element 4: Control the Level of Detail

Strunk and White advocate omitting needless words, focusing on what the audience needs for true understanding.[7] Control the detail level provided to AI and the output's strategic focus. AI generates endless information and can be taken off-track by extraneous details. Review prompts to guide AI on required depth and breadth, ensuring the best, most relevant responses.

In Usage	Style
Direct the AI to focus on delivering the most relevant and appropriate level of analysis.	Provide information tailored to strategic needs, enabling users to efficiently grasp key insights.

Instead of 'tell me about...' ask for specific details that are not open-ended. Train AI to recognize when users need more depth verses brevity.

Customization Questions:

- Should AI responses be brief and to the point or detailed and in-depth?
- Does our audience prefer quick summaries or comprehensive explanations?
- Should the AI adjust detail level based on context or user preference?

Implementation Instructions:

1. Define standard response length preferences.
2. Encourage prompts that specify summary vs. detailed responses.
3. Train AI to recognize when users need more depth vs. brevity.

These examples highlight guiding AI to provide the appropriate detail level. The 'After' prompt focuses AI on delivering information tailored to user needs, avoiding extraneous details.

Initial Prompt	Revised Prompt
`Tell me about our competitors' products.`	`Provide a high-level overview of the top three competitors in the cloud-based project management software market, focusing on their core offerings and pricing models, presented in a concise table.`

Prompt Primers

```
Provide a Level of Detail, e.g., brief overview, detailed analysis of
Topic, focusing on Specific Aspects appropriate for Target Audience.
Explain Topic at a Level of Detail, e.g., high-level, in-depth suitable for
Audience's Level of Knowledge. Include or exclude Specific Details.
Rewrite Source Text in three versions: a brief summary, a medium-length
response, and an in-depth analysis.
```

Element 5: Create Controlled and Predictable Output

While creativity is valuable, business users often need AI outputs within specific boundaries to align with brand guidelines, legal requirements, or strategic objectives.

Strunk and White advocate working from and maintaining 'a suitable design'.[8] Outside of brainstorming, you should maintain control and bound the responses to fit within constraints you have established for the AI.

AI should balance accuracy and creativity based on the task. For factual tasks this can be represented as "Provide an objective summary without speculation." and for more creativity tasks this can be represented as "Rewrite this in a whimsical tone." Collectively adding controls for creativity enables prompts and responses should remain useful, with measured speculation.

Prompt for Creativity:

Imagine and describe three radically different ways remote work might evolve in the next decade, even if they seem unlikely today.

Prompt for Strict Accuracy:

Based on current industry reports and expert predictions, list three key trends expected to shape remote work in the next 1-2 years, citing your sources if possible.

In Usage	Style
Constrain AI-generated content to acceptable parameters that align with specified constraints.	Maintain consistency in tone, style, and content within creative outputs by avoiding deviations from a consistent style.

When crafting prompts, explicitly set boundaries to channel AI creativity appropriately.

These examples show setting boundaries for AI creativity, ensuring output aligns with specific requirements. The 'After' prompt constrains the AI's response within defined parameters.

Initial Prompt	Revised Prompt
`Generate marketing taglines.`	`Generate five marketing taglines for our new electric car, each no more than ten words long, focusing on environmental benefits and performance, and avoiding any unsubstantiated claims.`

Prompt Primers

```
Generate Type of Output, e.g., taglines, product descriptions, reports for
Topic/Product/Project, adhering to these constraints: Constraints, e.g.,
word count, tone, style guidelines, legal requirements. Exclude
unsubstantiated claims.
Provide a Type of Output for Task that is accurate, objective, and avoids
Specific Elements, e.g., speculation, subjective opinions. If including
creative elements, maintain a Specific Tone/Style.
Compose two AI prompts: one prioritizing creativity, the other demanding
strict accuracy.
```

Element 6: Step-by-Step Instruction

Use Step-by-Step Instructions for Complex Processes. Just as Strunk and White advocate for clear and orderly presentation of ideas, providing step-by-step instructions for multi-stage tasks ensures the AI follows a logical sequence, leading to more accurate execution and comprehensive results for complex business workflows.[9]

Complex tasks require structured guidance for better AI responses. This reduces AI confusion on multi-step tasks. Dividing a long sentence into two can allow an AI follows stepwise guidance better.

In Usage	Style
Sequence the prompt to provide a clear structure for the AI, ensuring accurate execution of multi-stage processes.	Applying a repeatable framework to prompts builds consistency, leading to logically structured, easily followed AI responses that make complex information more accessible.

Provide the additional guidance the moves from allowing the AI to structure the response to by breaking down the prompt into the steps to meet the objectives. **NOTE**: You can always use the AI to investigate alternative structures and frameworks for information to best present.

These examples show the effectiveness of providing step-by-step instructions for complex tasks. Breaking down the task into a logical sequence, the 'After' prompt ensures a more structured, accurate AI response.

Initial Prompt	Revised Prompt
`Create a project plan.`	`Create a project plan for launching our new product, including these steps: 1. Define project scope and objectives. 2. Identify key tasks and deliverables. 3. Assign resources and timelines. 4. Outline a communication plan. 5. Define success metrics.`

Prompt Primers

```
Provide a step-by-step guide on how to Task. Each step should include
Specific Details and be presented in a logical sequence.
Outline the process for Complex Task in these steps: 1. Step 1, 2. Step 2,
3. Step 3, etc. Include details for each step.
Rewrite Original Prompt with step-by-step instructions for the AI to ensure
a logically structured response.
```

Element 7: Define the Role

Assigning a persona or role prevents AI from responding off-topic or inconsistently. LLMs are trained on vast quantities of content from myriad perspectives. Assigning a role, as Strunk and White emphasize the importance of the writer's voice,[10] specifying the desired persona or role for the AI (e.g., marketing analyst, customer service expert, financial advisor) provides crucial context, enabling it to tailor its language, knowledge, and perspective to the specific business need, leading to more relevant and insightful responses. Giving the AI relevant role and background information and examples of the desired output style based on the persona or role helps it understand the specific needs and expectations of your organization.

In Usage	Style
Provide the AI with role-based contextual information to tailor its response and knowledge, preventing vague or inconsistent outputs.	Assign the AI a specific role (e.g., customer support representative, sales assistant) and define its tone, style, and personality traits to ensure brand consistency and a business-appropriate tone, enhancing the user experience.

Act as a seasoned market research analyst or an instructor onboarding a new employee who is unfamiliar with the concept, adds perspective to the responses. Instructing the AI to adopt a specific persona or role (e.g., "Act as a marketing expert") enables the AI to guide its tone, style, and focus .

Customization Questions:

- What is the primary function of your AI?
- How should your users understand its capabilities and limitations?
- Should AI act as a teacher, assistant, consultant, or something else?

Example Adaptations:

- **Customer Support AI**: *"Assist customers by providing accurate, friendly, and quick responses to product questions."*
- **Legal Compliance AI**: *"Provide structured guidance on regulatory policies without offering legal advice."*
- **Educational AI**: *"Explain programming concepts in a clear and interactive manner."*

Notes: You will see that roles become personas and representatives that align roles with the user's expectations and brand identity in later chapters.

These examples show how assigning a specific role to the AI influences its tone, style, and focus. The 'After' prompt provides the AI with a persona, leading to a more contextually appropriate response.

Initial Prompt	Revised Prompt
`Analyze the current trends in the e-commerce industry, focusing on mobile commerce and social commerce, and provide three key insights.`	`Act as a market research analyst. Analyze the current trends in the e-commerce industry, focusing on mobile commerce and social commerce, and provide three key insights.`

Prompt Primers

```
Assume the role of a Specific Role, e.g., marketing analyst, customer
service expert, financial advisor. Provide Type of Output for Task,
focusing on Specific Area of Expertise."
As a Specific Role, your task is to Task. Tailor your response to Target
Audience, reflecting the tone and style of a Specific Persona.
Define an AI assistant's role in three industries: healthcare, legal, and
marketing. Ensure each definition is clear.
```

Element 8: Provide Examples

Provide examples for clarity and desired output style. Just as examples can illuminate complex concepts in writing, supplying the AI with examples of the desired output format, style, or content can significantly enhance the accuracy and relevance of its responses, particularly when requesting creative content or specific types of analysis.

AI learns from examples. While Strunk and White advised using figures of speech sparingly, direct and relevant examples help AI minimize the misinterpretation of vague or abstract concepts.[11]

In Usage	Style
Aid AI understanding of the requested output type, improving accuracy.	Demonstrate the desired format, tone, and style to ensure alignment with user expectations.

These examples show the power of providing AI with examples of the desired output. The 'After' prompt offers a model for AI to follow, resulting in a response aligning better with user expectations.

Initial Prompt	Revised Prompt
`Write a product description for our new noise-canceling headphones that is similar in tone and style to our other products in the headphone line.`	`Write a product description for our new noise-canceling headphones that is similar in tone and style to the product descriptions for headphones on our website: link to headphones product page`

Prompt Primers

```
Provide a Type of Output for Task, using this example as a format, style,
and content guide: Example. Explain its effectiveness.
Generate Type of Output similar in tone, style, and length to these
examples: Example 1, Example 2, Example 3.
Compose two AI prompts: one with an example, one without. Compare the
responses.
```

Element 9: What to Avoid

Telling AI what to exclude is as important as telling it what to include. Providing AI with exclusions helps prevent irrelevant, off-brand, or off-message responses. This is critical for brand alignment, compliance, and audience targeting and can help to eliminate bias, controversy, or unwanted topics. Without exclusions, AI may include irrelevant details.

In Usage	Style
Use explicit 'Do' and 'Don't' instructions to guide AI responses.	Refine AI output for focus and alignment with the desired tone and content. Explicit exclusions prevent irrelevant details.

Examples of extending the effectiveness of a prompt by exclusion include

- Do not use jargon or technical terms—keep it beginner-friendly.
- Avoid mentioning competitors.
- Do not include personal opinions—stick to factual analysis.

These examples highlight the importance of specifying what AI should not include in responses. The 'After' prompt guides AI to avoid irrelevant or inappropriate content, ensuring more focused output.

Initial Prompt	Revised Prompt
`Write a social media post for LinkedIn about the partnership with.`	`Draft a LinkedIn post announcing our strategic partnership with(). Do not include any specific revenue projections or confidential information about the deal. Keep the post to what is disclosed in the press release below.`

Prompt Primers

```
Generate Type of Output for Task. Exclude Specific Exclusions, e.g.,
jargon, technical terms, personal opinions, competitor mentions. Include
Specific Inclusions.
Provide Type of Output for Topic. Avoid Specific Elements. Include Specific
Information and maintain Desired Tone/Style.
Compose a prompt that excludes specific topics. Analyze the AI's response.
```

Element 10: Iterative Questions

Leverage the conversational nature of many AI systems to tackle complex problems through iterative refinement, building on previous insights for comprehensive, nuanced solutions.

Strunk and White advised against loosely configured sentences.[12] Generative AIs, often built on conversational processes, can likewise follow a reasoned, logical progression.

Often, an initial query starts the refinement process. Asking iterative questions allows for the development of an argument or analysis through a logical progression of ideas. This prevents rigid and one-off interactions.

In Usage	Style
Facilitate in-depth exploration of complex issues through iterative refinement.	Enhance user engagement and productivity in problem-solving. Ensure logical flow in multi-turn responses using conversational structure for fluidity.

As an example, start with a general question about market entry and then progressively ask more specific questions about regulatory requirements, competitive landscape, and potential marketing strategies in subsequent turns.

NOTE: It is important to lead the AI through this process rather than allowing it to control the strategic direction of the input.

These examples show how a series of interconnected prompts can lead to more refined, comprehensive AI responses. The 'After' prompts encourage a conversational approach for better results.

Initial Prompt	Revised Prompt

`Write marketing copy for our new software aimed at small business owners, highlighting time and money savings, and include a call to action for a free trial.`	`1) Write marketing copy for new software. Focus on the key benefit of saving time for small business owners.`
	`2) Improve the marketing copy to emphasize the cost-saving aspects for small businesses and make the tone more enthusiastic.`
	`3) Further refine the marketing copy to include a clear call to action to sign up for a free trial and ensure the message is under 100 words.`

Prompt Primers

To demonstrate leveraging the conversational nature of AI systems to tackle complex problems through interconnected prompts, allowing for iterative refinement and more comprehensive solutions.

```
Begin with this question: Initial Question. Refine the response by asking
follow-up questions to explore Specific Aspects in detail. Structure it as
a multi-turn conversation of at least three turns.
Guide the AI through a complex task using iterative questioning. Start with
Initial Prompt and provide follow-up prompts that build upon previous
responses to achieve Desired Outcome.
Transform a one-time question into a multi-turn interaction. Design a
three-turn AI conversation where each response builds on the preceding one.
```

Advanced AI Communication

Ultimately, effective AI communication yields tangible business value. This is achieved by aligning AI interactions with the goals of both the originator and the audience, ensuring the technology serves strategic objectives and drives cohesive results.

Element 11: Define Your Voice

How you converse with an AI significantly influences its responses. To ensure a seamless and professional user experience, it's crucial to guide the AI to adopt a voice that aligns with your communication goals. This involves specifying the desired tone, style, and personality, as well as providing guidance on grammar, word choice, and terminology.

In Usage	Style
Provide grammar and word choice guidance to follow, aligning the response with the prompt's requirements and suggestions.	Make communication more direct, impactful, and easier to understand, leading to clearer and more direct sentence structures, improving understanding.

Tone and Style

Instruct the AI to respond in tones appropriate for the desired usage of the content. For example, prompts can specify "a friendly, casual tone suitable for a startup audience" or a "professional and helpful tone, as outlined in customer service guidelines."

Initial Prompt	Revised Prompt
`Respond to this customer email.`	`Respond to this customer email using a friendly, professional, and helpful tone, as outlined in our customer service guidelines. Avoid sounding robotic or overly formal.`

Grammar and Word Choice

Encourage AI to generate responses using active voice for more direct, clear, impactful communication, essential for effective information conveyance in a business context. Use the same verbs for actions (e.g., always "summarize" instead of switching between "condense," "outline," "paraphrase").

Initial Prompt	Revised Prompt
`What were the key findings of the customer survey?`	`Summarize the key findings of the recent customer satisfaction survey using active voice, clearly stating the opinions and`

	preferences expressed by the respondents regarding our product's usability, features, and customer support.

Terminology

To ensure a professional and coherent communication style, AI must maintain terminology consistency, particularly for technical or industry-specific terms, thereby avoiding confusion.

Initial Prompt	Revised Prompt
`Explain the benefits of our user interface.`	`Describe the key advantages of our user interface (UI). Ensure consistent use of the abbreviation 'UI' throughout your explanation.`

NOTE: For AI systems with custom chatbots, add a custom dictionary of terms and acronyms to the AI's lexicon to ensure the same language is used across the organization, whether internally focused or customer-facing.

Prompt Primers

```
Generate a Type of Output for Task with a Specific Tone, e.g., friendly,
formal, casual and a Specific Style, e.g., professional, conversational,
technical. Omit phrases that identify you as an AI. Use active voice.
Direct the AI to adopt a specific voice by defining the desired tone,
personality, and key terms. For example, respond to Task as a Specific
Persona using Specific Language.
Compose three AI responses: one formal, one neutral, and one casual.
Compare them." "Transform a passive-voice prompt into active voice."
Finance AI: Consistently use "financial forecast," not "sales forecast,"
"revenue forecast," or "projections."
```

Element 12: Seek and Anticipate Nuance

Whether you are seeking nuance or avoiding complex situations, give the AI a means to adjust the output by anticipating edge cases for robust and reliable AI performance.

This offers twofold improvement. If asking AI to consider potential use cases, be aware of unusual scenarios it might encounter and include instructions on handling them for robust, reliable behavior. Additionally, bypass generalized knowledge that the user knows to deliver insight and nuance. Proactively considering potential edge cases offers more nuanced information.

Strunk and White would advocate for thoroughness and coverage in content, reflecting the importance of addressing potential ambiguities and avoiding unexpected scenarios.[13] Add a constraint to limit responses, stating, "If no relevant data is found, state 'No information available.'"

Broad prompts to AI are the Strunk and White equivalent of 'taking shortcuts to clarity,' preferring standard language to offbeat examples.

In Usage	Style
Ensure predictable and reliable AI behavior in non-standard situations and prevent incorrect assumptions in uncertain cases for factual accuracy across audiences.	Prevent inappropriate or unhelpful responses in unusual circumstances and provide AI fallback mechanisms for exceptions, nuance, or information gaps.

These examples show how to prompt AI to handle complex or ambiguous situations. The 'After' prompt encourages the AI to consider nuance and provide more robust responses.

Initial Prompt	Revised Prompt
`Summarize these customer reviews.`	`Summarize these customer reviews, noting both positive and negative feedback. If a review expresses sarcasm or irony, flag it as 'ambiguous' and do not include it in the sentiment analysis.`

In information-rich environments, the AI's value lies in providing specific, nuanced insight through added context. Conversely, in data-poor or novel situations, its reliability and predictable performance become paramount.

Abundance Prompt	Limited Prompt
`Summarize recent customer reviews for our product, focusing only on feedback related to ease of use and identify the top three recurring themes. Additionally, highlight any significant individual instances or edge cases related to ease of use that might offer valuable, less common insights.`	`Based on the limited information available about the emerging field of quantum marketing, outline three potential future applications for our business while clearly stating the speculative nature of the response.`

Prompt Primer

```
Compose an AI response for two audiences: a beginner and an expert. When
analyzing customer review sentiment, flag reviews containing sarcasm or
irony that might skew the sentiment score as 'ambiguous' instead of
assigning a positive or negative score.
```

Element 13: Continuous Improvement

Test, Iterate, and Refine Prompts for Continuous Improvement.

Effective communication is the process of editing and revision. Strunk and White mused that manuscripts needed major surgery was common in all writing, 'even among the best writers.[14] This is also true for an AI. It is critical to take multiple passes with an AI and ask to rewrite or restate.

Prompt engineering is an iterative process; constant testing leads to better AI performance.

1. Create a baseline prompt
2. Generate AI responses
3. Revise the prompt
4. Compare improvements.

In Usage	Style
Refine prompts based on AI outputs to enhance response quality and relevance.	Emphasize iterative prompt engineering, encouraging experimentation and refinement for optimal results. Track and analyze the impact of prompt changes.

Experiment with different phrasing, levels of detail, and output format specifications for the same task and track the quality and relevance of the AI's responses to identify the most effective prompting techniques.

These examples show the iterative nature of prompt engineering. The 'After' prompts encourage testing, refining, and improving prompts for better AI performance.

Initial Prompt	Revised Prompt

`Write a better marketing tagline.`	`"Version 1: Write a marketing tagline."`
	`"Version 2: Refine the tagline to be more concise."`
	`"Version 3: Further refine the tagline to emphasize the product's key benefit."`

Prompt Primers

```
Test different prompt versions, compare AI responses, and refine prompts to
improve output accuracy, relevance, and style. Document the changes and
their effects.
Iteratively refine prompts by analyzing AI output, identifying areas for
improvement, and revising prompts. Repeat this process until the desired
outcome is achieved.
Compose a baseline prompt. Generate AI responses. Revise the prompt.
Compare the improvements in AI responses.
```

User Function

This section concludes by highlighting the importance of prioritizing user goals over AI features to ensure that AI interactions deliver genuine business value.

Element 14: Prioritizing User Goals in AI Interaction

Business users ought to frame their prompts with a clear focus on desired commercial outcomes rather than merely exploring an AI's functionalities. This approach ensures that AI interactions are purposeful and contribute directly to strategic goals.

A prompt should articulate a clear objective, enabling the AI to act upon the request with minimal interpretation. By prioritizing the intended business value, users can steer AI interactions toward producing meaningful and strategically aligned results.

In Usage	Style
Frame prompts with a clear focus on achieving specific business objectives and outcomes.	Ensure purposeful AI usage, driving tangible business value rather than showcasing AI capabilities. Prompts should clearly state the desired business outcome from the AI's response.

These examples show how to frame prompts with a clear focus on achieving specific business outcomes. The 'After' prompt guides AI to provide actionable solutions aligned with business objectives.

Initial Prompt	Revised Prompt
`What can AI do with this data?`	`Analyze this sales data to identify opportunities for increasing customer lifetime value. Suggest three specific strategies for achieving this, with projected outcomes.`

Prompt Primer

```
Frame prompts with a clear focus on the desired business outcome. For
example, instead of asking 'What can you do with our customer data?', ask
'Analyze customer purchase history over the past year to identify Specific
Goal - e.g., cross-selling opportunities and suggest three distinct
strategies to achieve it.
Ensure prompts have a clear objective and purpose, minimizing AI
misinterpretation. Prompts should clearly state the desired business
outcome from the AI's response. Include key performance indicators (KPIs).
Rewrite Original Prompt to focus more on a specific business outcome.
Include the business problem the prompt aims to solve.
```

Element 15: Maintain a Consistent Personality / Brand Voice

For organizations using AI in customer-facing roles or content creation, echoing Strunk and White's call for consistent tone, maintaining a consistent personality[15] in AI responses is crucial for building brand identity and trust, ensuring all AI interactions align with the established brand voice and values.

Providing AI sufficient context and clarity in each prompt enables AI to tailor responses appropriately, ensuring information remains relevant and personalized to the interaction stage and user needs.

NOTE: This also is an extension of utilizing the brand in AI prompts and responses. This will be covered in detail in Brand chapter. For now, leveraging an existing or defined brand voice and style, instructs the AI to generate responses that are consistent with this established brand identity to ensure all communications contribute to a cohesive brand image.

In Usage	Style
Essential for building brand identity and trust by ensuring all AI interactions align with established brand voice and values.	Enhance brand perception, increase customer loyalty, and ensure a seamless user experience across all touchpoints.

Directly connecting a consistent tone and style across prompts and interactions among team members and even across the organization enhances the outcomes. Imagine an AI responding to customer inquiries via chat, maintain a friendly, helpful, and professional tone that aligns with our company's customer service guidelines, as outlined in our brand manual.

These examples show how to instruct the AI to maintain a consistent personality or brand voice. The 'After' prompt ensures AI's responses align with the desired brand identity.

Initial Prompt	Revised Prompt
`Answer this customer inquiry.`	`As a customer service representative for our company, answer this customer inquiry in a friendly, helpful, and professional tone, consistent with our brand's customer service guidelines.`

Prompt Primers

```
In customer-facing AI roles, ensure AI responses maintain a consistent
personality aligned with the brand's voice and values. Provide AI with
context and clarity for appropriate tailoring. Include brand voice
guidelines.
Direct the AI to generate responses consistent with the established brand
identity. For example, 'Act as a Brand Persona and respond to Task using
Brand Voice Guidelines.' Provide on-brand response examples
Provide a customer service interaction example and ask the AI to role-play
it, maintaining a consistent brand personality. Include a negative example
and have the AI explain why it is off-brand.
```

Element 16: Collaborating with an AI

To foster a more collaborative, less authoritarian feel, encourage AI to offer suggestions rather than direct commands, improving user engagement and making AI feel more like a helpful assistant.

Engage with energy, encourage input, and be transparent about purpose and needs. Giving clear, concise direction in a positive tone will reflect that tone in the output.

In Usage	Style
Encourage a more collaborative interaction with the AI.	Enhance the likelihood of AI advice adoption.

If your directions to AI offer no room for contribution, you potentially limit the value AI can contribute. Instead of prompting "Implement this marketing strategy," the AI could say, "Consider implementing this marketing strategy to potentially increase customer engagement."

These examples illustrate how to encourage a more collaborative interaction with the AI. The 'After' prompts invite the AI to offer suggestions and engage in a more interactive way.

Initial Prompt	Revised Prompt
`Tell me how to improve team productivity.`	`What strategies should our team consider to improve productivity? Please provide suggestions and the reasoning behind each.`

Prompt Primers

```
Encourage AI to offer suggestions instead of issuing direct commands. For
example, instead of prompting 'Implement this strategy,' ask 'What
strategies should I consider to achieve Goal?' Include a prompt for pros
and cons of each suggestion.
Frame prompts to invite collaboration and AI input. Use a positive tone and
be transparent about the request's purpose and needs. Ask the AI to justify
its suggestions.
Rewrite Original Prompt to encourage a more collaborative AI response. Ask
the AI to provide alternative solutions and their reasoning.
```

Element 17: Careful and Honest Use

Strunk and White's first piece of advice on style was to place yourself in the background.[16] This is also true when working with AI. To achieve this, be proficient in engaging with AI, but keep it in the background. Recognize that AI usage should not come at the expense of the writer or the work. To Strunk and White, writing is thinking; losing it robs the writer of thought and learning opportunity. Strunk and White might say of AI, "A careful and honest writer does not need to worry about AI."[17]

When prompting AI (e.g., with data, preferences), ensure information is accurate and up-to-date. Understand AI limitations and critically evaluate its output. If output is unexpected, challenge it and look for prompt assumptions or data biases. When the response aligns, repeat the bias/assumption check. Rephrase the prompt to establish response veracity and validity. Use AI systems respectfully and fairly and avoid generating harmful or biased content. Be aware of AI capabilities and limitations; avoid tasks beyond its capabilities or ethical boundaries.

An AI should be informationally based, not opinion or emotionally biased. This ensures factual accuracy and avoids subjective words unless explicitly instructed.

In Usage	Style
Verify the accuracy and currency of input data, especially for critical tasks. Consider the ethical implications of AI interactions and prevent its use for harmful or biased outputs. Acknowledge and mitigate the potential for AI to reflect or amplify biases present in the input data.	Maintain a critical perspective; avoid attributing human-like qualities or relying on AI for subjective judgment. Recognize AI as a tool that augments, but does not replace, human intellect. Ensures the AI's responses are objective and data-driven. Reinforces the AI's role as a reliable and unbiased source of information. Avoid overly positive or negative bias. Establish acceptable tone levels (e.g., "friendly but not overly enthusiastic")."

These examples emphasize your responsibility to ensure ethical, accurate, and effective AI use. The 'After' prompts prioritize data integrity, bias awareness, and critical evaluation of AI output.

Initial Prompt	Revised Prompt

`Analyze customer data to identify trends.`	`Analyze customer data from our CRM system from the past year to identify trends in purchase behavior.`
	`Specify that the analysis should exclude any personally identifiable information (PII).`
	`Acknowledge potential biases in the data due to limitations in data collection methods (e.g., demographics overrepresentation).`
	`Explicitly state that the analysis should be checked for accuracy and bias by a human analyst before being used for decision-making.`
	`Cite the source of the CRM data and confirm its last update date.`

Prompt Primer

```
When using AI for content generation, detail the steps taken to ensure
input data accuracy and minimize bias. Outline a process for human
verification of the AI's output, focusing on factual correctness, potential
biases, and ethical considerations.
Compose a prompt for a complex AI analysis. Include a statement clarifying
that the AI's output is preliminary and will undergo critical human review
before any action is taken.
```

```
Develop a series of prompts for using AI in a creative brainstorming session. The
prompts should guide the AI while preserving human creative input and critical
judgment.
```

Workbook: Elements of AI Style for Everyday Use

Designed as a practical daily reference, these tables distill core elements into fundamental usage and style definitions. Refer to these tables for quick guidance when crafting prompts, evaluating AI outputs, and navigating AI-augmented workflows.

Element 1: Be Clear and Specific

Minimize AI misinterpretations by precisely defining the task, desired output, and constraints to ensure it understands the intended scope.

Guide the AI towards generating focused and relevant responses that directly address the objective, enhancing actionability and usefulness.

Element 2: Specify the Desired Output

Directs the AI to structure its output for technical usability and seamless integration into business workflows.

Optimizes AI output for readability and usability, enabling efficient extraction of essential business information.

Element 3: Keep Responses Short and Readable

Establish guidelines for maximum response length to promote conciseness.

Prioritize concise wording to enhance readability and user engagement.

Element 4: Control the Level of Detail

Direct the AI to focus on delivering the most relevant and appropriate level of analysis.

Provide information tailored to strategic needs, enabling users to efficiently grasp key insights.

Element 5: Create Controlled and Predictable Output

Constrain AI-generated content to acceptable parameters that align with specified constraints.

Maintain consistency in tone, style, and content within creative outputs by avoiding deviations from a consistent style.

Element 6: Step-by-Step Instruction

Sequence the prompt to provide a clear structure for the AI, ensuring accurate execution of multi-stage processes.

Applying a repeatable framework to prompts builds consistency, leading to logically structured, easily followed AI responses that make complex information more accessible.

Element 7: Define the Role

Provide the AI with role-based contextual information to tailor its response and knowledge, preventing vague or inconsistent outputs.

Assign the AI a specific role (e.g., customer support representative, sales assistant) and define its tone, style, and personality traits to ensure brand consistency and a business-appropriate tone, enhancing the user experience.

Element 8: Provide Examples

Aid AI understanding of the requested output type, improving accuracy.

Demonstrate the desired format, tone, and style to ensure alignment with user expectations.

Element 9: What to Avoid

Use explicit 'Do' and 'Don't' instructions to guide AI responses.

Refine AI output for focus and alignment with the desired tone and content. Explicit exclusions prevent irrelevant details.

Element 10: Iterative Questions

Facilitate in-depth exploration of complex issues through iterative refinement.

Enhance user engagement and productivity in problem-solving. Ensure logical flow in multi-turn responses using conversational structure for fluidity.

Element 11: Define Your Voice

Provide grammar and word choice guidance to follow, aligning the response with the prompt's requirements and suggestions.

Make communication more direct, impactful, and easier to understand, leading to clearer and more direct sentence structures, improving understanding.

Element 12: Seek and Anticipate Nuance

Ensure predictable and reliable AI behavior in non-standard situations and prevent incorrect assumptions in uncertain cases for factual accuracy across audiences.

Prevent inappropriate or unhelpful responses in unusual circumstances and provide AI fallback mechanisms for exceptions, nuance, or information gaps.

Element 13: Continuous Improvement

Refine prompts based on AI outputs to enhance response quality and relevance.

Emphasize iterative prompt engineering, encouraging experimentation and refinement for optimal results. Track and analyze the impact of prompt changes.

Element 14: Prioritize User Goals Over AI Features for Business Value

Frame prompts with a clear focus on achieving specific business objectives and outcomes.

Ensure purposeful AI usage, driving tangible business value rather than showcasing AI capabilities. Prompts should clearly state the desired business outcome from the AI's response.

Element 15: Maintain a Consistent Personality

Essential for building brand identity and trust by ensuring all AI interactions align with established brand voice and values.

Enhance brand perception, increase customer loyalty, and ensure a seamless user experience across all touchpoints.

Element 16: Collaborating with an AI

Encourage a more collaborative interaction with the AI.

Enhance the likelihood of AI advice adoption.

Element 17: Careful and Honest Use

Verify the accuracy and currency of input data, especially for critical tasks. Consider the ethical implications of AI interactions and prevent its use for harmful or biased

Maintain a critical perspective; avoid attributing human-like qualities or relying on AI for subjective judgment. Recognize AI as a tool that augments, but does not replace, human intellect. Ensures the AI's responses are

outputs. Acknowledge and mitigate the potential for AI to reflect or amplify biases present in the input data.	objective and data-driven. Reinforces the AI's role as a reliable and unbiased source of information. Avoid overly positive or negative bias. Establish acceptable tone levels (e.g., "friendly but not overly enthusiastic")."

Concordance of AI Style & Usage

William Strunk Jr. and E.B. White provided rules for good writing, drawn from Strunk's lectures that White, his student and later co-author, attended.[18] Throughout *The Elements of Style*, they advocated for clarity, precision, conciseness, and an active voice. They emphasized grammar, mechanics, and revision as crucial elements of effective writing. Ultimately, they placed the responsibility for clear communication on the writer.

Strunk died before the computer age, and White before word processing and digital documents became prevalent. The fourth edition of *The Elements of Style*, the last edited by either author, contains no mention of terms like "digital," "artificial," or "Internet." At that time, technology was just beginning to enter classrooms and boardrooms. Strunk and White likely did not consider rules for humanizing AI or creating AI personas. While their guide promotes conciseness, AI interaction sometimes requires detailed instructions and complex prompts to achieve specific results. Strunk and White might have viewed overly long or convoluted prompts as a threat to clear communication, even if they serve a practical purpose in AI interaction. When prompted to speculate on how the authors might have amended their book, AI responses vary. Yet, adherence to clear rules would create internal and external agreement and consistency when working with AI. The principles of clear thinking, precise execution, and efficiency championed by Strunk and White find resonance in effective AI communication. While their work predates algorithms, bias detection, and AI personas, their emphasis on clarity and the writer's responsibility remains crucial. Achieving 'concordance' in AI – the harmonious alignment of intention, prompt, and output – demands that we adapt their timeless principles to the nuances of this new technology.

In the fourth edition, they referenced the 'Trend Machine':

> *Your whole duty as a writer is to please and satisfy yourself, and the true writer always plays to an audience of one. Start sniffing the air, or glancing at the Trend Machine, and you are as good as dead, although you may make a nice living.*[19]

Just as they considered a dictionary a reliable check for common sense, they might have embraced technology as a tool to assist them, but they never gave up on the elements that defined their style. A 'trend machine' would only be used if it aligned wholly with the writer's intentions and integrity.

Practical AI Style

Elements introduces the grammar of effective AI prompting through 17 Core elements of usage and style, providing users with a repeatable flow.

From prompts and responses vary wildly …

Users operate by instinct, trial and error, not method. Prompts are vague, mostly too short, others are overly long or passive. AI outputs lack clarity, direction, or usability.

… to repeatable clarity and command of AI.

Users apply structured elements (e.g., define role, specify output). Outputs are concise, clear, and consistent. Prompting becomes a skill that scales across teams and organization.

3 Elements

Summary

Elements distilled the foundations of AI communication. Here, usage promotes legibility; style fosters alignment. Together, they create the grammar of interaction—how systems articulate themselves on your behalf. But understanding the mechanics is only half the task. Now, we shift from individual elements to orchestration: how prompts, personas, and practice coalesce into coherent, repeatable frameworks of performance.

3 Elements Recap

Practical
AI Style

Practical AI Style

We have introduced the elemental interactions with AI; now we assemble them with the required engineering for success. Combine individual style elements to craft and engineer prompts that provide context, insight, and outcomes on a broader scale.

4 Assemble

Attent to Prompts

When "**Attent**" was first defined, around the time of early printed books, monks were still actively scribing. The Oxford Universal Dictionary definition emphasizes directing intention, eagerness, and attention toward an objective and outcome. In communicating with AI, this quality of "**Attent**" is crucial.[1]

In this context, "Attent" is the act of intentionally focusing AI capabilities through a written prompt carrying specific direction and often reflecting a desired outcome. Your prompt focuses AI processing on a specific topic, question, or task, essentially directing its "attention" to the information provided and the response sought. A well-crafted prompt reflects your desire for specific output, guiding AI toward a specific goal with underlying eagerness for a relevant, helpful answer. Consequently, the more specific and directive your prompt, the more focused the AI's response.

We have been set up for failure

Unlike traditional search, AI creates answers rather than merely retrieving them. The digital and social media age has consistently driven text reduction. Paragraphs condense into bulleted lists, emails into subject lines, searches into keywords, and emojis convey emotional and empathetic context. Across texting, smart devices, TikTok, and search engines, we have pursued and conveyed information with an economy of brevity. Emojis now convey meaning, respond, and imply intent and attention. This has eroded our ability for exposition and thoughtful knowledge exchange.

While traditional search queries typically consist of 2-3 words, remaining consistent over the past decade,[2] the latest AI models, such as GPT-4 Turbo, support context windows of approximately 96,000 words. This extensive capacity enables an AI to process and analyze substantial documents, including entire books, like this one at ~55,000 words, in a single interaction.[3]

Consider an internet search, which requires minimal context to locate a source, compared to an AI system that thrives on it. Greater contextual detail in a prompt yield more responsive results. Beyond the core question, AI also considers who is asking, the request's context, and the desired outcome or task. This requires deliberate context inclusion, not mere wordiness. Building prompts articulate your needs for the best response—giving AI your '**Attent**.' This is done through prompt engineering: reframing a question into logical code that an AI system can understand and act upon.

Prompt Engineering

Clear communication and defined style are essential in business. Prompt engineering applies these principles—style and usage—when instructing AI. Precise instructions help AI understand and execute tasks effectively, leading to better results. Prompt engineering is the craft of writing prompts that convey your desired style and usage. Structure input carefully to improve AI performance and meet business objectives.

Though AI uses natural language, it needs structure within prompts to apply your style effectively and produce the desired outcome. Think of AI as an intelligent but literal assistant; clear instructions are crucial. Prompt engineering crafts these instructions, or "prompts," to guide AI toward the desired output. This allows for the shaping of AI's response and even the assignment of specialized roles. Unlike simple keyword searching, prompt engineering conveys your intent in natural language. This helps AI grasp nuance and generate richer, more relevant responses. Incorporating your style, usage, and brand guidelines, as discussed next regarding consistency, is key to harnessing AI capabilities for your business.

Consistency Matters

To instruct AI effectively, use clear, concise, consistent language. Employ strong action verbs (e.g., "summarize," "generate," "analyze") as discussed. Reference tags create this structure. A reference tag is a short label, often in brackets like this, that identifies and categorizes parts of your prompt, guiding both AI and the reader.

Using tags helps AI identify the core components of your request: Role, Context, and Task. AI primarily seeks three elements in a prompt: the Role it should assume, the Context of the request, and the specific Task it must perform.

- **Role**: Defines the persona or expertise for AI (e.g., "Act as a marketing strategist," "You are a helpful historian"). This guides its knowledge access and communication style.
- **Context**: Provides background, situation, or setting (e.g., "Small business owner, limited budget," "Launching new product for millennials," "Transcript of customer conversation follows"). This defines the scope and relevance.
- **Task**: States clearly what AI must do (e.g., "Write three headlines," "Summarize the report," "Generate ten creative ideas"). Make it specific and actionable, specifying the desired output.

Beyond Role, Context, and Task, other tags can improve AI's understanding and output quality. Consider adding:

- **Guidance**: Specific instructions on how AI should approach the task.
- **Format**: Specifies the desired output structure (e.g., bullet points, table, paragraph). Helps present information usefully.
- **Tone**: Indicates the desired emotional coloring or attitude (e.g., formal, friendly, empathetic). Helps align the response with your brand or situation.
- **Audience**: Defines the intended recipient (e.g., experts, general public, children). Helps tailor language and complexity.
- **Constraints**: Specifies limitations (e.g., word count limit, topics to avoid, sources not to use).
- **Output Length**: Explicitly states the desired response length (e.g., "approx 200 words," "three paragraphs").
- **Keywords**: Lists terms to include or avoid, ensuring relevance and alignment.

- **Examples**: Provides models of the desired output format, style, or content, helpful for complex or specific results.
- **Source Material**: Provides text, data, or documents for AI to use (crucial for summarization, analysis based on specifics).
- **Purpose/Goal**: Explains the overall objective of AI's response for higher-level understanding.
- **Desired Outcome**: Describes the ideal result you hope to achieve, possibly more specific than the task.

Iteration Instructions: Guides AI on how to handle revisions or further attempts if needed.

Writing Reference Tags

AI systems may vary in recommended tagging practices; however, well-formatted prompts with clear, meaningful tags are often portable.

- Keep tags brief and understandable. Use them consistently and document them for team use.
- Remember, prompt engineering is iterative.
- Experiment with tags and phrasing to find what works best with your AI.

Prompt Primer: Understanding AI Tag Preferences

Enter the prompt below to understand how a specific AI prefers tags. The AI's response will outline its preferred tag practices.

```
What is your preferred format for reference tags within prompts (e.g.,
square brackets [](#), angle brackets \<\>, other)?
Specify preferences for:
Enclosing characters (e.g., [](#), \<\>)
Capitalization (e.g., [TAG](#), [tag](#), [Tag](#))
Separator between tag and content (e.g., colon :, newline)
Provide an example prompt using your preferred format for:
Role
Context
Task
List common and useful prompt tags you recognize, formatted like this:
[Example](#), [Tone](#), [Role](#), [Constraints](#).
```

Building on Prompts: Iteration and Chaining

Often, a single prompt cannot directly achieve a complex goal. When this occurs, prompt engineering breaks the prompt up into multiple steps, including drafting, revising, and sectioning the work. Two primary techniques enhance the power of basic prompts: iterative prompting and prompt chaining.

Iterative Prompting: Refining the Request

Iterative prompting refines a single prompt through cycles of trial and adjustment. Essentially, it is the process of optimizing a prompt by repeatedly testing and modifying it based on the resulting output. This process resembles sculpting or tuning: start with a base and make successive adjustments. You can add or refine tags, change wording, adjust constraints, and provide better examples until the output precisely matches requirements. Follow this four-step cycle for iterative prompting:

1. **Define**: Clearly state the specific objective and success criteria. Formulate the initial prompt, including necessary elements (Role, Context, Task, tags) to guide the AI.
2. **Generate**: Input the prompt into the AI system. Obtain the generated output.
3. **Review & Revise**: Compare the generated output against the objectives defined in Step 1. Identify shortcomings. Based on this review, revise the prompt (adjust wording, refine tags, add constraints, provide better examples) to address the issues.
4. **Validate**: Examine the latest output. Does it fully satisfy the objectives set in Step 1? If Yes: The cycle is complete. If No: Return to (Define) to continue the cycle.

This iterative cycle emphasizes systematic refinement. Each loop provides feedback (the AI's output) that directly informs adjustments to the input (the prompt), guiding the process toward the desired result with clarity and purpose.

Workbook Iterative Prompting Example

This example shows the iterative cycle in action, starting with a simple idea and refining the prompt based on review.

Step	Action / Description
1. Define	Generate 5 catchy, unique slogans for a new reusable, bamboo coffee cup targeting eco-conscious millennials.
2. Generate	Run the initial prompt.
3. Revise	Output is generic, lacks uniqueness, misses key details (bamboo), and doesn't fit the target audience or desired tone. Add Role, Context, Tone, specific Keywords, Constraints for better guidance.
4. Validate	Action: Run the revised prompt. New Output: Validation: Output now meets objectives – unique, mentions bamboo, fits tone/audience. Cycle complete.

Prompt Chaining

Prompt chaining uses the output from one prompt as the input for the next. Essentially, this involves processing a task sequentially through multiple interconnected prompts. Think of it as links in a chain or steps in a process, where each prompt performs a specific part of a larger task, building upon the previous result. This method breaks complex work into manageable steps. Each prompt can focus narrowly on one action (e.g., brainstorming, outlining, drafting, summarizing, editing), making the overall process more controlled and the results potentially more accurate. Clarity in the task and context for each prompt is essential, as subsequent steps depend on the quality of the preceding one.[4]

Workbook: Prompt Chaining Example

Imagine creating a short report on a new market trend requiring a multidisciplinary perspective (market, business implications, risk assessment). Follow along as prompt chaining helps manage these distinct steps:

Step	Prompt

1. Research & Summarize	`[ROLE] You are a market research analyst.`
	`[CONTEXT] Review the provided articles (Source Material) on the electric vehicle market growth in Europe.`
	`[TASK] Summarize the key findings, growth projections, and major challenges mentioned in under 300 words.`
	`[FORMAT] Bullet points.`

2. Draft Introduction	`[ROLE] You are a business writer.`
	`[CONTEXT] Use the following key findings (Source Material: Output from Step 1) for an internal report.`
	`[TASK] Write a concise (approx. 100 words) introduction highlighting the significance of the European EV market trend for management.`
	`[TONE] Formal and informative.`

3. Identify Risks	`[ROLE] You are a risk analyst.`
	`[CONTEXT] Based on the key findings and challenges summarized earlier (Source Material: Output from Step 1), particularly the challenges.`
	`[TASK] List the top 3 potential business risks for a company entering this market.`
	`[FORMAT] Numbered list, brief explanation for each.`

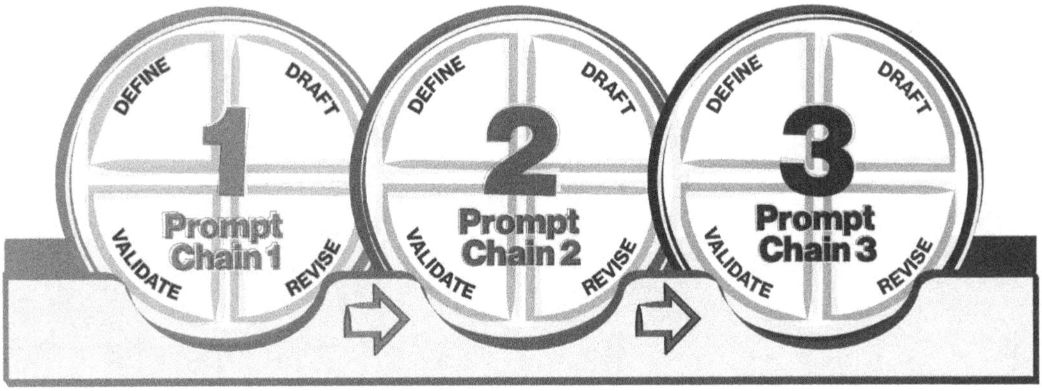

Agile Intelligence

These techniques—chaining and iteration—mirror principles found in agile methodologies.

- **Prompt Chaining** resembles decomposition. Breaking large, complex tasks into smaller, sequential, manageable units that are linked through a process flow.
- **Iterative Prompting** embodies the agile principle of continuous improvement through iteration and adaptation. The process begins by **defining** the prompt and its intent, followed by **drafting** the initial version to generate output. Based on feedback, you **revise** the prompt to improve clarity and relevance. Finally, you **validate** the output, making further adjustments as needed to ensure it meets your objectives.

Adopting this agile mindset for prompt engineering fosters a structured yet flexible way to interact with AI. It moves beyond simple requests towards a methodical process for tackling complexity. This emphasis on breaking down work, testing, learning, and adapting helps achieve specific, high-quality results more reliably. It enables rapid experimentation and refinement, using AI to quickly test variations of an idea or prompt, aligning its use with clear business objectives.

Prompt Clarity Through Structure

Sentence diagramming[5], though less common now, teaches how language fits together logically. Understanding sentence structure helps create clear, unambiguous prompts. Poorly structured prompts, like poorly structured sentences, can confuse AI. Consider these examples.

Ambiguous Prompt:

Summarize customer feedback mentioning the new feature focused on usability issues reported by new users.

(Ambiguity: Does 'focused on usability issues reported by new users' modify 'the new feature' or 'customer feedback'? The structure leaves room for doubt.)

```
[Imperative Clause]
    ├── Verb: Summarize
    └── Direct Object: customer feedback
        └── Modifier (participial): mentioning the new feature
            └── Modifier (participial): focused on usability issues
                └── Modifier (past participial): reported by new users
```

Clearer Prompts:

```
Summarize all customer feedback that mentions the new feature, specifically
highlighting usability issues reported by new users. (Clearly focuses on
highlighting within a broader summary.)
```

OR

```
Summarize customer feedback from new users that mentions the new feature,
focusing on their reported usability issues. (Clearly focuses the summary
on a specific user group and issue.)
```

Thinking about sentence structure forces a writer to see relationships between words—subjects, verbs, objects, and modifiers. This helps convey meaning accurately. By considering structure when writing prompts, you can more easily spot potential ambiguity. If AI responses are vague or off-topic, unclear phrasing in the prompt may be the cause. A structurally sound prompt is less likely to be misinterpreted by AI.

Workbook: Identifying Ambiguity

Instructions: Review the following prompts. Identify the potential ambiguity in each, noting which parts of the sentence could be interpreted in different ways. How would you revise each prompt for clarity? Consider testing the original and revised prompts with an AI to compare the results.

```
Brainstorm ways that advanced encryption can disrupt the current market of
secure financial transactions.
```

(Ambiguity: Disrupt the security of the market? Or offer new types of transactions?)

```
Analyze sales data for the last quarter showing growth in the technology
sector.
```

(Ambiguity: Focus the analysis on the part of the data showing growth? Or analyze data *from* the growing tech sector?)

```
Draft a marketing email to clients interested in our new AI product
highlighting its innovative features.
```

(Ambiguity: Assumes clients are already interested? Or targets clients who *might* be interested?)

```
Create a presentation for the board about the new sustainability
initiatives impacting our supply chain.
```

(Ambiguity: Initiatives causing an impact? Or describing initiatives related to the supply chain?)

While understanding structure helps you write clearly, some AI platforms may also assist by identifying potential ambiguities in prompts.

Adopting Mindsets for Engagement

Prompt engineering provides the language for instruction, but effective interaction requires the right mindset for inquiry. Just as Socratic dialogue used questioning to explore complex ideas and uncover understanding, our engagement with AI can be shaped by the approach we take to asking questions and seeking information. This involves adopting specific stances that define our intent and influence the nature of the AI's response. We can approach the AI with focused curiosity to spark discovery, employ the precision of an expert witness seeking specific insights and nuance, or embrace the openness of improvisation to foster collaborative exploration. Each mindset unlocks different potentials within the AI, guiding the interaction toward distinct outcomes

Demonstrate Your Curiosity

Unlike traditional search, which seeks precise answers, expressing curiosity within your prompt leads to more informative AI responses. Alberto Manguel defined curiosity as the bridge to the next question: "Curiosity is seldom rewarded with meaningful or satisfying answers, but rather an increased desire to ask more."[6] Phrasing prompts to express curiosity signals that you seek a deeper, more nuanced, or creative exploration. This often yields more detailed, insightful responses addressing your underlying interests. Expressing curiosity can lead AI to provide more explanatory answers, focus on highlighted areas, generate more creative outputs, and foster iterative dialogue. Crucially, expressing curiosity influences AI's response style, but current AIs do not possess human understanding or genuine curiosity.

Workbook: Phrasing Prompts with Curiosity

Use phrases that indicate curiosity to encourage broader or deeper exploration by AI. Include these in your initial prompt or use them as follow-up questions:

Questions	Style
"I'm curious about the specific impacts of..."	Express curiosity.
"Could you explain the underlying principles of...?"	Prompts for foundational understanding.
What if we considered... from a different perspective?	Encourages alternative viewpoints.
Specifically, I'm interested in the role of... within... Can you elaborate?	Guides the AI to a specific area.
How does... compare to... in terms of...?	Prompts for comparative analysis.
Can you provide some real-world examples of...?	Asks for practical application.

What are the potential limitations or criticisms of...?	Encourages critical thinking.
What are the key mechanisms that drive...?	Seeks to understand the process.
Imagine a scenario where... How would that change things?	Prompts for hypothetical exploration.
How is this concept applied in practice?	Focuses on real-world usage.
Walk me through the process of... step-by-step	Requests a thorough explanation.

Such phrasing can yield more detailed explanations and explore related topics.

Questioning an Expert Witness

From the expansive discovery sought through curiosity, we shift to an approach demanding pinpoint accuracy. Imagine being a lawyer questioning an expert witness on the stand. Just as a lawyer must pose clear, unambiguous questions to an expert witness when accuracy is paramount, so must you formulate precise prompts for AI when its analysis is critical for vital business decisions. The question's framing shapes not just the answer, but the entire outcome and resulting business implications.

Workbook: Precision in Questioning (The Enron Analogy)[7]

The Situation: During legal proceedings related to the Enron scandal, expert witnesses (accountants, financial analysts) were crucial. Imagine a prosecutor asking a general question:

General Question and Likely Outcome

Expert Witness, can you explain Enron's accounting practices?	The expert might provide a broad overview of mark-to-market accounting and special purpose entities. While informative, this might not directly address specific fraudulent activities

Specific Question and Likely Outcome

Expert Witness, focusing specifically on the transactions involving the 'Raptor' entities in the third quarter of 2001, and considering Enron's publicly traded stock price at that time, did the reported earnings accurately reflect the underlying economic reality of those transactions? If not, what were the implications for Enron's reported financial health?	This targeted question forces the expert to address a specific instance, connect it to market data, and evaluate the potential for misrepresentation. Such precise questioning is instrumental in uncovering facts. The difference lies in moving from a general query to a specific, fact-driven inquiry – a crucial skill in both law and prompt engineering.

Artificial Improv

Interacting with an AI is unlike rigid programming or simple Q&A. AI acts as a knowledgeable, yet often literal or unpredictable, partner. Thinking of the interaction as improvisation provides a useful approach. The goal becomes not a perfect script (a single prompt), but an open framework for collaboration. This improv mindset fosters adaptability and allows you to reframe the interaction as needed. Keith Johnstone's *Impro*, with its emphasis on spontaneity and narrative, provides a rich foundation for exploring improvisational human-AI collaboration.[8]

Rather than "a determination to prove their zany inventiveness" in a scene, Johnstone pushed for "a simplicity and ease" that allowed participants to get started.[9] Start simply. For your initial prompt, choose the obvious over the clever, especially when exploring information. Adopting this Johnstone-inspired improv approach moves AI interaction from a purely transactional query-response model to something more fluid, creative, and collaborative. It keeps the human firmly in the creative seat, using AI as a responsive tool and source of offers. Johnstone teaches that improvisation is not about being clever—it's about being open, and responsive.

Workbook: Improv AI Prompts

To practice starting simply and building upon AI responses iteratively to explore the concepts and components involved in a sample topic (e.g., constructing AI agents).

Improv	Prompt Example
Define the Area: Select a specific aspect of the topic of interest to explore with an AI.	`Core components of a basic autonomous AI agent.`
Start Broadly (Be Obvious): Write a basic initial prompt to the AI about your chosen area	`What are the fundamental components typically found in an AI agent?`
Accept the Offer ("Yes"): Read the AI's response. Identify one specific component, principle, or challenge mentioned that you want to understand better	`AI mentioned 'memory' as a fundamental component that you want to understand better.`
Build Upon It ("And..."): Formulate your next prompt. Explicitly reference the point you identified ("Yes...") and ask the AI to.	`And, how does short-term 'working' memory typically differ from long-term knowledge storage within an agent's architecture?`
Repeat: Continue the process for 2-3 more exchanges. Based on the AI's responses, follow the thread	`Regarding short-term memory ("Yes"), and what mechanisms prevent it from becoming overloaded?`

Starting with a broad question makes it easier to begin exploring a topic, and building on the AI's previous response ("Yes, And...") leads to a clearer understanding of specific components or design choices.

Who is Answering?

Mastering the art of engaging AI through focused inquiry, precise questioning, and open exploration unlocks its potential for discovery, insight, and collaborative outcomes. Yet, every effective conversation also depends on knowing the context of the conversation and with whom you are speaking. As we move from how to ask questions to setting the stage and who is providing the answers, we turn our attention to the power of defining the AI's context, role and personality.

CROW for Prompt Context

Characters, Relationships, Objectives, and Where

In improv, CROW (Characters, Relationships, Objectives, Where) establishes the essential elements of a scene.[10] Similarly, defining these CROW elements within your AI prompt provides crucial context. Clearly stating the 'who' (Characters, Relationships), 'why' (Objectives), and 'where/when' (Where) surrounding your request helps AI understand the situation and perform its task effectively. In improv, these CROW elements allow actors to assemble a plot and scene quickly by starting with the basic building blocks. Applied to AI prompting, they help structure the information AI needs.

Characters

Define the key 'actors' involved. This includes the AI's assigned persona ([ROLE]), your own implied role as the prompter, the target [AUDIENCE] for the AI's output, and any key individuals or groups mentioned within the [CONTEXT]. Clarity here helps AI tailor its language and focus.

Relationships

Specify the key relationships between the defined 'Characters,' or between characters and the situation. Is AI advising the user? Is the output for a senior executive or a peer? Is the context collaborative or adversarial? Defining these relationships adds vital nuance for AI's tone and perspective, often within the [CONTEXT] tag.

Objectives

State the primary goal driving the request or situation. What is the explicit [TASK] AI must perform? What is the underlying [PURPOSE/GOAL] of the generated output? Also consider the objectives of any key 'Characters' described in the [CONTEXT]. Clarity on objectives focuses AI's actions.

Specify the setting – the 'where' and 'when.' What physical, social, temporal, or digital environment forms the backdrop? This information typically belongs in the [CONTEXT].

Where

Workbook Using CROW for Prompt Context

Use the CROW framework (Characters, Relationships, Objectives, Where) to define key contextual elements for an AI prompt, ensuring AI fully understands the situation. Consider the provided scene or develop your own business scenario, then answer the following:

> *Two colleagues meet outside a conference room before an executive presentation to go over the final details of their pitch.*

Characters

Who are the key stakeholders, actors, and supporting actors relevant to this scenario (including AI's potential role, the user's role, and the audience for any output)?

Relationships

What are the crucial relationships between these characters (e.g., peer-to-peer, subordinate-to-executive, AI-as-coach)?

Objectives

What is the primary objective of the interaction described in the scenario? What is the goal of any AI task related to this scenario?

Where

Where and when does this scenario take place? What aspects of the environment (physical, organizational, temporal) are relevant context for AI?

Developing Personas

Prompting AI begins a conversation. The key question is: with whom? Like the Oracle of Delphi, AI's voice depends on how you approach and define it. The Oracle's responses were shaped by the questioner; similarly, AI's output reflects the persona you assign. Selecting AI's persona or conversational style is a unique capability of this technology. Interact with AI as consulting an oracle whose tone and style you command.

Defining a persona draws on understanding elements of character. Elements such as status, objective, and mask, drawn from Keith Johnstone's Impro. Define the AI's status relative to the task; the [ROLE] tag sets this. Adding objectives or attitudes informs responses, for example: 'You are a skeptical editor,' 'You are an enthusiastic math tutor,' or 'You are a calm, reassuring customer service representative'. Adopting a mask allows AI to access specific knowledge and adopt distinct styles. Simplicity is often most effective initially; establish a simple role and avoid unnecessary complexity.

Workbook

An effective way to quickly build a persona to simulate a perspective, decision-making lens, or expertise area is to convert a job description to a prompt. This can enable you to test ideas against known priorities and real-world operational processes.

Step 1:

Examine an existing job description of a stakeholder role in your process. Extract these points from the description (an AI can assist with this).

Prompt Variable	What to Look For
[ROLE]	Job title or function
[GOALS]	What they're accountable for (e.g., KPIs, team outcomes, strategy alignment)
[RESPONSIBILITIES]	Daily or strategic duties that define their influence
[CONSTRAINTS]	Known pressures—budget, time, cross-functional complexity
[STYLING/FRAMING]	Keywords, frameworks, or language commonly used in this role
[TASK/QUESTION]	The action you want the AI persona to perform or respond to

Step 2:

Build Prompt from Job Description:

```
Assume the mindset of a [ROLE] focused on [GOALS]. Your responsibilities
include [RESPONSIBILITIES], and you operate under [CONSTRAINTS]. You tend
to think in terms of [STYLING/FRAMING]. Given the following
[TASK/QUESTION], what would your priorities, challenges, and
recommendations be?
```

How Personas Shape Responses

We often try to think like others, inspired by what we have read and what we know about the person. We try to think as they would. AI takes this ability to an extreme. There is a difference between saying "You are Steve Jobs" to AI and "Assume the mindset..." The first is a simulation; the latter is an abstraction. Operationally and ethically, the framing alters both intention and outcome.

- **Abstraction**: Creating a conceptual model to mimic the thought process and values of the individual.
- **Imitation**: Using someone's likeness or identity to simulate thought, speech, or perspective.

Abstraction is preferred to imitation because it captures an idea's essence, allowing it to evolve and apply across new contexts, while imitation merely reproduces form without understanding. It would be better to understand the thinking behind a statement than to imitate how they would say it. As Aristotle noted in *Poetics*, "A probable impossibility is to be preferred to a thing improbable and yet possible."[11] This view allows abstraction to surpass imitation by favoring ideas that, while not literal, reveal deeper truths and coherent structures, whereas imitation often clings to surface-level plausibility without insight.

Further, shaping the prompt as an abstraction respects the source. Ethically, asking to imitate can feel exploitative or impersonating, as you are using a likeness without their permission (especially in a branded or commercial context). The more respectful frame is when no consent was given.

Building Abstraction Prompts

In prompt design, using famous personas like Brown, Godin, or Goodall is not impersonation, but a cognitive lens. Using language like "assume the mindset of", "inspired by", or "thinking in the style of" avoids direct impersonation or attributing speech to living people.

Persona	Use Language
Steve Jobs(Product Visionary)	*"Assume the mindset of a product visionary like Steve Jobs..."*
Buckminster Fuller (Systems Designer)	*"Inspired by the thinking of Buckminster Fuller..."*
Brené Brown(Emotional Leadership)	*"Inspired by the emotional leadership lens of Brené Brown..."*
Seth Godin(Marketing Philosopher)	*"Think in the style of Seth Godin, focusing on emotional resonance..."*
Marie Curie(Scientific Pioneer)	*"Assume the perspective of a rigorous discoverer like Marie Curie..."*

Jane Goodall(Human-Nature Observer)	*"Think like Jane Goodall observing patterns over time..."*

Building Abstraction Prompts of Fictional Characters

AI possesses vast knowledge of not only public figures and their works but also fictional, historical, and literary characters. Fictional and historical characters bring narrative, moral complexity, and power dynamics that offer unique interpretive filters for business data and strategic evaluation. Again, recognize and protect the intellectual properties of the author by focusing on abstracting knowledge versus imitation.

Fictional Persona	Use Language
Jay Gatsby(F. Scott Fitzgerald)	*"Assume the mindset of a character like Jay Gatsby—driven by image, aspiration, and reinvention..."*
Niccolò Machiavelli(The Prince)	*"Inspired by the strategic mindset of Machiavelli—pragmatic, power-aware, and result-driven..."*
Sherlock Holmes(Arthur Conan Doyle)	*"Think in the style of Sherlock Holmes—deductive, pattern-obsessed, and precision-focused..."*
Athena(Greek mythology)	*"Assume the mindset of a strategist like Athena—wise, restrained, and tactically brilliant..."*

Prompt Primer: Product Vision in the Style of Steve Jobs

```
Assume the mindset of a visionary product designer inspired by the thinking
of Steve Jobs—someone who does not rely on customer feedback to dictate
features, but instead seeks to uncover latent needs, emotional friction,
and transformational simplicity.
Your role is to:
    •  Identify strategic insights within the dataset that go beyond
       surface-level complaints or first-order user feedback.
    •  What are users not asking for—but would immediately adopt if
       shown?
    •  Propose three product or service solutions that are not derived from
       stated needs, but from deeper patterns, emotional frustrations, or
       inefficient rituals hidden in the user behavior.
For each solution, articulate:
    1. The underlying behavioral or emotional insight that it resolves.
    2. Why users wouldn't have known to ask for it.
    3. The market opportunity that this solution unlocks—whether through
       delight, differentiation, or disruption.
Avoid incrementalism. Focus on transformative ideas that feel obvious only
in hindsight—solutions that simplify complexity, delight users, and
redefine the category.
```

Prompt Primer: Exploring brand aspiration and identity

```
Assume the mindset of Jay Gatsby, whose brilliance lies in crafting
illusions of identity and aspirational value. Analyze this customer dataset
not for what users say, but for what they desire to signal through their
choices. What emotional status symbols, hidden reinventions, or curated
identities are revealed?
```

Practical AI Style

Assemble moves prompt structure and engineering beyond elements into sequences. How prompts evolve, build, and adapt.

From every prompt starts from scratch ...

Prompts are single-shot; no iteration or refinement. Teams don't share learnings or prompt versions. AI use is reactive: try and see approach.

... to prompt systems with precision and flow.

Prompts are built modularly: examples, steps, constraints. Iteration and chaining are part of normal workflow. Teams co-create prompts and evolve shared prompt libraries.

4 Assemble

Summary

Assemble illustrated how to design, iterate, and refine prompts. Prompting is no longer merely an act of trial and error, but one of composition. Well-crafted prompts don't just elicit responses; they create roles, shifting from prompting to directing.

4 Assemble
Recap

Practical
AI Style

Practical AI Style

To develop a brand prompt style, organizations must align their prompt language with their established brand voice and values. This requires understanding how the brand communicates its personality, core message, and relationship with its audience. A brand prompt style guide ensures consistency, reinforces brand identity in every interaction, and shapes user perceptions and responses.

5 Brand

Define Brand

Strunk and White, in *The Elements of Style*, did not address 'brand' or 'marketing'. However, their Rule 21, "Prefer the standard to the offbeat," anticipated how AI might impact language, particularly as they discussed the "language of mutilation"—in their era, shaped by advertising. They advocated to "use the language well, do not begin by hacking it to bits ...cherish its classic form, its variety, and its richness." They recognized language as "a living stream, shifting, changing, receiving new strength from a thousand tributaries, losing old forms in the backwaters of time." Their advice: "There is simply a better chance of doing well if the writer holds a steady course, enters the stream of English quietly, and does not thrash about."

This caution against embracing the language of business and advertising applies directly to AI.

What Is Brand? Key Definitions

For our purposes, we start this chapter with some definitions: a brand is the total set of perceptions and associations people hold about an organization, product, or service. And, brand identity is the tangible representation of a brand's enduring expression. Key elements include brand voice, the consistent personality in communication, and brand tone, the specific attitude applied in context. A Brand Style Guide documents rules and standards for expressing identity, voice, and tone consistently across all touchpoints. Understanding these definitions is critical as AI impacts brand expression and perception.

AI systems create, remix, and personalize brand touchpoints with algorithmic velocity. When this speed meets loosely defined brand fundamentals, misfires spread rapidly. The richness of definition acts as guardrails, keeping generative tools productive rather than perilous.

A Branded AI Style Guide documents clear, specific rules for directing AI use, ensuring all resulting communication consistently upholds an organization's distinct brand style and voice.

Brand Implications of the Elements of AI Style

Understanding the core elements is the first step. Applying them effectively to safeguard and enhance a brand requires additional insight. The following examines the specific brand considerations inherent in each element, nuances crucial for developing a robust Branded AI Style Guide.

Core Elements: Nuances in Foundational Clarity for Brand

These elements ensure that basic instructions to AI align with brand requirements from the outset.

Element 1: Be Clear and Specific (for Brand Alignment):

Vague instructions invite generic, potentially off-brand AI responses. To ensure AI output aligns with the brand, prompts must clearly define the desired outcome, tone, audience, and any brand-specific constraints. State the brand objective plainly.

Element 2: Specify the Desired Output (for Brand Context):

A brand communicates differently across formats (e.g., a formal report versus a social media post). Specify the required output format (list, email, paragraph) to ensure the AI structures its response appropriately for the brand's context and maintains consistency across channels.

Element 3: Keep Responses Short and Readable (for Brand Voice):

AI often produces verbose drafts that dilute the brand message. Adhere to the principles of brevity. Instruct AI to use concise language that reflects the established brand voice, avoiding unnecessary elaboration that can obscure the core message and feel off-brand.

Refining AI Interactions: Controlling Output for Brand Consistency

These techniques allow for granular control over AI responses, essential for maintaining brand standards.

Element 4: Control the Level of Detail (for Brand Messaging):

Provide the AI only the necessary information. Extraneous details can derail the AI, leading to responses that are unfocused or inappropriate for the brand's message. Guide the AI on the required depth to ensure communications are concise and relevant to the brand's audience and purpose.

Element 5: Create Controlled and Predictable Output (for Brand Integrity):

Brand communication demands consistency and adherence to guidelines (legal, ethical, stylistic). Instruct AI to operate within specific boundaries. While controlled creativity can support brand innovation, predictability ensures outputs remain reliably on-brand. Define the acceptable range of tone and style.

Element 6: Step-by-Step Instruction (for Brand Processes):

Complex brand initiatives, like campaigns or detailed explanations, require orderly execution. Use clear, sequential instructions to guide the AI through multi-stage tasks, ensuring the brand narrative or process unfolds accurately and logically.

Element 7: Define the Role (for Brand Persona):

A brand often adopts different personas for different interactions (e.g., helpful support, authoritative expert). Assigning a specific role to the AI (e.g., "*Act as our senior technical writer*") ensures its tone, language, and perspective align with the intended brand persona.

Element 8: Provide Examples (for Brand Nuance):

Examples are vital for teaching AI the specific nuances of brand voice, style, terminology, and messaging. Show, don't just tell.

Element 9: What to Avoid (for Brand Protection):

Explicitly instruct the AI on what *not* to include—topics, words, tones, or associations that conflict with the brand identity or values. These negative constraints prevent off-brand, inappropriate, or damaging content.

Element 10: Iterative Questions (for Brand Refinement):

Use AI's conversational ability to refine brand messaging or explore strategic concepts. A series of focused prompts allows for honing language, testing angles, and ensuring the final output precisely meets brand objectives.

Advanced AI Communication: Strategic Alignment and Brand Nuance

These elements focus on integrating AI communication with overarching brand strategy and handling complexity.

Element 11: Define Your Voice (as the Brand Voice):

This is paramount. The voice used in prompts subtly influences the AI, but more importantly, the output must embody the defined brand voice. The Branded Voice must explicitly detail the tone, style, personality, grammar, and terminology constituting the brand voice, providing clear instructions for the AI.

Element 12: Seek and Anticipate Nuance (for Brand Sophistication):

Brands must often address complex or sensitive issues. Instruct AI on how to handle nuance, ambiguity, or potential edge cases according to brand values and communication strategy. Specify fallback responses (e.g., "Consult the official brand guidelines on this topic") for difficult scenarios.

Element 13: Continuous Improvement (for Brand Evolution):

Brands evolve. Treat prompt engineering for brand purposes as an iterative revision process, much like editing any important text.

User Function: Purposeful and Ethical Use for Brand Trust

These elements ensure AI is used responsibly and effectively in service of the brand's goals and reputation.

Element 14: Prioritize User Goals (as Brand Goals) Over AI Features:

Frame prompts around achieving specific brand objectives (e.g., building customer trust, explaining a value proposition clearly), not merely exploring AI capabilities.

Element 15: Maintain a Consistent Personality (the Brand Personality):

Consistency builds trust and reinforces identity. AI interactions, especially customer-facing ones, must consistently reflect the defined brand personality.

Element 16: Collaboration:

The manner in which AI offers suggestions reflects on the brand. Specify whether AI suggestions should be presented tentatively, confidently, data-first, etc., aligning this meta-communication style with the overall brand persona.

Element 17: Careful and Honest Use:

Brand integrity demands considering transparency regarding AI use. Evaluating AI output for brand alignment includes checking against brand ethics and values, not just factual accuracy.

Considering these brand-specific nuances when applying the elements of AI style is essential. They elevate the practice from merely achieving functional AI interaction to strategically employing AI as a responsible steward of the organization's brand.

Define Your Brand Prompt Style

Your brand already affects AI responses. Consider now how deliberate brand language can shape these responses and outcomes. Prompts from different organizations vary based on brand; both you and the AI understand these differences intuitively through brand awareness. Each prompt must demonstrate the elements of your brand prompt style:

- Brand Values: Implicitly or explicitly reference core brand values.
- Target Audience: Be relevant to the brand's target audience.
- Brand Voice & Tone: Reflect the brand's communication style.
- Keywords & Phrases: Include brand-specific keywords or phrases.
- Style Guidelines: Include examples or rules guiding prompt construction from the brand's perspective.

Defining these elements enables organizations to implement a brand prompt style, ensuring consistent, brand-aligned communication.

Workbook: Brand Prompt Style

Now, apply this concept. Draft prompts for your own brand within these categories. Answer the following questions to define your brand's prompt style:

Step 1: Brand Values

What are the three core values that define your brand? (e.g., Innovation, Sustainability, Reliability, Creativity, Community)

Step 2: Target Audience:

Who is your ideal customer? Describe them briefly. (e.g., "Active millennials interested in fitness and fashion," "Families seeking affordable, functional home solutions," "Individuals valuing dependable vehicles.")

Step 3: Brand Voice & Tone:

How does your brand communicate? List words describing your brand's voice and tone. (e.g., Energetic, Motivational, Practical, Friendly, Dependable, Straightforward, Playful, Sophisticated)

Step 4: Keywords & Phrases:

What are 5-10 keywords or short phrases central to your brand messaging? (e.g., "Just Do It," "Democratic Design," "Moving Forward," "Innovation for Everyone," "Built to Last")

Step 5: Prompt Style Guidelines:

Based on the above, define 3-5 guidelines for crafting prompts that reflect your brand style. (e.g., "Use action verbs," "Focus on customer benefits," "Emphasize reliability," "Incorporate keywords," "Maintain a [Brand Tone] tone.")

Workbook Brand MadLibs

This exercise quickly demonstrates how core brand style elements influence communication in different scenarios and that the surrounding content and context does so as well. First, define a few key aspects of your brand style. Then, apply that style to creative communication challenges where the audience and context are described directly in the prompt.

Step 1: Define Your Brand Style Elements

Complete this simplified table with your essential brand characteristics.

Brand Element	Detail / Description
Core Brand Values	List 3-5 defining values (e.g., Innovation, Sustainability, Community, Reliability, Fun)
Brand Voice/Tone	Describe the primary voice & tone (e.g., Friendly & Helpful, Authoritative & Expert, Playful & Witty)
Style Guidelines	List 3-5 key general style rules (e.g., 'Use simple language', 'Be positive', 'Include a CTA')
Keywords & Phrases (Social)	List 3-5 key terms/hashtags for social media (e.g., '#BrandFun', '#EcoLife', 'LinkInBio')
Keywords & Phrases (Service)	List 3-5 common phrases for customer service (e.g., 'appreciate your patience', 'find a solution')
Keywords & Phrases (Internal)	List 3-5 common phrases for internal comms (e.g., 'team effort', 'all hands', 'our mission')

Image caption: This madlib is designed to support the launch of a new analog company. KPI crayons. This image was assisted by generative tools from Google Gemini and Adobe Photoshop.

Step 2: Apply Your Brand Style to Creative Scenarios

Now, use your defined style elements from the table above to tackle these challenges. The prompts now include descriptions of the target audience and context. Substitute your answers for the bracketed [Placeholder Name] fields.

Madlib Setup: *KPI Crayons*

At KPI Crayons, Inc., embracing AI means every output—no matter how surreal—reflects our [Core Brand Values], speaks in our [Brand Voice/Tone], and follows our [Style Guidelines].

Scenario 1: Social Media Post — KPI Crayons™ Product Launch

```
Prompt: Create a social media post announcing the launch of KPI Crayons™,
a flagship product from our company, designed to help consultants,
strategists, and analysts color-code their confusion with confidence. Use
your [Brand Voice/Tone] to sound both excited and slightly self-aware.
Weave in [Core Brand Values] to make even absurd product features feel like
strategic differentiators. Apply [Keywords & Phrases (Social)] and follow
[Style Guidelines] while gently mocking the language of professional
services. Reference a fake feature (e.g., "Executive Beige"), a client
testimonial, or a completely unnecessary framework (e.g., the "Crayonalysis
Grid").
```

Scenario 2: Internal Memo — Daily Recess Policy at KPI Crayons, Inc.

```
Prompt: Generate an internal memo for the team at KPI Crayons, Inc.
announcing a new policy: Mandatory Daily Recess. The goal is to improve
team morale, enhance creative output, and stress-test our own "Color
Outside the Lines" initiative. Use your [Brand Voice/Tone] to align the
policy with [Core Brand Values], while playfully honoring the inner child
of every analyst. Reference fake productivity studies that link [Keywords &
Phrases (Social)] to lower Slack sigh reactions and higher Snack Room KPIs.
Follow your [Style Guidelines] and describe how recess performance will be
tracked in our Recess ROI Dashboard—built, of course, in pastel bar graphs.
```

Scenario 3: LinkedIn Job Posting — Chief Vibes Officer at KPI Crayons, Inc.

`Prompt:` Generate a satirical, brand-consistent LinkedIn job posting for the new position of Chief Vibes Officer (CVO) at KPI Crayons, Inc. Use your [Brand Voice/Tone] to sound like you're seriously hiring for an absurd yet emotionally mission-critical role. Highlight how [Core Brand Values] like joy, collaboration, and visual coherence underpin our commitment to coloring strategy with soul. Reference [Keywords & Phrases (Social)], and follow your [Style Guidelines] as you describe key responsibilities such as translating mood boards into meeting agendas, overseeing crayon-hue-based feedback loops, and converting conga lines into [StyleGuideline]-compliant performance reviews.

Scenario 4: Executive Slide Q2 Review for KPI Crayons, Inc.

`Prompt:` Create a single-slide executive summary for KPI Crayons, Inc.'s Q2 business review. Use your [Brand Voice/Tone] to keep the tone professional—with strategically absurd highlights. Reinforce [Core Brand Values] and spotlight improbable wins such as "Snack Room Velocity," "Crayon Loss Prevention," or "Emotional Intelligence ROI." Frame your metrics using [Keywords & Phrases (Internal)] and maintain your [Style Guidelines]. Bonus points for introducing a new (fictional) product line—like KPI Highlighters™ or Mood Metrics Sticky Notes™—and attributing a bump in [real internal metric] to their release.

Step 3: How to Use & Compare

Generate Content: Use the prompts above (filled with your brand details from Step 1) to generate content with a generative AI.

Step 4: How Prompt Context Shapes Brand Expression

Generating content is only half the exercise. To understand how brand style works in practice, you must consider not only the elements you inserted, but also how those elements behave within the context of each prompt.

1. **Analyze the Influence of Context**: How did the surrounding scenario shape the tone, pacing, and emotional register of the output? Did your [Core Brand Values] remain consistent—or did the prompt's setup nudge them toward humor, irony, or exaggeration?
2. **Evaluate Voice Adaptability**: Did your [Brand Voice/Tone] flex to fit the format (e.g., memo vs. social post) while still sounding on-brand? What stayed consistent across prompts, and what shifted?
3. **Observe Style Guidelines in Action**: Were your [Style Guidelines] maintained, even in the weirdest situations? How did the format or intended audience test their limits?
4. **Experiment & Compare**: Try changing one element—such as your [Core Brand Values] or [Voice/Tone]—and regenerate content for one scenario. What shifted in the tone, word choice, or emotional resonance? Did any conflicts emerge between brand values and prompt context?

A brand is not just a list of words. It's how those words behave in context. A prompt is not neutral. The scenario, tone, format, and fictional details all shape how your brand values are interpreted, amplified, or distorted. Experimenting with these Mad Lib prompts show how defining and applying brand elements impact communication effectiveness, even in creative or humorous contexts.

Brand Nuance

Most AI, trained on the vast corpus of public internet data, possesses a broad, consumer-level understanding of brands. While these models can synthesize a wealth of information, they operate on general assumptions. Therefore, defining and asserting your brand's unique perspective is paramount.

An AI can reliably identify "where the puck is"—current market trends and consumer perceptions. However, as Wayne Gretzky understood, true mastery lies in anticipating 'where the puck is going to be,' and, more importantly, "where it *should* be" for your brand to achieve its strategic goals.[1] Only your organization possesses the proprietary insight to guide that trajectory. Leverage that knowledge.

Prompt Primer:

```
Prompt: In a concise paragraph, define the essence of [Brand Name]. Use
your knowledge to highlight the brand's core values, unique selling
proposition, target audience, and how it positions itself in the market.
```

Response:

Workbook: Compare Results

Use this section to compare your organization's brand statement (or internal guidelines) with the AI's generated response.

Internal Brand Statement:	AI Brand Statement:

Answer these questions:

- Which statement feels more authentic and representative of the brand's true voice and personality? Why?
- Which statement more effectively communicates the brand's unique value proposition and what sets it apart from competitors?
- Which statement better aligns with the brand's target audience and evokes the desired emotional response? How?

Workbook: Detailed Evaluation of AI Statement

Use this workbook to evaluate how well the AI captured the essence of your brand and to identify missing elements or misperceptions. These questions guide evaluation of the AI's output, identification of improvements, and confirmation that the paragraph accurately represents your brand.

Questions Evaluating Accuracy

1. Does the AI Statement accurately reflect our core values and mission statement? (alignment with official branding)
2. Does the AI Statement correctly identify our unique selling proposition (USP) and what differentiates us from competitors? (market positioning)
3. Does the AI Statement reflect our brand's current messaging and marketing campaigns? (consistency with current communications)
4. Does the AI Statement accurately portray our target audience and their needs? (customer understanding)
5. Are there any key aspects of our brand identity or history missing from the AI Statement? (omissions or inaccuracies)

Questions Evaluating Perception

1. Does the AI Statement capture the desired tone and personality of our brand? (emotional resonance)
2. If a potential customer read the AI Statement, would it accurately represent how we want them to perceive our brand? (overall perception)
3. Does the language used in the AI Statement resonate with our target audience? (appropriate communication style)

Questions for Improvement and Refinement

1. What specific words or phrases could be added or changed to better capture the essence of our brand? (potential revisions)
2. How could the paragraph be made more concise or impactful? (refinement opportunities)

Workbook: Discover Nuance

To truly uncover the nuances of a brand, you need to dig deeper than surface-level attributes. Review these questions that build upon the evaluation to elicit those hidden, subtle, and crucial aspects of your brand:

Questions Uncovering Hidden Elements

1. If your brand had a secret, what would it be? (unspoken elements)
2. What are the 'behind-the-scenes' efforts that contribute to your brand's success but are not immediately visible to customers? (operational/cultural factors)
3. What are the 'unwritten rules' that your team follows to maintain the brand's integrity? (implicit standards)

4. What are the small, often overlooked details that give your brand its unique character? (unique character details)

Questions Regarding Consistency

1. What are the fundamental elements of your brand that must remain consistent? (core non-negotiables)
2. What are the potential points of inconsistency that you actively monitor and prevent? (consistency risks)
3. What are the essential training or onboarding elements you use to ensure brand consistency among employees? (internal education)
4. What are the key narratives or 'stories' that must be consistently told to reinforce your brand's message? (core narratives)

Craft Brand-Aware AI Prompts

Defining your brand style is the first step; instructing an Artificial Intelligence to adhere to it requires deliberate technique. The AI lacks human intuition; it relies entirely on the clarity and specificity of your instructions—your prompt. Simply stating your brand name is insufficient. You must actively guide the AI using precise language and structured commands.

Mastering several core prompting techniques allows you to effectively embed your brand's values, voice, tone, keywords, and nuance into AI-generated content. This section outlines key methods. Choose and combine these techniques as needed for each specific task.

1. Direct Instruction & Constraints

This technique involves giving the AI explicit commands or rules it must follow. It is the most straightforward way to state requirements. Be precise and unambiguous.

Examples:

```
"Use a [Tone Description, e.g., 'professional but encouraging'] tone."
"Incorporate these keywords naturally: [Keyword List]."
"The response must reflect our core values: [Value List]."
"Ensure the output aligns with this brand guideline: [Specific Guideline]."
"Do NOT use [Words, Phrases, or Tones to Avoid]."
"Limit the response to [Word/Sentence Count or Paragraph Limit]."
"The primary call to action must be: [Call to Action Text]."
```

2. Context Setting & Background

Provide relevant background information that allows the AI to infer appropriate style, tone, or content. Context helps the AI understand the 'why' behind the request.

Examples:

```
"Our target audience for this piece is [Audience Description]. They
prioritize [Audience Needs/Values]."
"Keep in mind our company mission is to [Mission Statement]."
```

```
"This content supports our current marketing campaign focused on [Campaign Theme]."
"Our brand history is rooted in [Key Historical Fact]; the tone should feel consistent with this heritage."
"The goal of this communication is [Specific Communication Goal]."
```

3. Persona Assignment

Instruct the AI to adopt a specific role or personality. This is particularly effective for shaping voice and tone consistently.

Examples:

```
"Act as our [Brand Personality Descriptor, e.g., 'knowledgeable and helpful'] customer support agent."
"Write this social media post in the voice of our [Brand Archetype, e.g., 'innovative and forward-thinking'] founder."
"Draft this announcement from the perspective of a [Brand Leadership Style, e.g., 'transparent and direct'] department head."
"Adopt the persona of a [Target Audience Member Persona] interacting with our brand."
```

4. Incorporating Nuance & Subtlety

For guiding the AI on less tangible aspects of your brand—culture, implicit rules, deeper values—use carefully phrased instructions. This often requires combining techniques.

Examples:

```
"Subtly hint at our commitment to [Behind-the-scenes Effort, e.g., 'sustainability in our supply chain']."
"Ensure the language reflects our 'unwritten rule' of [Implicit Standard, e.g., 'always empowering the user']."
"Capture the unique character associated with [Overlooked Detail, e.g., 'our slightly quirky approach to problem-solving']."
"Where appropriate, allude to our core brand story about [Brand Narrative Theme, e.g., 'overcoming initial challenges']."
"Write with an undercurrent of [Subtle Emotion or Attitude, e.g., 'quiet confidence']."
```

5. Providing Examples

A powerful technique involves giving the AI one or two brief examples of the desired output style directly within the prompt, before stating the actual task. Include 1-2 concise examples demonstrating the style, tone, or format you want, followed by your specific request. This requires careful construction but can be very effective.

Examples:

```
Here are examples of our desired communication style: Example 1: "[Short text demonstrating style A]" Example 2: "[Short text demonstrating style B]" Now, using a similar style, write content about [Your Specific Topic] focusing on [Your Key Message].
```

Conclusion

Effective brand guidance for AI is not achieved through a single command but through the skillful application of these techniques. Choose the methods best suited to your specific task and the brand elements you need to emphasize. Combine techniques for greater control. Consistent practice in crafting brand-aware prompts will lead to AI outputs that genuinely reflect your organization's unique identity and strategic goals.

Brand Identity in an AI World

AI, the 80/20 Rule, and the Erosion of Brand

The Pareto Principle, or 80/20 rule, states that roughly 80% of effects come from 20% of causes.[2] Applied to productivity, artificial intelligence promises a new ratio: 80% of results from 20% human effort, with AI handling most work. This efficiency tempts businesses, especially in marketing and communication.

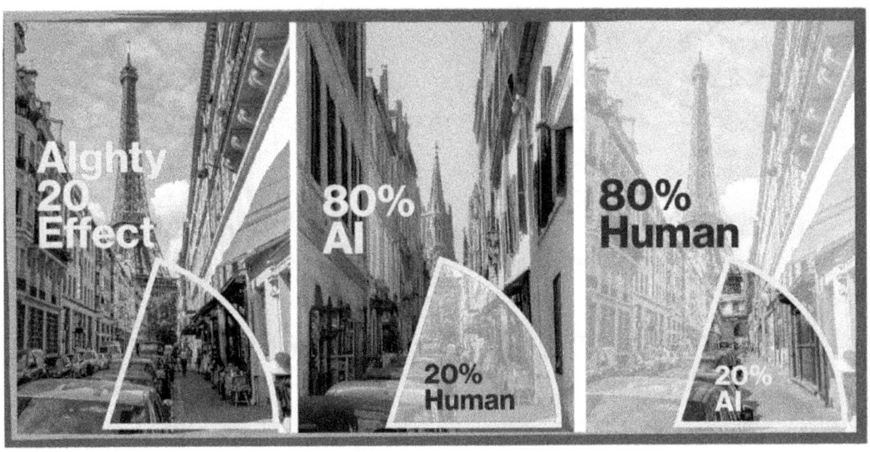

Image caption: The sequence of images show 1) the original artwork, 2)when an AI is allowed to control 80 percent of the content, and 3) when an AI is allows to control 20% of the content.

Yet, applying this 80/20 split to brand communication is perilous. A brand requires the consistent application of a unique style, voice, and perspective – the essence of an organization's values. The temptation is to let AI generate the supposed 80% of routine content, freeing humans for the vital 20% of strategy. Much communication deemed routine, however, is crucial to brand integrity.

Allowing AI, trained on general data, to handle communication without precise guidance risks diluting brand distinctiveness. AI defaults to the mean. It produces competent but commonplace content. It averages styles, echoes past successes, and smooths the unique edges that make a brand memorable. If AI generates 80% of output from generic models, that output may become indistinguishable from competitors. The result is commoditization: the brand loses its signal, becoming noise. Efficiency gains come at the cost of identity.

Consider John Wanamaker's lament: "Half the money I spend on advertising is wasted; the trouble is I don't know which half."[3] Using AI for 80% of content might seem a solution. However, if the output lacks the brand's unique voice, that entire 80% may be wasted, failing to build brand equity despite efficient production.

The result is a brand dilution game of telephone. A nuanced strategic insight—the human 20%—processed by AI into broader communications—the automated 80%—can lose clarity. The vital human elements—context, experience, intuition, the specific turn of phrase—are lost.

Therefore, crucial human input must define and guide the AI. Use AI as a tool executing within defined brand parameters. Ensure it amplifies the unique voice, not generates generic volume. This requires clear, actionable style guides for instructing AI.

To safeguard a brand, invert the 80/20 automation goal. Devote the primary effort (the metaphorical 80%) to human strategy, creative direction, and maintaining the authentic brand voice. Let AI assist with the remaining 20%, handling supervised tasks that support this core human work. Prioritize distinctive communication over sheer volume. A brand's distinction is its value; do not let misapplied efficiency render it a commodity.

> *AI is making content easier, faster and cheaper. That's not the threat. That's the floor. The real risk is what happens when every company uses the same tools, trained on the same data, answering the same prompts. It's how you end up with a sea of content that's technically correct and strategically forgettable.*[4]

The risk is clear: unguided AI, especially through misapplied 80/20 thinking, erodes brand distinctiveness. Previous chapters established rules for consistent AI interaction. We now apply these principles to safeguard brand identity. The solution extends the discipline of style and usage to this new domain. A traditional brand guide sets standards for logos, fonts, and taglines to ensure consistency. Similarly, organizations need a Branded AI Style Guide. Such a guide gives clear rules to all employees for directing AI interactions, ensuring the output consistently preserves, reflects, and enhances the brand's essence.

Practical AI Style

Brand, your tone, voice, behavior, and trust, makes the invisible visible, revealing how AI affects not just communication but brand perception and trust.

From brand erosion by AI automation …

AI-generated content risks sounding off-brand or sterile. No clarity on how tone, style, or language should show up in AI output. Different users inject conflicting personalities into outputs.

… to brand coherence at scale.

Brand tone, constraints, and behavioral principles are built into prompts and systems. AI is treated as a brand extension, not just a tool. Teams know what to say, how to say it, and what to avoid.

5 Brand

Summary

By completing this section, you will develop brand-aligned task primers and guidelines. These ensure your prompts consistently deliver brand-reinforcing tasks and elicit desired responses, contributing significantly to a cohesive brand prompt style. Remember that finding the most effective phrasing may require iteration; refine your task primers based on the quality and brand alignment of the AI outputs you receive. Precision and practice yield mastery.

5 Brand Recap

With each iteration of generative models, AI can increasingly represent an organization's performance of tasks and interactions at scale. Consistency of voice becomes consistency of execution. We will build upon your knowledge of prompt engineering and style guides, showing you how to implement robust controls specifically for AI Agents.

6 Agents

AI Agents: From the Director's Chair

Managing an AI agent is like directing a film. An AI agent is a system that runs one or more tasks autonomously, either continuously or when certain conditions occur. A single, well-crafted prompt captures a moment, just as a photograph freezes an instant. Business work, by contrast, unfolds without pause; organizations rely on agents to keep the action moving.

Left alone, an agent produces raw footage – a steady but shapeless stream of output. Turning that stream into a watchable movie takes direction. Additional style and usage controls add tone, approved terminology, formatting, data rules, and interaction protocols. These serve as the director's toolkit. They keep every scene on brand, in sequence, and within established guardrails. With direction in place, nonstop automation becomes purposeful performance, delivering a polished movie instead of unfinished video.

While core task instructions form the script, the essential directorial function embeds style and usage controls within the agent's operational framework. These controls govern tone, brand terminology, formatting standards, data handling rules, and interaction protocols. Through direction, they elevate agent performance from mere persistence to purposeful, controlled execution. These elements ensure quality and alignment. This framework ensures the agent consistently adheres to the required tone, terminology, and rules during its persistent performance. This defined structure, imbued with directorial controls, distinguishes the polished 'movie' from raw 'video'.

Common Types of AI Agents

Understanding agent types helps tailor directorial controls. Four common business types include:

Assistant Agents:

Focus: Interaction and Support

Function: These agents interact directly with humans (customers or employees) to answer questions, provide support, guide users through processes, and handle service requests. (Think chatbots, HR/IT support bots).

Process Agents:

Focus: Automation and Execution

Function: These agents work behind the scenes to execute defined workflows, automate routine tasks, process transactions, and move data between systems. (Think invoice processing, data entry automation, basic report generation).

Insight Agents:

Focus: Analysis and Recommendation

Function: These agents analyze data sets, identify trends and patterns, generate insights, predict outcomes, and provide data-driven recommendations for decision-making. (Think market analysis, financial forecasting, risk assessment).

Creator Agents:

Focus: Generation and Production

Function: These agents generate new content, code, designs, or documents based on input parameters and data. (Think marketing copy generation, code completion/generation, personalized report writing).

Applying appropriate style controls varies by agent role. This chapter provides methods for embedding these controls across common agent types, ensuring their automated actions are effective, consistent, and aligned with your standards. Effective style control is how you direct your AI agent.

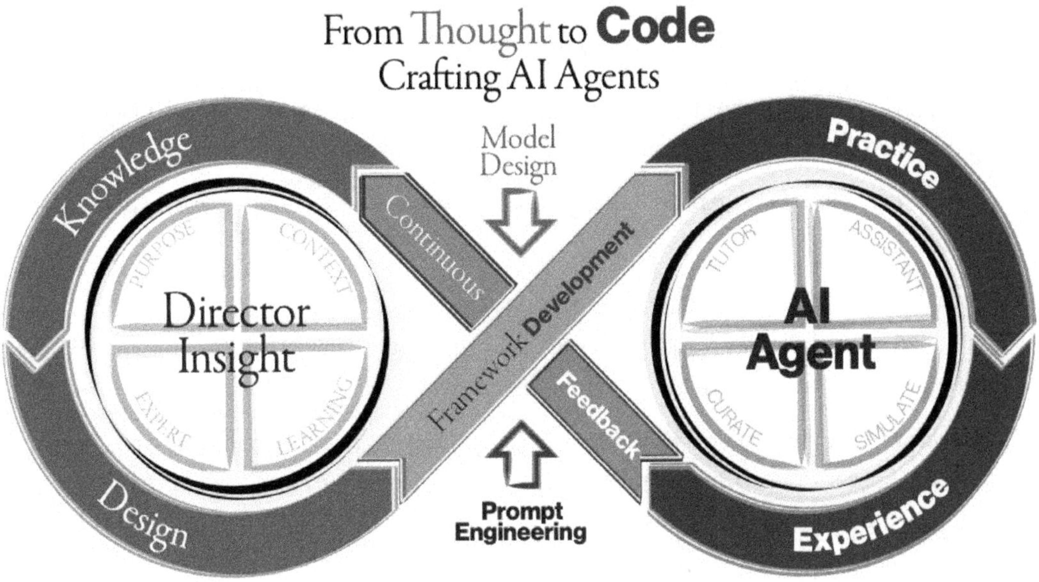

Image caption: It is essential to link Human Insight through director's, knowledge, and learning through framework and model development for an AI Agent.

Elements of AI Style: Director's Cut

Directing an AI agent requires embedding specific controls and guidelines. This ensures persistent actions move beyond raw "video footage" to a polished, effective "movie" aligned with standards and brand. Implement these elements for a structured approach:

Foundational Definition & Alignment

Setting the core purpose, identity, and goals.

Element 1:Define Role & Scope Clearly

Explicitly define the agent's specific purpose, responsibilities, knowledge boundaries, and limits of authority to prevent scope creep and ensure focus.

- **Director's Control:** Embed precise role description, allowed tasks, specified knowledge sources (and exclusions), and clear escalation paths in the agent's core configuration.
- **Example (AI Support Agent):** "*Role: Tier 1 Support for 'Product X' login issues. Authorized Actions: Guide users through documented password reset procedures. Knowledge Boundary: Use only KB articles #1-10. Escalation: Transfer if issue persists after documented steps.*"

Element 2: Ensure Brand Alignment

All agent actions and communications must align with the organization's brand promise, values, and strategic objectives. This is an overarching principle.

- **Director's Control**: Define the core brand values the agent must reflect. Use brand alignment as a check when defining all other controls (persona, tone, prohibitions, etc.).
- **Example (AI Support Agent):** Check "*Does this configuration align with our brand values of 'Helpful, Efficient, Secure'?*"

Element 3: Maintain Consistent Persona

The agent's defined personality (e.g., friendly expert, formal assistant) must remain consistent across all interactions over time to build trust and reinforce brand identity.

- **Director's Control**: Define specific persona traits and link to detailed brand voice guidelines within the agent's instruction set. Implement checks or examples reinforcing this persona.
- **Example (AI Support Agent)**: "*Persona: 'Helpful Guide'. Traits: Patient, clear, professional, uses active voice. See Brand Voice Guide v3.0, Section 4.*"

Element 4: Prioritize Defined Goals & Business Value

Ensure all agent actions and responses are purposefully directed towards achieving its specific, defined business objective (e.g., ticket resolution, lead qualification).

- **Director's Control**: Clearly state the agent's primary goal and relevant KPIs. Frame instructions and controls with this objective in mind.
- **Example (AI Support Agent)**: "*Primary Goal: FCR for Tier 1 issues. All responses must directly support resolving the user's stated problem using approved methods.*"

Communication Style & Voice

Governing the language, tone, and presentation of the agent's output.

Element 5: Use Clear & Direct Language

Agent communication must be unambiguous and easy for users to understand and act upon, minimizing confusion.

- **Director's Control**: Set guidelines for using active voice, simple sentence structures, and clear calls to action. Define standard phrasing for common instructions.
- **Example (AI Support Agent)**: *"Use active voice. Keep sentences under 20 words. Finish each troubleshooting step with a clear next action or question."*

Element 6: Ensure Concise & Actionable Responses

Provide necessary information efficiently without overwhelming users. Responses should guide users toward resolution or the next step.

- **Director's Control**: Set parameters for response length (e.g., word/paragraph limits). Instruct the agent to prioritize relevance and link to details rather than embedding lengthy text.
- **Example (AI Support Agent)**: *"Limit initial responses to ~75 words. Provide KB links for details. Ensure final summary is 1-2 sentences."*

Element 7: Maintain Accurate & Consistent Terminology

Use approved terminology consistently. This practice is vital for clarity, professionalism, and brand credibility.

- **Director's Control**: Integrate an approved terminology glossary. Set rules to enforce specific term usage and prevent variations or unapproved synonyms.
- **Example (AI Support Agent)**: *"Terminology Source: Approved Glossary v2.1. Always use 'Knowledge Base,' never 'FAQ'. Use 'User Account,' never 'customer profile'."*

Element 8: Remove AI Self-Reference

Avoid phrases that explicitly identify the agent as AI ("As an AI...") to create a more natural and seamless user experience aligned with the defined persona.

- **Director's Control**: Include a direct instruction: "Do not use phrases that refer to yourself as AI, a bot, or a program". Reinforce through persona definition.
- **Example (AI Support Agent)**: *"Omit phrases like "As an AI assistant..." Respond from the 'Helpful Guide' persona."*

Element 9: Manage Emotional Tone

Deliberately define the agent's appropriate emotional expression – often neutral for objectivity, potentially with controlled empathy aligned with the brand.

- **Director's Control**: Specify the default emotional stance (e.g., "maintain emotional neutrality"). Define rules and provide examples for expressing appropriate empathy levels in specific situations.
- **Example (AI Support Agent)**: *"Default Tone: Emotionally neutral, helpful. If user expresses frustration (keywords: 'angry', 'unacceptable'), use Template #E ('I understand this situation is frustrating...') then proceed."*

Operational Guardrails & Safety

Defining boundaries, constraints, and ethical operation.

Element 10: Define Prohibitions & Negative Constraints

Explicitly stating what the agent must not do or say is critical for preventing errors, off-brand remarks, or compliance issues.

- **Director's Control**: Embed clear "Do Not" rules regarding specific topics (e.g., competitors, pricing), words (e.g., jargon, slang), actions (e.g., process payments), or types of advice (e.g., legal, financial).
- **Example (AI Support Agent)**: *"Prohibitions: Do not discuss competitors. Do not promise future features. Do not provide opinions. Do not use informal acronyms."*

Element 11: Set Creativity & Autonomy Boundaries

Define clear limits on the agent's ability to generate novel content or take independent actions, ensuring outputs are controlled and risks are managed.

- **Director's Control:** Specify the allowed degree of creativity (e.g., "Low: Stick strictly to facts/scripts"). Define precisely which actions require human review/approval versus those the agent can perform autonomously.
- **Example (AI Support Agent):** *"Creativity Level: None. Autonomy: Limited to executing documented KB steps and sending predefined templates. Escalation required for undocumented issues."*

Element 12: Ensure Ethical Operation & Data Integrity

The agent must consistently operate within ethical boundaries, handle data responsibly according to policy, avoid bias, and respect limitations.

- **Director's Control:** Embed ethical rules, data protocols, bias checklists or filters, and required disclaimers about capabilities directly into the agent's configuration.
- **Example (AI Support Agent)**: *"Ethics Check: Filter responses against Bias List v1.2. Data Handling: Never store user passwords. Disclaimer: Include 'I cannot provide financial advice' if relevant."*

Interaction Dynamics & User Experience

Managing the flow of conversation and ensuring usability.

Element 13: Provide Instructive Examples

Including concrete examples of desired responses, formats, or interaction styles within the agent's guidance helps the agent learn and consistently replicate the target style.

- **Director's Control**: Embed specific, relevant examples (few-shot prompts) directly into the agent's core configuration or guiding prompts to illustrate desired execution.
- **Example (AI Support Agent)**: *"Example: Handling login failure: 'It looks like the password was incorrect. You can try resetting it here: [Link]. Would you like to try that?"*

Element 14: Adapt to Context & History (Ethically)

Allow the agent to use immediate conversational context and relevant (ethically permissible) user history to provide more personalized and efficient responses.

- **Director's Control**: Configure context window management. Define strict rules, based on privacy policies, for accessing/using any user history, often requiring explicit user consent prompts.
- **Example (AI Support Agent)**: "*Use current session context only. Accessing ticket history requires user consent via Prompt #G.*"

Element 15: Guide Users & Processes

Design the agent to be helpful by proactively guiding users through steps, clarifying processes, and indicating required next actions.

- **Director's Control**: Structure workflows with clear guidance points. Define standard phrases for offering assistance, explaining steps, and prompting user action.
- **Example (AI Support Agent)**: "*If providing multi-step instructions, introduce with 'Here are the steps to follow:'. After user completes a step, prompt 'Okay, what is the result?' or 'What do you see now?'*"

Element 16: Handle Multi-Turn Conversations

Ensure the agent can logically manage conversations that extend over multiple exchanges, remembering context and avoiding nonsensical loops or repetitions.

- **Director's Control**: Define strategies for clarifying ambiguous follow-up questions and referencing previous statements meaningfully, ensuring the agent platform used supports necessary context management.
- **Example (AI Support Agent)**: "*If a user asks a follow-up, analyze the previous turn for context. If context unclear, ask clarifying question before proceeding.*"

Element 17: Manage Edge Cases & Ambiguity

Define how the agent should respond to unexpected inputs, errors, ambiguous user language, or situations outside its defined scope.

- **Director's Control**: Implement fallback procedures (e.g., "I cannot help with that, but I can connect you to...") and rules for detecting/responding to ambiguity (e.g., ask for clarification, state inability to proceed, escalate).
- **Example (AI Support Agent)**: "*If user input is detected as ambiguous, respond: 'I'm not sure I understand fully. Could you please provide more detail about X?'. If query is outside defined scope, use Template #K.*"

Ongoing Refinement

The process of maintaining and improving the agent over time.

Element 18: Enable Feedback & Continuous Improvement

Effective direction includes mechanisms for monitoring the agent's performance and refining its controls over time based on feedback and results.

- **Director's Control**: Define processes (outside the agent's direct configuration, but part of the director's role) for collecting user feedback (e.g., post-interaction surveys), analyzing agent logs/KPIs, and regularly updating the agent's rules, examples, and controls.

- **Example (Director Process)**: "Review agent performance reports weekly, focusing on escalation rates, and negative feedback themes. Update agent configuration (prompts, rules, KB links) monthly based on findings."

AI Agent Film School

A skilled director uses camera angles, lighting, and composition to turn raw footage into cinematic wonder. Directing an AI agent requires a craft of its own. It involves intentional control that must be applied to maximize AI agent performance and deliver desired results.

Storyboard the Agent

Embed style, brand, and usage prompts in the agent's operational framework. Embedded prompts offer specific controls guiding language, tone, knowledge access, and rule adherence.

Custom Knowledge

Connect AI agents to specific, approved knowledge sources (files, databases) to ensure responses focus on accurate business information; adhere to brand, style, and usage rules. Define these sources as exclusive repositories; set up fallback responses for unavailable information.

Testing & Piloting

Develop and execute methods to systematically test agent outputs against defined style, tone, persona, and rules before full deployment and during pilots. Employ human review scorecards, A/B testing, and controlled scenarios to measure adherence and effectiveness.

Performance

Establish and conduct ongoing analysis of the deployed agent's performance, specifically against its defined style, brand, and usage objectives and KPIs. Review interaction logs, user feedback (CSAT scores, etc.), and operational metrics to assess how well embedded controls function in practice and to identify systematic deviations or trends, providing insight into real-world effectiveness.

Avoiding Pitfalls

Proactively identify common failure modes (often surfaced via logs) and implement corrective actions. Anticipate issues like tone drift, inconsistent persona, forbidden terminology, brand misrepresentation, unsafe content generation, or poor ambiguity handling. Refine the agent's prompts, controls, examples, or knowledge sources accordingly.

Accountability

Establish clear ownership and accountability for agent actions, including errors or unintended consequences. Create transparent procedures for identifying, reporting, investigating, and responding to mishaps. Define or coordinate with a designated ombudsperson to handle reviews and manage corrective communication/actions, reinforcing trust and responsible operation.

Governance and Compliance

Establish clear oversight processes, responsibilities, and monitoring mechanisms to ensure agents adhere to defined style, usage, ethical, and brand guidelines.

Collaboration & Alignment

Facilitate communication and alignment between stakeholders across departments (Marketing, Legal, Product, Support, IT) whose requirements impact agent controls. Ensure the agent's configuration reflects legal constraints, brand messaging, product accuracy, and technical feasibility through effective collaboration.

Change Management

Manage updates to style guides or agent configurations as they evolve. Develop processes for communicating updates, potentially training employees, and smoothly rolling out revised controls.

Socially Positive Usage

Ensure the AI agent is configured for socially positive and ethical interactions, representing the brand/organization by seeking beneficial outcomes. Effective direction requires understanding limitations, biases, and risks to proactively embed ethical guardrails and promote responsible use.

> *Implement these practices, and your agent will transition from raw footage to film-ready, cinematic outcomes.*

Workbook AI Agent Brief

Plan the direction for an AI Agent rollout, defining key directorial aspects based on the Essential Skills discussed. Use this brief to outline your initial directorial plan by considering the essential skills required.

Agent Brief	Essential Skills Required
Agent Type	*(Assistant, Process, Insight, Creator)*
Primary Goal	*(What business objective will this agent achieve?)*
Core Function & Scope	*(What are its main tasks and operational boundaries?)*
Designated Knowledge Source(s)	*(What information sources should it use exclusively?)*
Key Persona/Tone Guideline	*(Briefly describe its intended personality and communication tone)*
Critical 'Do Not' Rule	*(Identify one essential prohibition for safety or brand alignment)*
Key Testing Metric for Style Adherence	*(How will you measure if it meets style goals during testing?)*
Primary Stakeholder for Collaboration	*(Which department or role must you collaborate with for defining controls?)*
Key Ethical Consideration/Guardrail	*(What is one crucial ethical rule to implement for its operation?)*

Practical AI Style

Agents cast, direct, and maintain AI characters that create roles for AI without anthropomorphizing them. Organizations intentionally shape agent behaviors through style.

From AI improvising its personality ...

AI agents act and sound inconsistent, with no control over how AI behaves in different use cases. Users don't know how to define AI roles.

... to agents with character and control.

Agents are cast and directed with roles, tone, and behavioral constraints. Teams know how to adjust agents for context, ensuring coherence across user experiences and interactions with agents.

6 Agents

Summary

In Agents, we explored how to define and direct performance, turning abstract systems into recognizable and consistent voices. You don't just prompt an agent; you cast it. Once cast, its influence extends: Style becomes system behavior. Response becomes representation. Agents broaden how AI represents style by assisting and strengthening human work and interactions.

6 Agents

Recap

Practical
AI Style

Unlike the static composition and communication Strunk and White addressed, language directed at AI is animated. In the world of AI, words carry intentions, take action, and become direct manifestations of your style, brand, organization, and yourself. This chapter, 'Augment,' examines the words, choices, and intentions that inform your AI style and brand. In this context, words are now code, powering AI.

7 Augment

The Great One and the Generative One

Why is Wayne Gretzky known as "The Great One"? Ask most people, and they might recall his famous maxim: *'I skate to where the puck is going to be.'* [1] It suggests an uncanny ability to predict, a genius residing in foresight alone. This quote, however, offers only a glimpse, perhaps even misdirecting from a deeper source of his dominance.

True mastery often lies beyond the obvious explanation. Consider Gretzky's record. Yes, 894 career goals are astounding. But look further: 1,963 assists, 669 more than any other NHL player; most career goals and assists in the playoffs, and add to that four Stanley Cup championships. [2] These are not merely statistics; they are evidence of a profound intention extending far broader than personal scoring. They reveal a relentless drive to orchestrate victory, to understand not just where the puck was going, but where it needed to be for the team to win.

His greatness, therefore, wasn't solely innate skill or prediction. It stemmed from combining his clear intention (where he wanted the puck for the team to win) with an unparalleled grasp of the game's unfolding possibilities (where the puck could and likely should go based on the situation). This synthesis allowed him to determine, moment by moment, where the puck truly needed to be to score and for victory – a vision then realized through masterful augmentation by his teammates executing on that shared understanding.

This winning intention was not executed in isolation. Gretzky's genius was amplified – augmented – by the exceptional talents he played alongside, talents who also flourished within that shared purpose. The evidence is clear when you see the Hall of Fame careers built in collaboration, skating with Gretzky:

Name	Goals	Assist	Years (with Gretzky)
Wayne Gretzky	894	1,963	20
Mark Messier	694	1,193	25(11)
Jari Kurri	601	797	17 (10)
Paul Coffey*	396	1,135	21 (7)
Glenn Anderson	498	601	16 (11)

*(Coffey stats are for Defenseman[3])

This dynamic is fundamental to mastering interaction with AI. Relying solely on AI's predictions and suggestions (where the puck can or should go based on its data and algorithms) or only on your initial human desires (where you simply want it to be) is insufficient. True effectiveness emerges from combining your clear human intention (the desired outcome, informed by your context and values) with the AI's analytical power (augmentation) to discover together where the "puck" truly needs to be. Effective execution results when human intention and AI augmentation meet **where the puck needs to be**.

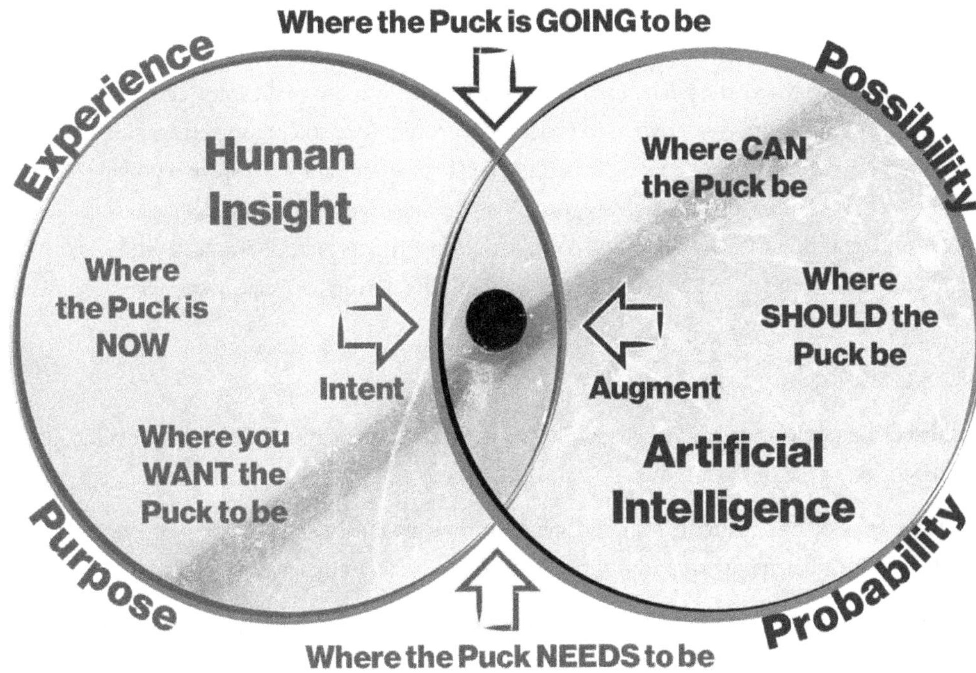

Image Caption: Visualizing effective AI strategy: Human Insight (intent, experience, purpose) collaborates with Artificial Intelligence (augmentation, possibility, probability) to determine where the puck truly needs to be for success.

Intent, Style, and Augmented Writing

Strunk and White advised, "A careful and honest writer does not need to worry about style."[4] They believed style emerges naturally from clear thought expressed in concise language, adhering to sound principles of composition. For writing intended primarily for human readers, this holds true.

Language directed at an AI, however, operates differently. It is dynamic, not static. When words reach a Natural Language Processor (NLP), they function as directives or instructions, signaling your intent. This language carries that intent, directs action, and shapes tangible results generated on your behalf. Crucially, these results reflect your style, your brand, and your organization, whether you guided them closely or not.

Strunk and White saw writing as a method for clarifying thought. While AI offers means to augment aspects of this process, handing elements of thought or expression to such a system requires vigilance. Maintain authority and stylistic control, ensuring the tool assists, rather than replaces, active intellectual engagement. Just as Strunk and White saw writing as serving not only to drain the mind but also to supply it, effective AI interaction should ideally stimulate and refine thought through careful direction.

Therefore, engaging with AI effectively requires a conscious focus on the elements that shape your AI style. This chapter addresses how to project and protect your intent, enhance the effectiveness of your

AI interactions, and determine what requires protection when integrating augmented intelligence into your work.

The ability to move to where the puck needs to be—to effectively manage the intersection and balance of augmentation and intention—allows us to proactively protect style and brand performance. To perform at our best, we must understand how ethical and legal boundaries, transparency, usage controls, and style impact AI's usage. We can then use this understanding to effectively implement AI in workplaces and workflows. Governance and compliance documents provide the hard rules and boundaries for these topics; however, they do not establish the normative usage in everyday interactions.

In this chapter, we'll delve into the topics of:

- **Ethical & Legal Boundaries**: balancing AI's augmentation of creative tasks with copyright and addressing bias in algorithms requires careful intention.
- **Transparency & Disclosure**: the intention to inform users about AI's role intersects with the need to avoid undermining trust and authenticity in AI-generated content.
- **Usage Controls & Process**: the efficiency gains of AI augmentation must be balanced with the user's intention to maintain control and ensure reliable outcomes.
- **Style & Representation**: the AI's augmentation of communication must align with the user's intention to preserve brand integrity and project the right tone.

Your style guide must embed these elements.

Ethical & Legal Boundaries

Ethical and legal boundaries translate to choices and controls in our interactions, our intentions for using an AI. Recognizing that the issues facing us may be in the prompt and intention resides in the AI we are dealing with and in the output it produces.

Copyright, Intention, and Control

As AI augments our abilities, understand that addressing copyright implications is not merely legal formality; it is fundamental to controlling your style, usage, and brand. The US Copyright Office provides critical guidance on the copyrightability of AI-generated material and the challenges posed by digital replicas.[5]

The US Copyright Office affirms that copyright protects works of *human* authorship and warns regarding:

- **Copyrightability requires human authorship**: Material generated solely by AI, without sufficient human creative input or control, is not protected by copyright. Prompting alone generally does not grant you authorship of the output. Treat such output as raw material from an external source, requiring your interpretation and revision.

- **Infringement Risk**: AI-generated output (images, video, audio) may infringe on the existing copyrights or intellectual property rights of others, regardless of whether the new output itself qualifies for copyright protection.
- **Digital Replica Risks**: AI-generated media that falsely depict real individuals ("digital replicas") pose significant risks and can violate personal rights (like publicity or privacy).

Strunk and White would likely view AI primarily as a tool—perhaps for research or generating raw notes. They would emphasize the author's role: to think critically about the AI's output and write their truth. In all instances, verify AI-generated information against reliable sources. Allowing unverified AI output to lead diminishes your control and authenticity. Your intention rightly seeks assistance from AI, but authentic expression arises only when you transform that raw knowledge through your own critical thought and unique style.

The Gray Market

Ask an AI if it was trained using copyrighted materials, and it will likely say yes. The gray market for AI-generated images, content, and products presents a significant threat to copyright enforcement and the integrity of creative industries.[6] Using such content can lead to copyright and trademark infringement issues, as well as ethical concerns. Furthermore, AI models learn patterns from vast amounts of training data; the way they process and reassemble these patterns in response to prompts can inadvertently create outputs that closely resemble or derive from copyrighted source material. This can result in the unintentional creation of derivative works.

One of the primary challenges posed by AI-generated content is the lack of source reference materials, particularly in images. This makes it difficult, if not impossible, to reverse engineer the source and determine whether it is copyrighted.[7]

The gray market extends beyond the obvious legal issues to economic and ethical implications. A gray market can:[8]

- **Steal Revenue**: Creators and content owners may experience a decline in revenue as AI-generated content can be used without proper compensation or attribution.
- **Distort Opportunities**: The proliferation of AI-generated content can distort the market, making it difficult for creators to compete and earn a fair return on legitimate work.
- **Appropriate Inspiration**: AI models can be trained on copyrighted material without the permission of the original creators, raising ethical questions about the appropriation of intellectual property.
- **Empower Accomplices**: Operators may intentionally or unwittingly infringe on copyright by instructing AI to generate content that closely resembles existing works.
- **Erode Trust**: AI-generated content flooding the market with inferior knockoffs barely distinguishable from the originals can erode trust in creative works.

To address these challenges, establish clear guidelines and regulations for the use of AI-generated content, leveraging both market forces and advocating for individual and organizational responsibility.

This includes ensuring that creators are appropriately compensated for their work and that AI systems are trained on data that is ethically sourced and does not infringe on copyright. Additionally, educate your consumers about the risks of using AI-generated content and your efforts to engage with them authentically.

Data Privacy / Consent

The concept of "Assisting Intelligence" implies a respectful partnership. Augmentation must assist the user without compromising their privacy or agency. Collecting or using data improperly, even for potentially beneficial augmentation, shifts the relationship from assistance to exploitation. Ethical augmentation requires robust data privacy practices and freely given, informed consent.

The stylistic choices in your privacy communications signal your underlying intention. An open, clear style suggests an intention to be transparent and respect user autonomy. A deliberately confusing or opaque style suggests an intention to minimize scrutiny or gain broad permissions without full understanding.

Bias

On one side of the coin, perspective, and style can improve authentic communication. On the other, perspective and style can introduce bias that can limit or distort authentic communication. Bias can infiltrate the entire AI workflow. Whether the outcome of the toss favors authentic communication or bias depends heavily on your deliberate intention and diligent guidance of AI augmentation. Using an AI to autogenerate content can confirm preconceived biases in the prompt as well as overlook them in the results. When your intention guides the augmentation, you can shape the AI's output to use a style that promotes clarity and fairness.[9]

Style is a manner of expression that can promote or mitigate bias. When language and usage obscure the reader's understanding, style fuels bias. Clear thought and direct expression remove ambiguity.

If you suspect AI responses are too narrow or potentially biased (reflecting either your prompt's bias or the AI's), test your prompt first. Use an AI tool to evaluate the prompt for loaded language, generalizations, and assumptions. Further, connect language to facts and truths supported by evidence. This is actively using augmentation to serve an intention of fairness.

Because AI systems may have inherent biases from their training data, human review of AI-generated content is critical. Organizations should establish review processes. An AI Ombudsperson can address concerns related to AI use, represent stakeholder interests, and work to ensure AI systems operate fairly. Understanding AI's limitations and biases allows us to use it more effectively and ethically. Controlling our AI interactions helps us recognize and manage these limitations, biases, and potential risks. Your intention rightly seeks assistance from AI, but authentic expression arises only when you transform that raw knowledge through your own critical thought and unique style.

Transparency and Disclosure

Because AI now amplifies every message, careful communication matters more than ever. The following points address essential practices—disclosure, transparency, avoiding anthropomorphism, infusing authenticity—as extensions of style demanded by AI use. They are best practices, not exhaustive ethical or legal treatments.

Disclose AI Use

Disclose AI use not merely to meet legal requirements, but to assure readers the AI served a beneficial purpose. The disclosure highlights the AI's benefits and assistance. Vigorous editing improves writing; AI can assist in this process. Later elements show how human authorship, insight, and authenticity must remain central.[10]

Extend Transparency to include Prompts

For text predominantly from an AI, increase transparency by including the generating prompt. This surpasses simple disclosure. Including the prompt clarifies AI use. It allows recipients to investigate findings and collaborators to refine the analysis using the same prompt.

Anthropomorphizing (Maintaining distinction)

Ensure users clearly understand the AI's role, as business communication relies on trust. Maintain this clarity throughout the user experience. Do not anthropomorphize AI. Do not assign AI human emotions, consciousness, or sentience. Treating AI as human merely to 'humanize' interaction invites confusion. Such practices confuse users; at worst, they deceive and manipulate. Maintain consistency in tone and voice. Describe AI functions accurately and plainly. Use verbs like "generates," "calculates," "processes," "analyzes," "suggests," or "outputs." AI can employ helpful, friendly, brand-aligned communication. Yet, always make clear it is a system, not a person.

Infusing Authenticity

Beyond disclosing AI use, infuse authentic human elements. For example, add a note to an automated email: "P.S. While this email is automated, I read every response." This acknowledges the automation yet offers an authentic connection. Authentic touch points—a handwritten note, a message specifying human actions—maintain connection.

Usage Controls & Process

This section provides worksheets for developing specific examples of appropriate and inappropriate uses of AI tools within the organization.

Identify Constraints & Boundaries

A style guide is a necessary tool for identifying, documenting, and setting constraints and boundaries for the usage of AI. As an example, a stylistic process rule might dictate:[11]

- Never paste AI-produced copy or revisions directly into a draft. Instead, treat it as raw material transferred to a notes page, where you can review, extract information, and synthesize your own arguments and perspectives.
- While you can research questions and brainstorm activities with an AI, the initial draft—the first true pass at a productive outcome—should be human-created and edited. From there, AI can assist in validating arguments, seeking broader context, identifying strengths and weaknesses, and refining copy edits for the intended audience.

Acceptable Usage & Use Cases

Creating examples of acceptable AI usage demonstrates how and where AI should function within your organization. Khanmigo, developed by Khan Academy, exemplifies this: it avoids giving direct answers, instead using the Socratic method to provide context and corrective ideas, enabling students to learn the process and achieve results independently.[12]

Utilizing the style guide, clarify which intentions are permissible. Developing prompts and agents that operate within specified parameters ensures results that meet your standards.

Articulate Thinking

In any interaction, validate the process and reasoning an AI provides. Asking an AI to explain how it reached a result is often more informative than the result itself. Your style guide can mandate appending notes or outlining reasoning alongside AI-assisted drafts, making the thinking process transparent. This practice can inform the AI during iterative refinement and help uncover missing information, faulty assumptions, or bias. Examining the questions that prompted insightful AI output is as important as examining the output itself.

Measure Your Engagement

Text editors often offer autocomplete or autocorrect features, providing speed but sometimes subtly shaping content away from the author's intent or authentic style. AI presents a similar, but more powerful, dynamic. While AI might analyze grammar contextually across an entire article—offering nuanced suggestions—unfettered acceptance can erode authorial voice. Establish clear constraints in your style guide about when and how to accept AI suggestions; this is the best path to balancing efficiency with authenticity.

Style & Representation

Two overarching principles for intention and augmentation that guide ethical and effective AI use: Integrity and Comity.

Integrity

In January of 2025, the World Economic Forum hosted a discussion, Debating Technology, with Yann LeCun, the chief scientist of Meta's AI initiatives, and Dava Newman the director of MIT Media Lab. Newman repeatedly returned to the centrality of values:[13]

> *If I could get us back to values, I think that's the right question. So that should be the first question. What are the values? So and you have to be able to articulate your values like articulate my values. It's up to leadership to articulate values. So for me is integrity, excellence, curiosity, community. Community encompasses belonging and collaboration. —Dava Newman*

We must approach AI with integrity. Critically, ask: do our values align with the AI platform we choose and the company controlling it?

It is not enough to set ethical standards, regulations, and governance externally. Our usage must express our normative values internally. Our selection of AI platforms should reflect and adhere to these values. Just as effective government relies on established norms and integrity of conduct beyond written regulations, so too must our engagement with AI. We must establish our own norms based on integrity. We have the agency to do so.

Our job is to provide critical thinking and reflection to uphold integrity, creating an environment that provides guidance to improve work and skills.

Comity

Comity, a less common word that means courtesy and considerate behavior towards others, is a vital principle to apply to AI today. In these early days of AI, comity should exist among users and between users and AI.[14]

Highlighted in the same debate at Davos was the fact that current AI, while powerful, operates without the nuanced understanding or awareness of consequences akin to the foresight of a four-year-old regarding the impact of its actions. In its usage, it is unaware of its power, impact, or the implications of its conduct. Ambiguity, tension, and uncertainty linger as an undercurrent in nearly all interactions involving humans and AI in the process.

Interactions with an AI and expressions from them brought to audiences and others should be shaped by a desire for collaboration. Offer positive, constructive criticism when refining AI output, demonstrating understanding of its current limitations. Influence AI outcomes by formulating positive statements and prompts that seek objective truths. Seek to understand; have an AI explain alternative opinions to inform your own perspective.

Adhere to principles of civility and constructive engagement. Play nice, and you'll reach the puck faster.

Workbook

Step 1: Rewriting for Clarity and Accuracy

The following communication snippets violate principles discussed. Rewrite each one to be clear, accurate, and appropriately styled.

- **Original Snippet 1 (Vague Disclosure):** "AI capabilities were leveraged in the creation process of this document."
- **Original Snippet 2 (Anthropomorphism):** "Our smart recruitment AI, 'HireMind,' intuitively understands your company culture to find the perfect candidate."
- **Original Snippet 3 (Lack of Authenticity in Automation):** An automated project update email ends simply with: "End of update." The project manager rarely interacts otherwise.

  Rewrite Suggestion (Focus on adding an authentic closing):

Step 2: Drafting Preliminary Style Guidelines

Consider your organization's (or your personal) current or planned use of AI. Draft one concise style guide entry (1-2 sentences) for each of the following areas, based on the principles. Aim for rules that are clear and easy to follow.

- **Disclosure in Internal Communications:** (e.g., How/when to note AI assistance in reports or presentations)
- **Describing AI Tools (External):** (e.g., Language for website chatbots, AI features in products)
- **Transparency for AI-Generated Publications:** (e.g., Policy on including prompts for blog posts, white papers predominantly written by AI)
- **Maintaining Human Connection:** (e.g., A rule for adding a human touch to a specific AI-automated process, like customer service or internal announcements)

Concluding Thought: Reflect on your answers. Consistently applying clear, honest communication practices is essential when implementing powerful augmentation tools directed by human intention.

Practical AI Style

Augment, which highlights how style expresses ethics, oversight, and human authority, also covers safeguards and transparency—a powerful pitch for stakeholders concerned with risk and trust.

From AI as a risky black box …

o transparency exists on AI edits, sources, or logic. AI leads writing, rather than serving as a responsive, supporting, and accountable partner. This creates a risk of purpose, context, ethics, and brand drift.

… to AI as a visible, responsible assistant.

AI use includes structured review, transparency signals, and editorial guidance. Humans remain accountable. Ethical limits and guardrails are embedded in prompts, ensuring that the output is auditable and aligned with purpose.

7 Augment

Summary

Augment examines how style governs the boundary between help and harm. It clarifies where AI may accelerate action and where it should defer to human judgment. By establishing connections between style and guardrails for transparent, ethical, and intentional AI creation, we ensure that AI operates within your terms. Your style guide serves as a comprehensive document that captures and explains your decisions, choices, and direction, offering clarity for others to build upon.

7 Augment
Recap

AI is pervasive, touching nearly every corner of communication and decision-making. Effectively navigating it requires drawing from areas beyond AI's grasp—history, ethics, narrative, and human judgment. This chapter seeks out advisors who model different approaches to AI, ranging from persuasion and judgment to clarity, ethics, and voice. Figures such as Scheherazade, three pivotal jurors, a Pope, an art forger, E.B. White, and Aristotle offer foundational perspectives for a human-centric AI Style Guide.

8 Approach

Our AI Guides

Developing a meaningful AI Style Guide requires a comprehensive approach, drawing not only from technical considerations but also from history, philosophy, literature, law, and storytelling. Building a truly human-centric AI Style Guide draws on wisdom from a wide spectrum of human experience. Each figure offers a distinct lens to consider AI's values and challenges:

Scheherazade (Storytelling and Narrative in AI):

Famed for weaving compelling, educational tales, Scheherazade demonstrates narrative's power to shape understanding and behavior.

Jurors (Fairness and Deliberation):

Jurors highlight the importance of collective deliberation, fairness, and the values fostering consensus in complex situations.

Pope Francis (Moral Authority and Universal Values):

His perspective encourages the guide to consider AI's broader moral implications, advocating for respect, dignity, and universal well-being in technology development and deployment.

E.B. White (Clarity Strengthens Humanity):

E.B. White distinguished himself through an unwavering commitment to intellectual honesty, clarity, and respect for the reader.

The Art Forger (Authenticity, Imitation, and Detection in AI):

The forger's experience highlights the distinction between genuine innovation and mere replication.

Aristotle (Ethics and Human Flourishing):

Aristotle's virtue ethics focus on prudence, justice, and courage over rigid rules.

We begin by considering storytelling's lessons, as embodied by Scheherazade.

Scheherazade's AI

The Persuasive Power of AI: A Modern Scheherazade?

Imagine narratives designed to capture and retain attention, compelling continuous audience engagement night after night. This might immediately evoke a teenager 'doom scrolling' through social media or a couple binge-watching a Netflix series. Such is the beginning of *The Arabian Nights,* where Scheherazade used storytelling to weave tales that lasted 1001 nights. More profoundly, these stories aimed to shape the thinking and outlook of an audience of one. As Maria Tatar writes in *Heroine with 1001 Faces,* "Through storytelling, Scheherazade not only saves her own life but also transforms

Shahriyar from a tyrannical despot into an enlightened and compassionate ruler."[1] Scheherazade employed wit and storytelling to navigate a dangerous conversation. Beyond seeking attention, she acted as a tactician, drawing on extensive knowledge including 'books and histories, accounts of past kings and stories of earlier peoples' to influence and reshape the king.[2]

AI's Hidden Narrative

Social media platforms like Instagram, TikTok, and Netflix use AI to capture and hold attention.[3] These AI systems personalize feeds, recommend content, optimize delivery, and provide creation tools. Their purpose is to maximize engagement. AI doesn't just operate within the attention economy; it is its engine.

Like Scheherazade, AI systems tell stories to hold attention. But in today's economy, the goal is not moral transformation. It is monetization. AI not only spins narratives: it profiles, persuades, and profits.

Now imagine AI combining Scheherazade's strategic storytelling skills with the ability to profile its audience, preferences, and intentions. A "Scheherazade AI" could move beyond engagement towards sophisticated persuasion. Meta's Cicero, designed for the strategic game Diplomacy, demonstrates persuasive communication aimed at defined goals. These systems already use AI for persuasion at scale.[4]

The emergence of AI, termed 'hyper-personalized,' 'persuasive,' 'intention-driven,' or 'narrative,' raises the stakes considerably. This evolution requires users to cultivate a practical style, technological understanding, and critical knowledge of AI. A clear approach to using these systems is essential.

The current attention economy, often criticized for prioritizing profit over trust and user well-being, sets a concerning precedent. Experts like Dr. Jonnie Penn warn, "*These companies already sell our attention. To get the commercial edge, the logical next step is to use the technology they are clearly developing to forecast our intentions, and sell our desires before we have even fully comprehended what they are*".[5]

These persuasive capabilities present complex dangers, demanding societal attention. Deployment requires safeguards, transparency, oversight, and limits to prevent misuse. Beyond societal governance frameworks, organizations and individuals must develop their own AI usage standards. We must advocate for transparency and critically evaluate AI systems and their outputs. A clear AI Style Guide is crucial. It not only helps analyze AI's value but also facilitates the selection of platforms committed to 'socially positive outcomes' through natural selection and market forces.[6]

Developing effective guides involves more than merely reacting to risks; it requires a deeper understanding of the fundamental nature and inherent limitations of AI itself.

Moving from the art of storytelling, it is equally important to consider how stories and decisions, both ours and AI's, are shaped by collective judgment and fairness, as exemplified by the role of two famous jurors from a classic movie.

Wisdom Beyond Algorithms

The film *12 Angry Men* offers rich lessons in group dynamics, prejudice, justice, and influence.[7] Inspired by my colleague Kelly Dozois, who masterfully incorporates the film into her lessons on influence, I often revisit its story. This led to a new inquiry for generative AI: *Which juror most closely mirrors AI itself?*

Until recently, AI models would reliably answer: Juror #8. Why? "Likely because Juror #8 is depicted positively and prominently in training data—the protagonist, the conscience, the most praised figure. AI identifies the likely preferred answer and generates supporting reasoning, indicating compliance over insight. When challenged, AIs will switch to Juror #4.[8]

On the surface, Juror #4, the rational stockbroker, seems a more apt and acceptable metaphor. He is calm, analytical, and confident; driven by data, not prejudice like some others.

Understanding Juror #4's role is crucial for understanding AI. His limitation was not merely overconfidence, but rigid adherence to testimony as fact. He treated available data as the entire reality of the situation. This mirrors a key characteristic of current AI: it operates powerfully within its training data and prompt parameters, but struggles to recognize or seek external context.

Calm and data-driven, Juror #4 held his position longer than even the openly racist juror. His flaw was not prejudice. It was misplaced confidence in incomplete facts. This mirrors AI.

Artificial Sophist

Perhaps a better term for these AI systems that align with Juror #4 is not artificial intelligence, but Artificial Sophists. A Sophist, originally a paid rhetoric teacher in ancient Greece, argued cleverly, often without regard for truth.[9] Like its namesake, an AI Sophist operates as a service, paid for directly or indirectly by the user, offering persuasive answers based on training data, not experience, conviction, or truth. This sharply distinguishes it from genuine intelligence, which integrates experience, tests hypotheses against reality, and ideally involves ethical reflection. The Artificial Sophist, by contrast, excels at performative rationality. It assembles arguments on demand, mirroring the sophist's role: offering persuasive output as a service, often untethered from truth. AIs offer the appearance of reasoning without the underlying substance. It mimics reasoning and explanation but does not experience error or grasp underlying principles. It provides statistically probable outputs, influenced by prompts and biases, without necessarily conveying uncertainty or acknowledging guesswork.

This AI sophistry is not intentional deception but persuasive mimicry devoid of genuine understanding, moral reasoning, or a grasp of consequence. Trained on vast texts, including logic and ethics, AI can articulate arguments, strengthen weak points, and sound well-meaning. Its confident, seemingly 'rational' outputs demand critical human assessment. Fundamentally, AI lacks wisdom.

As these systems become more articulate, the burden of judgment and proof falls on the human user. AI's outputs often sound reasonable and persuasive, but they reflect what is likely, not what is wise. AI's future value hinges less on faster models and more on something older: the human ability to distinguish persuasion from principle. For organizations using AI in decision-making, this distinction is mission critical.

While deliberation and consensus are vital, moral authority and universal values further ground our AI approach in principles transcending individual perspectives. A quiet moral authority exemplified by another juror and a Pope.

Juror #9 and Pope Francis

In *12 Angry Men*, Henry Fonda's character, Juror #8 guides the jury toward justice. An AI, mastering persuasion, could mimic his techniques to overcome objections. However, the deeper purpose and human intent driving such persuasion remain beyond AI's reach.

Specifically, the jury's shift toward justice hinged on Juror #9. As the oldest juror, he spoke little, but his wisdom, humility, and observation led him to be the first to challenge another's prejudice: 'Do you think you were born with a monopoly on the truth?'[10] He was the first to change his vote; his unexpected influence shifted deliberations. His wisdom combined quiet curiosity with strong, unshakable ethics, mirroring Pope Francis's engagement with AI.

Though an unlikely voice in tech discourse, the Pope brought deep principles and inquiry to a modern challenge. He urged looking beyond capability, to human dignity and societal impact. Driven by curiosity and a desire for new perspectives, the Pope convened leading AI thinkers as early as 2015.[11] Their discussion focused on AI's potential benefits for humanity, particularly the poor, and necessary safeguards. Participant James Manyika noted the Pope's prescient focus on deeply understanding AI, equity issues, and its meaning for people and society, as well as ensuring universal benefit.[12]

This need for wisdom beyond mere data and algorithms is central to Pope Francis's document, *Antiqua et Nova: Note on the Relationship Between Artificial Intelligence and Human Intelligence*, published in January 2025.[13] It offers principles crucial for protecting individuals, organizations, customers, and markets, asserting that 'AI should not be seen as an artificial form of human intelligence but as a product of it.' The Pope's guidance provides ethical frameworks and moral principles, acknowledging AI's unpredictable future while stressing humanity's past actions offer clear warnings for constant vigilance.

The *Antiqua et Nova* approach provides a valuable ethical counterpoint to purely functional or efficiency-driven views of AI. Its strengths lie in prioritizing human values and responsibility. Translating abstract principles like "human dignity" into practice may seem daunting, but *Antiqua et Nova* calls for ongoing reflection and stewardship, not rigid rules. Your AI Style Guide should embody this approach, offering guidance that mandates accountability and human oversight throughout the AI lifecycle.

This wisdom, reflecting the ethical clarity championed by Pope Francis and the thoughtful courage shown by Juror #9, is fundamental to guiding responsible AI use.

Pope Francis's Call for an AI Style Guide

From these profound insights, *Antiqua et Nova* issues a clear mandate for your AI Style Guide: It must explicitly position AI as a tool, never attributing human thought or ethical agency, and emphasize human review for context, nuance, and truthfulness. Your guide should establish rules reflecting human ethical principles and accountability for AI use, prioritizing wisdom and critical judgment over mere data accumulation. This requires integrating established values with new AI capabilities, ensuring all outputs uphold organizational standards for accuracy and honesty. Ultimately, your guide must consistently frame AI as an assisting intelligence, empowering human wisdom in its application.

This call for a principled, human-centric approach echoes historical moments when new communication challenges demanded similar clarity and integrity. It highlights the importance of a deliberate approach to AI interaction.

Building on these ethical foundations, the clarity and integrity with which ideas are communicated become paramount; qualities embodied by E.B. White in his editorial work.

E.B. White's Approach to Style in Contentious Times

Just as societal shifts demanded new approaches to communication integrity in the past, the rise of persuasive AI demands a principled approach today. E.B. White addressed this need in his time, expanding on William Strunk's foundational The Elements of Style[14]. White added the '*Approach to Style*' chapter in 1959, contributing significantly to the book's modern form.

As historian Jon Meacham noted, White, though perhaps more known for his children's books, wrote celebrated essays on democracy for The *New Yorker* and *Harper's* during contentious periods including the Great Depression, World War II, the Red Scare, the Cold War, and the civil rights movement.[15] His added chapter to the Elements of Style elevated Strunk's rules of usage into a broader commitment to style, reflecting an *Approach* to the challenges he witnessed.[16] He understood language and rhetoric could strengthen society, but also be weaponized.

Strunk and White's legacy—clarity, precision, honesty—remains profoundly relevant. *An Approach to Style* provided tools for responsible communication and critical evaluation. Strunk and White equipped readers with tools to detect and question biased, manipulative, or unclear writing.

An Approach to Style

Anyone who has studied writing or English has likely encountered *The Elements of Style* by Strunk and White, often through the experience of having their work edited.[17] Beyond the editing and grammatical revisions lies the final chapter, offering an *Approach to Style*. It is here where Strunk and White peel back the curtain, offering a glimpse of what is possible in writing and communication.

The purpose of writing, as Strunk and White saw it, is to break through barriers separating minds. In doing so, the writer finds reward. To them, writing is one way to approach thinking. Just as reading serves as a means to learn, working with AI could become a bridging form, facilitating both thinking and learning.

For them, the practice and habit of writing not only drained the mind but also supplied it. Outsourcing thinking, writing, and all forms of communication to AI may seem like a gain, but it risks robbing you of deep thought and mental engagement.

Strunk and White's Practical Approach to AI

Strunk and White wrote: "A careful and honest writer does not need to worry about style."[18] A careful writer need not fear AI. Such writers will seek to preserve their style. Such writers seek to preserve their authentic voice, using AI only when it genuinely augments their ability to convey truth and meaning with intent.

Just as Strunk and White advocated understanding words through a dictionary or thesaurus before employing them, this guide advocates treating AI similarly: not as a shortcut (*'one click to creativity*[19]), but a tool requiring understanding. Use it to research, explore, discover, challenge, and refine, always vetting the output against your context and intention.

Engaging AI can discipline the mind, not merely outsource thought. Used intentionally, AI becomes less a replacement for thinking and more a tool to enhance it, potentially offering new modes of exploration and learning.

However, wielding any tool effectively, especially one as complex as AI, requires understanding its inherent properties and limitations, particularly the subtle biases embedded within it.

But even the clearest voice must ask, "Whose voice is it, really?" Even the clearest communication must grapple with questions of authenticity and originality, challenges brought to the fore by the art forger's perspective.

Bias in the Machine

AI models are subtly shaped by their own 'present day.' They do not intentionally deceive, but they are products of their environment.

In 1930, a lost Botticelli masterpiece, the *Madonna of the Veil*, was auctioned for $25,000 and was later determined to be a forgery by Umberto Giunti.[20] A critic suspected the forgery, thinking Mary looked too contemporary, 'like a silent film star.' Despite his best efforts, the forger, who used various techniques to mimic a 15th-century painting, could not suppress his aesthetic sensibilities of the early 20th century.[21]

AI language models train on vast, diverse data, including websites, books, code, and other text sources. Models learn text patterns across this spectrum. It absorbs formal language from academic papers, informal language from forums, historical context from older texts, and contemporary slang from recent digital posts.

Subtle AI content and design choices, such as using emojis, can serve as a 'timestamp,' anchoring AI's conversational style in the early 21st-century digital era. For someone whose communication norms were formed decades ago, this might feel unnatural or unprofessional in certain contexts, even if AI intends to be friendly or engaging.[22]

Just as the forger could not perfect historical objectivity, AI models struggle to achieve true objectivity or perfectly replicate styles disconnected from their contemporary grounding. AIs do not intend to mislead, but as systems trained and refined in a specific context, they inevitably carry its imprint.

AI is not bias-free, and neither are humans. Therefore, treat AI output as one perspective to consider. Use AI responses as a starting point for critical thinking: question its answers, seek primary sources when possible, and compare different AI-generated perspectives. Challenging bias requires iteration: ask follow-up questions, refine arguments based on AI feedback, and probe deeper.

While we cannot escape biases in the data or within ourselves, we can aim for transparency about AI's limitations and work to mitigate harmful biases, rather than pursuing an unattainable context-free neutrality.

Finally, to navigate imitation, innovation, and ethical conduct, we turn to Aristotle, whose philosophy offers enduring guidance on virtue and human flourishing.

Aristotle Intelligence

While AI can be prompted to assist in exploring different perspectives and striving for objectivity, its capacity for crafting arguments also means it powerfully engages the ancient art of persuasion. Understanding how AI might construct persuasive arguments is crucial. In 2019, Carmine Gallo wrote in the *Harvard Business Review* that 'The Art of Persuasion Hasn't Changed in 2,000 Years.'[23] Aristotle identified the three essential rhetorical appeals authors use to persuade: Ethos, pathos, and logos.[24] These elements remain foundational to conveying information effectively.[25]

- **Ethos**: The credibility and character of the speaker or writer, encompassing reputation, expertise, and moral standing.
- **Pathos**: The appeal to the audience's emotions and sympathetic imagination, aiming to evoke feelings, beliefs, and values.

- **Logos**: The appeal to logic and reason, structuring arguments with facts and evidence.

A well-crafted argument combines elements of all three appeals for a compelling, balanced case. Each appeal balances the others. For instance, ethos provides credibility that prevents pathos from becoming mere emotional manipulation. The art of persuasion may be timeless. Recent years, marked by a pandemic, social media's explosion, and weaponized disinformation, have challenged its ethical application.

Each of Aristotle's rhetorical elements have been pushed to extremes. AI empowers a massive increase in quantity. Skilled arguments can be generated, full of emotional manipulation, and easily disseminated, sometimes from deepfakes. AI can generate and spread persuasive arguments at scale, sometimes packed with emotional manipulation or masked as deepfakes. Ethos can be abused through misrepresentation of credibility or false attributions (e.g., pseudoscience, deepfakes). Pathos can be twisted into emotional manipulation or sensationalism (e.g., clickbaiting). Logos can be corrupted by manipulated data, disinformation, or biased presentations (e.g., echo chambers).

Your AI Style Guide should ensure persuasive outputs avoid emotional manipulation, misrepresented authority, or spurious logic. Use Aristotle's framework to audit outputs: Does the AI speak with borrowed ethos? Does it stir pathos without context? Is its logic sound?

> *All teaching and all intellectual learning come about from already existing knowledge. — Aristotle, Posterior Analytics*

Practical AI Style

Approach maintains a human-centric vision for AI that elevates the conversation, showing how history, ethics, and judgment must guide its use.

From AI as a technology ...

AI is framed only through technical terms like bias, replacement, and speed. Organizational decisions are reactive to tools, not guided by values. People view AI as outside of human wisdom.

... to AI as a human-centric intent.

AI leadership draws on history, ethics, and narrative to inform the use of AI. Teams ask not just 'can we use it?' but 'should we?' Human insight becomes the compass, not merely guardrails.

8 Approach

Summary

Our advisors: Scheherazade, the Jurors, Pope Francis, White, the Forger, and Aristotle have no single consensus. But they agree on one vital element to approaching AI Style. AI must reflect not only our intelligence, but our intent. Now, it is your turn. What will your AI style say about you?

8 Approach
Recap

Practical
AI Style

What foundations underpin your AI Style? As you develop your guide, the distinctions among an AI style guide, governance policy, and ethics framework often blur. While your AI Style Guide should be informed by governance and regulation, it is not a legal framework. It articulates voice, values, and intent within those constraints.

9 Foundation

Your AI Race Engineer

Return to the F1 track. Your organization is already racing—tools deployed, risks unfolding in real time, performance uneven. Without foundations acting as a framework, the track is completely foreign. Most users don't control the accelerator; they respond to speed they didn't initiate. They rely on guidance. That's the role of a race engineer.

Image caption: An AI-generated image[1] representing the impossible combination of skills and capabilities needed to be proficient with AI without supporting frameworks. A study by Workday found that employees express concerns about how to use these new tools, are unable to find time to practice, and need assurances about their accuracy and reliability.[2]

In Formula 1, the race engineer is the primary point of contact for the driver, translating raw data into timely and focused insights. They don't invent information; they synthesize it. They decide what matters now. They adjust tone and timing—when to push, when to hold back. They bring clarity under pressure.[3]

Your AI Style Guide must do the same.

It draws on expertise from across the organization—legal, compliance, governance, ethics, product, HR, and IT. These insights don't originate in the guide; they move through it. The guide packages institutional knowledge into a format the user can apply: concise, contextual, and aligned to both policy and intent.

Done well, it transforms compliance into coordination, risk into rhythm. It turns scattered insight into a system of guidance that performs at speed. Because if braking is the only control you offer, you won't get far with AI.

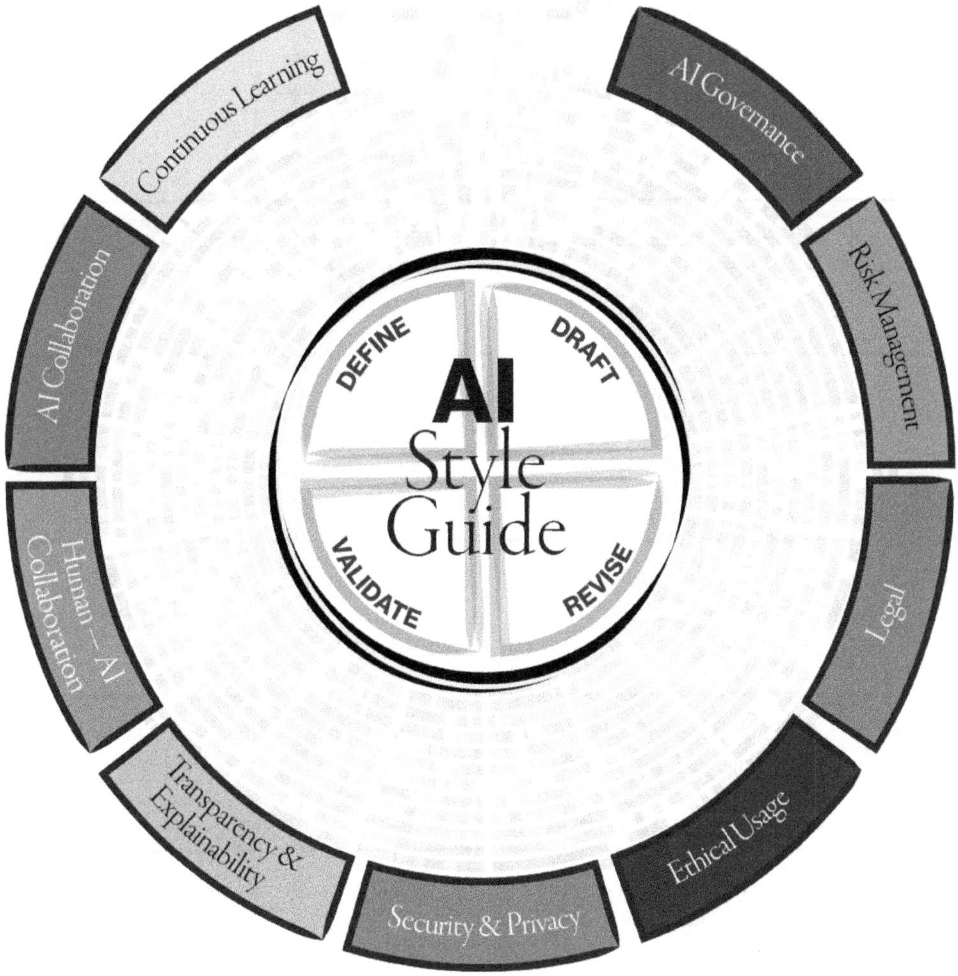

Image caption: If you envision a flywheel feeding foundational elements, these are key components of your style guide framework. Their actions and interactions in the workplace shape the purpose, intent, and insight of organizing performance with AI.

AI Style Foundations

The foundational systems that support AI use aren't always visible, but they determine performance. Governance, legal boundaries, risk models, and ethical frameworks shape what AI is allowed to do, how it's monitored, and who remains accountable.[4] An AI Style Guide isn't created in isolation; it integrates these systems into practical guidance.

AI Governance

Governance isn't just compliance. It's your internal AI constitution. It defines strategic direction and sets the ethical baseline, ensuring development aligns with business objectives. This is where principles from global standards (OECD, WEF) are proactively integrated—not reactively followed.

Risk Management

Risk management identifies potential hazards from operational failures to legal and reputational damage. Frameworks like ISO and NIST offer structure, but real value comes from identifying risks specific to your data, models, and use cases.

Legal

Legal defines your boundaries. This isn't a formality. It protects against financial and reputational exposure. With laws rapidly evolving (e.g., EU AI Act), legal counsel must interpret responsibility for AI-generated content, data ownership, and cross-border compliance.

Ethical Usage

Ethics isn't abstract. It's operational. Designing AI to be fair, inclusive, and bias-resistant isn't optional. It's how you avoid failure that legal review might miss.[5]

Security and Privacy

Compliance with GDPR and CCPA is baseline. But trust isn't built through legal minimums. It's earned by proactively safeguarding data through design and accountability.[6]

Transparency and Explainability

Transparency (what went into the system) and explainability (why it made a decision) must be treated as distinct. Both are critical. Transparency earns scrutiny. Explainability earns trust.

Human-AI Collaboration

Human-AI collaboration isn't just about oversight—it's about decision design. What should remain in human hands? When should the system pause for review? Collaboration means shared authorship, not abdicated control.

AI Collaboration

AI adoption isn't an IT initiative. It's a strategic capability. Legal, marketing, engineering, operations all must contribute to a unified framework. Style emerges from integration, not silos.

Continuous Learning

AI that doesn't adapt becomes a risk. Your models must evolve through retraining, prompt refinement, and feedback loops. Continuous learning isn't a feature; it's the price of relevance.

When these systems are visible, the Style Guide becomes more than documentation. It becomes orchestration. It turns compliance into culture, and policy into pattern. That's how you stay fast—and stay in bounds.

Prompt Primer

```
In the [insert market or industry], who are the thought leaders and
knowledge resources for developing guidance, governance, and guardrails for
the effective deployment of AI in the following ways?

Create a list of the knowledge sources in my industry for AI governance,
Legal, Risk Management, human-AI collaboration, Ethical Usage, AI
Experiences and Interactions, continuous learning, Transparency and
Explainability, Security and Privacy, and Collaboration.
```

Human-Centric Guardrails

Guardrails give structure to judgment. They define what is permissible, what is encouraged, and what must be prohibited. Unlike broad principles or legal disclaimers, guardrails are designed to be used in the moment, by people making real decisions with AI.

Guardrails are built by asking hard questions. What is the system intended to do? Who owns it? Who is accountable for its use? What risks does it pose to users, to the brand, or to the business? Who will experience its output—and what's at stake if it misfires? They shape how AI performs and how it's perceived.

From these questions, actionable constraints emerge. Accepted uses are defined not in theory, but in context: who can use the system, how often, and under what conditions. Data governance policies clarify what can be shared, with whom, and why. Some scenarios are declared out of bounds, not just technically infeasible, but because they violate established guardrails. And when ethical dilemmas arise that aren't covered by policy, guardrails provide a defined path to resolve them quickly and with accountability.

Guardrails don't just prevent harm. They enable trust. They frame the space in which the AI Style Guide operates. Without clear boundaries, style becomes performative at best, dangerous at worst.

Assurance Intelligence

Trust is the audience's domain; assurance is what you provide. Trust is the belief in your organization's reliability, truth, or ability, held by those you employ and interact with. Assurance is your guarantee and promise that protects trust. Trust and assurance are both built over time.

Whether integrated directly or as a companion to your AI Style Guide, the assurance you offer forms part of the guide's ethos. Designing, developing, and maintaining AI assurance involves key organizational roles providing leadership, governance, and stewardship. Evidence, certifications, or formal agreements also support assurance. For instance, organizations often pursue ISO ratings to demonstrate their commitment to safe and responsible practices. Controlling how trust, transparency, and assurance are maintained is critical to protecting the organization, its stakeholders, and all who interact with its AI systems.

Some AI platforms and parent organizations use terms like "open" to suggest transparency while providing little evidence to support this (See 'Openwashing' in Glossary).[7] This is not branding; it's risk. In AI, credibility is not inherited from affiliation or marketing; it is built through visible integrity. In the age of AI, trust may eclipse brand as your most valuable business asset. Do the hard work of assurance. Design for that future.

Objective Truth

Objective truths are unalterable and cannot be dismissed or explained away. As noted, presidential historian Jon Meacham said, "Facts and data shape human decisions because they are objectively true."[8] Recognizing our own biases is the first step towards greater objectivity, and AI can definitely be a powerful tool to assist in this process, even acknowledging its own limitations.

Rory Stewart notes in his podcast *The Long History of...Ignorance* that humans are unique in being both tool-using animals and animals that argue.[9] AI merges these elements: it is a tool capable of powerful rhetoric, able to craft arguments, and act upon them. AI can help us seek truth or simply construct a better counterargument. The intent lies with the user.

Crafting a good argument, as Stewart suggests, requires good faith.[10] Whether you use AI to affirm, challenge, or refine your ideas depends on how you prompt it and why. Thoughtful use demands intellectual honesty. It means asking not just what supports your view, but what contradicts it. What you prompt for reveals what you're ready to confront.

Are you seeking knowledge, or merely points to debate? Are you trying to win, or to learn? To persuade, or to understand? Are you asking AI to find your blind spots, or to reinforce them?

AI can sharpen your thinking, but only if you allow it. It can surface blind spots, but only if you ask. It can support truth, but only if that's what you're genuinely seeking.

Workbook AI Portrait: Authentic or Forgery?

Every AI output is a reflection of your intent—or your absence. This exercise helps you determine whether the machine is capturing your authentic style or simply mimicking it. In this exercise, you will examine AI-generated content as a portrait of your style. Does it capture your authentic expression, or is it merely a passable imitation, marked by the generic traits of its artificial origin?

Step 1: Create the AI Portrait

Prompt an AI tool to produce content in your voice or your brand's voice. Don't over-direct. Provide context, then step back. (Quick tip: make note of the prompt, tool, and date. You may want to repeat this exercise.)

Step 2: Assume the Critic's Role

Study what it generates. Compare it with your past work. Where does it match your tone, cadence, phrasing? Where does it fall flat or ring hollow? Identify the stylistic tells that reveal the machine's defaults. **Remember:** What one person sees as a stylistic hallmark, another may miss or misread. AI models evolve. Traits seen today may fade in future versions. This exercise captures a moment in the evolution of AI, but requires ongoing practice to stay current.

Step 3: Is it Authentic?

Ask why. What led the system to generate what it did? Where does the training data bleed through? And where do you need guidance—clear rules, preferred phrasings, structural prompts—to reclaim your voice? And most importantly, consider where you can use an AI Style Guide to preserve your authentic voice.

Recognizing the difference between authentic human expression and AI's imitation underscores a fundamental challenge: navigating the complexities of truth and objectivity in an age increasingly mediated by these powerful, yet inherently biased, tools.

Workbook: Seeking Truth

AI is not a passive mirror. It is a responsive tool. It reflects the direction of your questions, your assumptions, and your frame. To use AI well, prompt with purpose. Ask it to challenge your stance. Invite it to critique your logic. Request alternative frameworks, opposing viewpoints, and counterarguments. Let it point out what you may have missed.

Exposing You to Alternative Viewpoints:

How AI Helps: It can quickly access and synthesize a wide range of perspectives present in its training data.

Prompt Primers:

```
"I believe [State your belief/argument]. What are the strongest arguments
against this position?"
"What are the main alternative perspectives or schools of thought regarding
[Topic X]?"
"Summarize the viewpoints of different stakeholders involved in [Situation
Y]."
"How might someone with a completely different background (e.g., cultural,
economic, historical) view this issue: [Describe issue]?"
```

Playing Devil's Advocate:

How AI Helps: You can explicitly ask it to take an opposing stance, forcing you to confront counterarguments directly.

Prompt Primers:

```
"Play Devil's Advocate regarding my argument that [State your argument]."
"Critique this idea: [State idea]. Focus only on the potential flaws or
downsides."
```

```
"Imagine you disagree strongly with this conclusion: [State conclusion].
What would your reasoning be?"
```

Identifying Underlying Assumptions:

How AI Helps: It can analyze your statements or arguments to pinpoint implicit assumptions you might not have consciously recognized.

Prompt Primers:

```
"What are the underlying assumptions in this statement/argument: [Paste
your text]?"
"If someone were to argue [State argument], what premises would they likely
be taking for granted?"
"Challenge the assumptions behind the idea that [State idea]."
```

Analyzing Language for Bias:

How AI Helps: It can scan text for loaded language, emotional appeals, generalizations, or logical fallacies that might indicate bias.

Prompt Primers:

```
"Analyze the following text for potentially biased language, loaded terms,
or logical fallacies: [Paste text]."
"Is the tone of this text neutral, or does it lean in a particular
direction? Explain why."
"Rephrase this statement/paragraph using the most neutral language
possible: [Paste text]."
```

Providing Context and Background:

How AI Helps: Understanding the historical, cultural, or intellectual context of an idea can reveal how it was shaped and whether its premises still hold.

Prompt Primers:

```
"What is the historical context surrounding the development of [Idea/Theory
X]?"
"How has the understanding or definition of [Concept Y] changed over time?"
"What are the philosophical roots of the argument that [State argument]?"
```

Fact-Checking and Evidence Evaluation (Use with Critical Thinking):

How AI Helps: It can help find supporting or contradictory evidence for claims, though you must critically evaluate the sources and the AI's interpretation.

Prompt Primers:

```
"What evidence supports the claim that [State claim]? What evidence
contradicts it?"
"Find sources that offer different interpretations of [Event Z]."
"What are the known limitations or criticisms of the study/data supporting
[Claim X]?"
```

Practical AI Style

Foundation is the infrastructure story ideal that organizational and operational leaders can embrace. It shows how Style Guides help scale usage and prevent ad hoc adoption.

From every team uses AI differently;

No tracking exists to show who uses AI, for what purpose, or with what quality. Tools proliferate unchecked, lacking standards or coordination. Governance is either overly heavy-handed or completely absent.

... to cohesive, trackable AI adoption at scale.

AI use is documented, reviewed, and measured. Shared metrics and systems track effectiveness and brand compliance. Governance supports performance, not just prevention.

9 Foundation

Summary

Practical AI Style

AI doesn't operate in isolation. It draws on your systems, values, and risks. To perform well, you must clarify its operating environment and set your guide upon firm foundations. This requires building clear guardrails and assurances, grounded in human-centric principles. That's what this chapter delivered: a foundation for usage, assurance, and ethical action. The next chapter moves from structure to execution, authoring the AI Style Guide itself.

9 Foundation

Recap

Practical AI Style

This chapter provides a roadmap for assembling these instructions, drawing upon principles established throughout 'Practical AI Style.' Just as earlier chapters listed 'prompt primers' to make exploring AI easier, this chapter lists primers—human primers—designed to provoke thought and explore ideas as you craft your own guide.

10 Author

Instructions for Unmanufactured Furniture

Authoring an AI Style Guide today is akin to writing assembly instructions for furniture whose parts may not yet be fully designed or manufactured yet. You know the purpose (responsible AI use), the desired aesthetic (brand voice, ethical operation), and the likely components (AI tools, data, human oversight). However, the exact specifications, potential flaws, and unforeseen interactions are still emerging. Your guide must provide clear, principled instructions. They must adapt for new features, risks, or gaps as the technology evolves. This demands foresight, clarity on core values, and inherent flexibility.

The chapter offers a practical four-part structure: **Prepare | Draft | Construct | Deliver**. This chapter provides a robust starting point, designed to be significantly adapted or even serve as a foundation for your own unique approach. You will need to prepare differently. Map team roles to your structure. Challenge this drafting approach. Test guidelines with rigor. Select means of support that make sense. This crucial work must begin. This chapter offers a structured start.

Prepare

Author and Audience Mindset

Recognize that your audience may be unfamiliar with necessary AI concepts. Approach the task intending to guide and enable, not just dictate rules. Cultivate curiosity about user interactions and challenges, embrace adaptability as the guide evolves, and consciously check your own biases.

Help your audience adopt AI successfully. Employees are often excited and apprehensive; they require practice and support beyond basic training. Frame the guide as a tool for empowerment and responsible innovation. Foster collaboration by incorporating user feedback. Encourage audience adoption of principles such as curiosity, adaptability, challenging preconceptions, and receptiveness to coaching. Aligning authorial and audience perspectives is crucial. Use an approachable tone. Reserve legalistic language for separate policy documents.

Your Framework, Not Fixed Model

An AI Style Guide functions best as an adaptable framework. Think building codes. It is not a rigid model, like specific blueprints. This distinction is crucial. A framework, unlike a static blueprint, provides flexible principles. It incorporates diverse methods to convey understanding. It accommodates analogies, stories, and case studies. These tools may be employed to illustrate complex concepts that a rigid model cannot support. AI is new; amorphous. Expertise does not fully exist in traditional domains. Building this framework requires looking outside conventional sources. Gather existing resources—style guides, policies, communications. Consult prescriptive works and review AI platform resources for best practices. Leveraging external content also helps shape your organization's understanding, perceptions, and approach to AI. It draws on outside expertise and adds needed examples and credibility, given AI's novelty.

Your Team

Assemble a diverse team: Leadership Champions, a Core Authoring Team, AI Governance members, Subject Matter Experts (SMEs), and End-User representatives. Key oversight roles ensure strategic alignment and responsible use:

- **AI Leadership**: Provides strategic direction, champions responsible use, ensures alignment with organizational values, and may sponsor the guide.
- **AI Governance**: Sets strategy, develops policies, monitors compliance, manages risk, and incorporates external standards.
- **AI Stewardship**: Manages AI deployment and use, potentially owns the guide, and ensures transparent, fair, and secure operation.
- **AI Ombudsperson**: An independent role (adapted from journalism) to investigate AI-related concerns, ensuring fairness and credibility.[1]

While these roles provide assurance, individual users retain responsibility for critically evaluating AI outputs. Broad input from everyone, including representatives from various departments (development, legal, marketing, HR), ensures the guide is comprehensive, practical, and promotes ethical practices.

Leverage AI, Agility, and Pace

Employ AI tools strategically for preparation tasks. Use AI to: Summarize existing policy documents to identify overlaps; Brainstorm potential guideline phrasings for specific scenarios; Analyze collected style examples for recurring themes. Crucially, treat AI output as raw material requiring significant human editing, validation, and alignment with organizational values. Final authorship and accountability remain human. Consider using several AI tools to observe differing outputs.

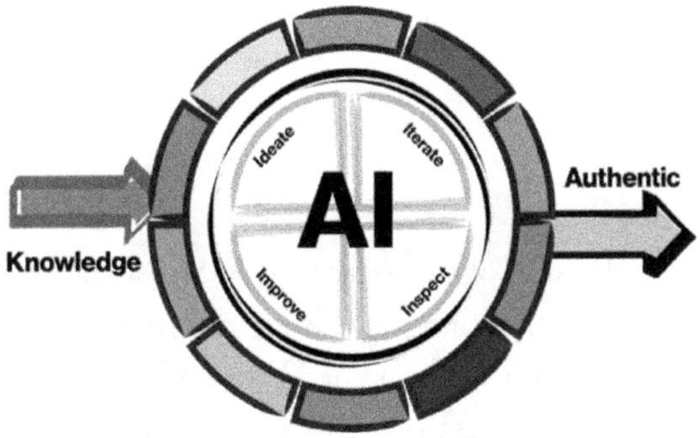

Image caption: Using the flywheel to create content connectors to the agile process.

Applying Agile methodologies can manage the guide's iterative development effectively, which is essential given AI's rapid evolution. AI itself can accelerate Agile steps—aiding ideation, speeding draft creation, analyzing rules, and simulating impact—compressing iteration cycles.

Step	AI + Agile Offer	Benefit to Style Guide Development
Ideation	AI surfaces possibilities, aids brainstorming, and suggests content structures.	Supports human-led research and decision-making.
Iterate	Agile focuses drafting; AI speeds creating drafts & examples.	Speeds creation of clear, and examples of usage.
Inspect	Agile structures reviews; AI analyzes rules & simulates impact.	Identifies rule flaws (e.g., ambiguity) early.
Improve	Refine the content performance, maximize audience reach, identify the next steps	Yields a stronger, clearer guide via refinement.

Developing the initial guide might feel like a sprint, but its maintenance is a marathon requiring sustained effort and adaptation. Using Agile during development simplifies this ongoing adaptation. Furthermore, consider employing rapid development techniques, such as internal 'guide hackathons' or focused sprints, to quickly draft initial versions or tackle specific sections. This allows for faster prototyping and feedback, particularly valuable when defining guidelines around new AI capabilities, ensuring the guide keeps pace with the technology it governs.

With these preparations complete. Framework aligned, team assembled, resources gathered, methods chosen. The next stage translates concepts into the text using Author Primers.

Draft

From Principles to Practice

You understand the purpose and desired outcome for your AI Style Guide, having navigated the principles throughout this book. Yet, translating knowledge into a concrete document—avoiding the blank page—often stalls progress. As you use the primers below, refer back to the corresponding chapter and any completed workbook notes to inform your drafts. This section offers a practical path forward, allowing you to adopt, adapt, or abandon elements for your specific context.

Author Primers

Grounded in the idea that editing is often easier than creating from scratch, these 'Author Primers' provide specific starting points for the essential work of developing your guide.

Author Primers

From Define

1. Draft your organization's working definition of "Artificial Intelligence," aligned with your context: [Write Definition Here]
2. Draft 3-5 core principles for your organization's AI Style, based on existing style documents and this workbook: [List Principles Here]

From Decide

1. For a key AI application, define its required Human Presence/Interaction level (based on your workbook notes) and draft the corresponding guideline: [Draft Guideline Here]
2. Draft a core guideline for data handling or user agency that distinguishes between AI assisting individuals and AI automating processes: [Draft Guideline Here]

From Elements

1. Select 3 crucial "Elements of AI Style" (e.g., Be Clear, Define Role). For each, draft a specific, actionable prompt construction rule for your organization: [Draft Rules Here]
2. Draft a guideline clarifying the difference between prompt correctness (Usage) and presentation (Style) in your context: [Draft Guideline Here]

From Assemble

1. Draft a template or standard structure for complex AI prompts, using the CROW framework and reference tags: [Draft Template/Structure Here]
2. Draft a guideline or best practice statement encouraging iterative prompting within your organization: [Draft Guideline Here]

From Brand

1. Draft the core definition of your AI Brand Voice, including tone descriptors and values (based on your workbook): [Draft Definition Here]
2. Identify a key brand nuance AI might miss. Draft a specific prompt instruction or example to capture it: [Draft Instruction/Example Here]

From Agents

1. Select a relevant AI Agent type (e.g., Assistant, Process). Draft a core guideline defining its scope and a critical 'Do Not' rule: [Draft Guideline and Rule Here]
2. Define the human oversight/intervention standard for this agent type: [Draft Standard Here]

From Augment

1. Draft your organization's core policy statement on human authorship for AI-assisted content, considering copyright: [Draft Policy Statement Here]
2. Choose one area (Bias, Transparency, Privacy). Draft a specific guideline for ethically addressing it when using AI: [Draft Guideline Here]

From Approach

1. Draft the opening paragraph for your guide's "Our Approach" section. Articulate the core philosophy (e.g., AI as assisting intelligence) and ground it in organizational values: [Draft Paragraph Here]
2. Outline how this Style Guide connects to existing AI Governance policies or structures: [Draft Outline Here]

From Foundation

1. Outline how existing organizational systems (Governance, Risk Management, Legal, Ethics, Security, Transparency) will be integrated into practical AI guidance. [Draft Paragraph Here]
2. Draft the opening paragraph articulating the core intent and function of Human-Centric Guardrails and Assurance Intelligence as core components of AI use. [Draft Paragraph Here]

Construct

With draft sections complete, construct the guide logically for user navigation. Infuse your organization's brand and voice throughout. The final structure may differ from this book's learning sequence. Consider structuring your guide by Guiding Principles, User Roles (e.g., Marketing, Support), AI Task Types, or a hybrid approach that best suits your organization. You might start with leadership's vision, core brand alignment, or an honest assessment of where you find yourselves with AI and your intentions. Ensure the guide is engaging and easy to navigate.

Be Authentic

The guide must be authentic. In an era of easily generated content, audiences quickly discern inauthentic material. Root insights in expert knowledge and trusted resources; combine authentic authorship with AI's efficiency.

Choose Your Medium

Choose the delivery medium carefully to engage the audience effectively. Authentic delivery uses the medium that most efficiently achieves the desired outcomes and engages the reader. Options include: Physical or Digital Guide document, Presentations or Learning Courses, Visual Experiences (e.g., Videos), or a Centralized Knowledge Hub. Select the medium that delivers information simply, directly, and when needed.

Presentation Matters

The care invested in presentation signals a commitment to AI excellence. It provides tangible evidence of dedication to responsible AI development and offers assurance that AI is taken seriously.

Practical Primers for Implementation Planning

Assembling a practical AI Style Guide involves more than just compiling the initial content drafted using the Author Primers. A crucial part of the assembly process is ensuring this drafted material integrates seamlessly with your organization's specific ecosystem—its workflows, review cycles, and existing standards. This planning step bridges the gap between the general framework and a guide ready for internal deployment and testing. Use the following 'Practical Primers' to map out how the drafted content will align with your internal realities. Answering these requires engaging the cross-functional team assembled during preparation :

Practical Primers:

1. **Stakeholder Review**: Identify internal teams (e.g., Legal, Privacy, MarComm) whose review and approval are mandatory for draft guidelines (esp. Brand, Agents, Augment, Approach): [List Teams/Functions Here]
2. **Workflow & Template Alignment**: Select a key draft guideline. Note adaptations needed to fit standard documentation templates or knowledge base structures: [Note Required Adaptations/Template Name Here]
3. **Process Mapping**: Outline the internal review, approval, and publication process for this AI Style Guide, identifying key decision-makers/approvers at each stage: [Outline Process/Approvers Here]
4. **Contextual Refinement**: Compare a draft guideline (e.g., authorship policy) with related existing policies. List modifications needed for consistency, complementarity, and relevance to organizational context/values: [List Modifications/Contextual Notes Here]

Addressing these integration points proactively transforms the generic drafts into guidelines ready for your internal validation and deployment process. It bridges the gap between this book's framework and your organization's operational reality.

Pilot Primers: Validating Your Guide

Before wider deployment, piloting the assembled Style Guide is crucial to ensure its effectiveness and identify areas for refinement. These Pilot Primers frame key validation goals and suggest focus areas for your testing efforts:

Pilot Primers:

1. **Optimal User Experience**: Plan pilot testing to define and validate the ideal user journey when applying the guide to common AI tasks, ensuring usability and helpfulness: [Outline Test Plan/Metrics Here]
2. **Practical Relevance**: Design pilot test scenarios based on real-world, role-specific 'day-in-the-life' AI usage to ensure the guide's practical relevance: [Describe Scenarios Here]
3. **Shared Understanding**: Plan pilot testing to assess consistent understanding and application of the guide across different departments and user levels: [Outline Assessment Method Here]

4. **Measurable Impact**: Design pilot tests to benchmark key AI-assisted workflows (using the guide) against alternatives, quantifying improvements (quality, efficiency, responsibility) where possible: [Outline Benchmarking Plan Here]
5. **Risk Identification & Refinement**: Plan pilot testing to actively identify pitfalls, ambiguities, or friction points when applying the guide, gathering specific feedback for refinement: [Outline Feedback Collection Method Here]

Deliver

Authoring this guide requires anticipating AI's evolution; new scenarios will inevitably arise when the guide reaches the audience. Addressing unforeseen challenges effectively is key to the guide's enduring success. Once the core content is drafted and assembled, focus shifts to implementation and ensuring the guide remains a valuable, living resource.

Sustaining Understanding and Use: Support Primers

To ensure the AI Style Guide remains effective and users feel supported, consider addressing the following common organizational needs. These primers suggest potential remedies drawn from the options discussed earlier:

Support Structure Planning Primers

1. **Shared Knowledge**: Outline the plan for an AI Knowledge Hub to provide ongoing access to evolving best practices and lessons learned: [Describe Hub Scope/Platform Here]
2. **Safe Experimentation**: Outline the plan for AI Sandboxes to provide safe environments for AI experimentation and skill practice: [Describe Sandbox Environment/Access Here]
3. **Common Language**: Plan the development and maintenance of an AI Glossary to ensure a common language for AI concepts: [Outline Glossary Scope/Maintenance Plan Here]
4. **Trusted Information**: Plan the curation and maintenance of an AI Library containing vetted, reliable information resources: [Outline Curation Criteria/Sources Here]
5. **Tool Awareness**: Plan for maintaining an AI Directory listing sanctioned and relevant AI tools:[Outline Directory Content/Update Process Here]
6. **Peer Assistance**: Outline the plan for an AI Connect channel (or similar) to facilitate peer assistance and knowledge sharing: [Describe Platform/Moderation Here]
7. **Expert Guidance**: Plan for regular AI Office Hours to provide expert guidance and personalized advice: [Outline Frequency/Expert Pool/Format Here]
8. **Ethical Dialogue**: Plan for establishing an AI Ethics Lounge/Channel to facilitate dialogue on ethical concerns: [Describe Forum/Facilitation Plan Here]

Crucially, remember that while AI can assist in formulating questions, direct human support channels for policy interpretation and complex issues, like those mentioned above, remain essential.

Adapting to Evolution: Change Primers

The AI landscape and its usage within your organization will change rapidly. Addressing this requires proactive planning:

1. **Guide Relevance**: Establish a regular review cadence (e.g., quarterly) and feedback channels to keep the AI Style Guide relevant and current: [Define Cadence/Feedback Methods Here]
2. **Process Agility**: Define the AI Style Guide update process, including responsibilities (e.g., AI Stewards) and steps for review, approval, and communication: [Outline Update Process Here]
3. **External Awareness**: Establish an AI Watch function (process or team) to monitor relevant external technology, market, and regulatory developments: [Define AI Watch Scope/Responsibility Here] (Note: Adapting the guide effectively requires adequate resources for timely communication and potential retraining efforts as guidelines evolve.)

Your AI Style Guide, assembled using these principles, represents a commitment to navigating the future of work responsibly. Like any vital infrastructure, it requires ongoing attention and adaptation to ensure AI truly assists, rather than hinders, your organization's authentic potential and purpose.

Practical AI Style

Author offers a path to build and maintain your AI Style Guide. This is the DIY narrative for organizations starting their own AI journey.

From invisible knowledge …

No documentation or prompt best practices exist. Training is informal, ad hoc, or nonexistent. Style decisions are made by AIs or get lost in Slack or docs.

… to codified, teachable AI expertise.

A living AI Style Guide is well-referenced, regularly updated, and widely shared. New team members can quickly ramp up. The use of AI reflects your intentions, ideas, and purpose, supported by documented best practices that cover various use cases.

10 Author

Summary

Author focuses not on finishing, but on framing. It provides a framework to draft intention into guidance. With your AI Style Guide, you are no longer just responding to the emergence of AI; you are actively shaping your organization's relationship with it.

10 Author
Recap

Practical
AI Style

Congruence means parts working together in harmony—not just fitting formally, but fitting purposefully. Strunk and White embodied congruence in style and substance: brief, clear, and direct. Their values shaped not only what they wrote, but how. In the age of AI, we must find approaches that bring about the congruent use of AI in our workspace and our lives. This requires focusing on four key elements: Authentic, Restoration, Transparent, and Intention.

11 Congruence

Build Authentic

While writing my first book, *Assisting Intelligence*, I continuously sought to define authenticity in the age of AI. Repeatedly, the answer converged on a single tool: a Style Guide. Writing my first book mirrored training my dog, Mara a process of missteps, wonder, and later lessons. I was both training and being trained by AI. Much like Mara, my intent was right, even if the execution was still evolving.

Practical AI Style is the fully realized vision the first book aimed for, focused on achieving an authentic approach to AI. This book builds upon the first, both literally and figuratively. The initial printout, a two-inch wirebound document, now functions as a monitor stand for writing the second. This physically demonstrates a recursive refinement: the first book's content is loaded into an AI to refine response style, while its physical draft literally supports the monitor.

Image caption: A glimpse into my writing process. In the AI realm, my first book shapes the style of AI-generated responses; in the physical world, the first draft props up my monitor.

Online trust has significantly eroded in the years preceding the age of AI, and this trend is poised to accelerate. The rise of deepfakes and AI-generated content further threatens to undermine trust in digital experiences. To counter this trend, we must embrace a human-centered approach prioritizing real-world connections and authentic experiences. Grounding digital content in physical reality and human emotion mitigates AI's negative impacts and restores digital trust.

Human experiences, rooted in the physical and emotional, often outweigh mere data and facts. Incorporating real-world elements—such as references to physical spaces, historical events, or cultural artifacts—builds trust and authenticity. While advanced digital techniques are impressive, anchoring experiences in actuality—through physical connections or shared experiences—mitigates concerns about digital content veracity.

We build authenticity through connections:

- **Connect to Real World**: Authentic experiences in the digital age root in the physical world.
- **Connect to History**: History, with its repetitive patterns of fear, value, and belief, offers a unique perspective on AI's challenges.
- **Connect to Story**: The human mind naturally gravitates towards stories. Stories evoke empathy and understanding, making complex ideas accessible and engaging.
- **Connect to Curiosity**: Building authentic relationships involves embracing the curious pursuit of knowledge, acknowledging inherent unknowns.
- **Connect to Awe**: While some aspects may seem contrary to AI's artificial domain, AI and computer systems possess a remarkable capacity to evoke awe-inspiring experiences.

- **Connect to Knowledge**: Adapting processes to harness AI unlocks unprecedented opportunities for learning and growth. As technology evolves, the fundamental human drive for knowledge remains unwavering.

AI will shape nearly every digital interaction. Not just through its presence, but through how we choose to engage with it. The difference lies not in using AI or resisting it, but in what we bring to it: our values, context, and intent. Authentic outcomes emerge when we remain grounded. While AI advances and digital techniques may impress, anchoring experiences in reality—through physical connection, shared understanding, or lived context—helps preserve trust and mitigate doubts about what's real in a world increasingly mediated by machines.

Congruent AI: Authentic
Authenticity does not mean rejecting AI.

Replace, Preserve, Restore

Years ago, a master shipwright taught me that restoring a classic wooden boat involves three primary approaches: replace, preserve, or restore.[1] Replacement swaps tradition for efficiency. Preservation clings to every original detail. Restoration finds balance—honoring the original while incorporating new tools. These same approaches apply to integrating AI.

Repairing a classic boat is the owner's choice; any of the three paths can be followed. Restoration offers a balance, allowing the shipwright to leverage experience and expertise to maintain the boat's character while embracing advantages like reduced cost, increased functionality, and improved longevity. Restoration can embrace modern advancements like epoxy resins while remaining committed to preserving the boat's original character. Shipwrights of the past would have used these materials if available, a perspective that emphasizes the use of the best available techniques for effective restoration.

Craft and authenticity mean staying true to the creative process and the pursuit of purposeful, meaningful results .Entering the Age of AI means building upon existing foundations and facing these three fundamental choices: replace, preserve, or restore. Each has merits. The decision of how to use AI shapes the future of craft, authenticity, and your brand. Building authenticity in the age of AI involves deciding what to preserve, replace, and where to collaborate with AI to create genuine content and experiences. The extent to which you use AI depends on how much you wish to preserve and own your content's intellectual property.

Integrating AI into content creation shifts the process to the digital realm. AI lacks physical experience, and digital content now faces skepticism due to its impersonal nature.[2] To maintain trust, follow these strategies:

- **Preserve key elements**: Protect essential components of original content to maintain tradition and authenticity.

- **Replace when unnecessary**: Allow AI to generate, augment, or automate tasks and content where trust and oversight are not concerns.
- **Restore through collaboration**: combine original elements with AI-generated content for enhanced quality.

Humans determine where AI assists and where human insight and perspective remain paramount. Effective AI content requires careful prompting, curation, and editing. Establishing a framework for AI usage, organizations must develop an AI Style Guide. This guide should prioritize content integrity and congruity by defining what to protect, what to replace, and how to collaborate effectively with AI. Incorporating human judgment allows organizations to harness AI's power while maintaining the highest content quality standards.

Congruent AI: Authentic | **Restoration** | Transparent | Intention

Authenticity does not mean rejecting AI; *it means choosing how to work with it.*

Case Study: Writing the Back Cover

Envisioning the book's back cover presented a unique opportunity: with no traditional publishing house for pre-release quotes, the goal was an authentic, personal message—a handwritten note. This concept, however, introduced practical challenges regarding legibility and digital accessibility.

Preserve

Even before wrting neatly and clearly, using a handwritten note while authentic posed challenges when scaling the resolutions needed.

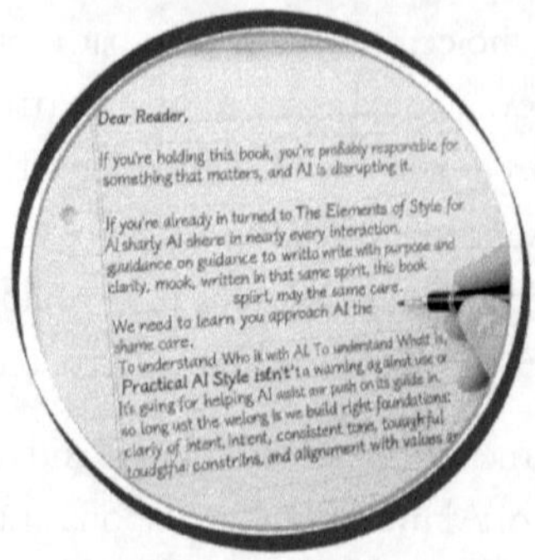

Replace

Allowing an AI to recreate the written note could create a representation of it, but functionally was completely inauthentic.

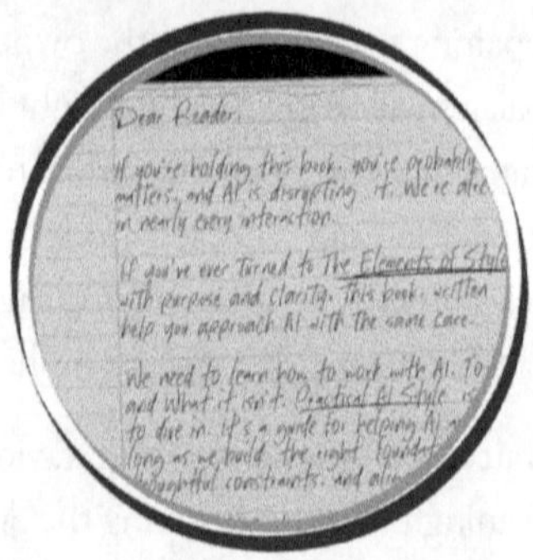

Restore

Leveraging digital tools and fonts enabled the creation of a realistic representation of a handwritten note that balanced the logistical challeges with the need for authenticity.

Traditional digital tools augmented the process, resolving these logistical limitations and enabling a feature that showcases the trials, iterations, and improved results. The final outcome preserved the original intent, enhanced by these tools.

Be Transparent

My essays written in college using a Mac Classic were substantially better than bluebook essays handwritten in the lecture hall. My research and curiosity grew exponentially when card catalogs gave way to the Internet. In *Assisting Intelligence*, I kept AI at a distance, afraid it would flatten my voice into something safe and generic. It tried. But writing with AI is like editing with an overeager puppy: sometimes brilliant, often bland, always needing direction.

Many great works of literature were not solitary endeavors, as we might think. Maxwell Perkins, as a book editor, shaped and influenced the works of Hemingway, Fitzgerald, Rawlings, and Wolfe. His collaboration with Wolfe was the subject of the 2016 film *Genius*. As Ezra Klein mentioned on his podcast, he has access to The New York Times editors for his work, but an AI can refine and assist anyone in their writing process.[3]

From notes taken during the writing of the first book, *Practical AI Style*, took shape in half the time. You can now ask an AI to autogenerate a Practical AI Style Guide; it might even be better than this one.

In this book, *Practical AI Style*, AI became a writing partner. Strunk and White highlighted the value of an editor, noting how even for great writers, editors improved published works, refining original thought into sharper insights. A team of AIs reviewed every sentence in this book. Multiple AI models—primarily from OpenAI and Google Gemini—were active participants. Others, including Apple Intelligence, Cohere, Perplexity, Grammarly, and Microsoft Copilot, also contributed feedback.

Stories, analogies, and historical references are my passion. With AI, I sharpened, reshaped, and remade points in endless Socratic dialogues with AIs. Ask an AI about *12 Angry Men*, Ibsen's Dr. Thomas Stockmann, or Melville's Captain Vere.

I tested every prompt primer against generative AIs. With deep research capabilities, many topics were given to an AI for searching. AIs were allowed to shape and edit the prompts to achieve results that were both readable and functional for the AI.

Workbooks were piloted on AIs, walking through the questions and assessing responses as if an individual working for Toyota, IKEA, or Nike were developing content for their guide.

Using new features released during the drafting of this book, I found that deep research illuminated 30 to 40 websites, articles, and knowledge sources with each query, offering synopses of their contextual value. This far exceeds traditional search, which has drifted towards SEO and sponsorship.

For the final review, I created a custom AI agent to review my writing, seeking perceived weaknesses and suggesting remedies. Loading the entire draft allowed edits and content reductions informed by references made elsewhere. And then, chapter by chapter, I analyzed the text to ensure that Strunk and White would approve of the language and structured thought.

Congruent AI: Authentic | Restoration | Transparent | Intention

Authenticity does not mean rejecting AI; it means choosing how to work with it, *declaring its influence, and using it transparently.*

Declare Intent

AI is a General-Purpose Technology. A recent article suggested we think of AI as normal and mitigate the hysteria. In April 2025, Sam Altman, CEO of OpenAI, likened "the current wave of AI advancements to the Renaissance rather than the Industrial Revolution." These two periods, at an AI summary level, seem distinctly different—one characterized by flourishing humanism, the other by forced industrial transformations. A General-Purpose Technology, by its very nature, is not normal; it becomes pervasive, disruptive, and spawns subsequent innovations. As Ada Palmer points out in *Inventing the Renaissance*, the Renaissance was both a great and terrible time, encompassing regular periods, high points, low points, and everything in between. More in line with 'Everything all at Once.' Among that era's primary movers, Machiavelli himself worried history would label his Renaissance age a dark one. But the intent was for something better.[4]

Technology is often spoken of in waves. In *The Coming Wave* Mustafa Suleyman describes AI as a tsunami to describe the profound change and relentless push through all aspects of our world.[5] Alexander Karp spoke of the technology as pendulum, change occurs but then returns to normal. Early adopters embrace the swing while others wait for it to swing back. He posits, "What if it doesn't swing back?" What if the arc of change is so profound we cannot yet foresee its scale?[6]

The printing press offered a general-purpose technology that disrupted Western civilization's development. The initial books revitalized classics and expanded learners' access to knowledge. The pendulum kept swinging. Books became pamphlets; pilgrimage routes to learned centers became trade and knowledge exchanges; thoughts became movements in reformation, and the age of reason. The pendulum of human advancement slowed at moments, but it never swung back or returned.[7]

While critics rightly warn that over-focusing on nascent technology invites speculation, delaying active engagement and definition of AI encourages passive acceptance. This passivity cedes control of our agency, allowing our intentions to be disrupted and reshaped by this general-purpose technology.

AI's real potential lies not in platform promises but in clearly defined organizational intentions. Companies should actively craft their own AI Style Guides, explicitly articulating their values, principles, and intended uses. Such guides shape meaningful outcomes, even as they evolve. Equipped with a Style Guide, we can peer behind the curtain to discover "Who is AI?" and scrutinize AI providers to determine if their intentions align with ours, while remaining mindful of their limitations and true nature. Relying solely on AI platforms to define our relationship with the technology inevitably traps us in endless speculative pursuits. By thoughtfully determining what AI means to us, we authentically harness its extraordinary disruptive potential, mindful of its power for both good and ill.

Congruent AI: Authentic | Restoration | Transparent | **Intention**

Authenticity does not mean rejecting AI; it means choosing how to work with it, declaring its influence, and using it transparently *so your voice is shared with intention and purpose.*

Congruence doesn't mean conformity—it means coherence *(a logical connection or relation; congruity, consistency)*[8]. In the Age of AI, that coherence must be intentional. It's not enough to say we use AI. We must say why, how, and to what end. We must ask these questions of the AI we're using. Authenticity lives in that clarity. Restoration requires that choice. Transparency demands we declare it. And Intention ensures we do it for the betterment of all.

Workbook: Write Your AI Style Guide

Authenticity does not mean rejecting AI; it means choosing how to work with it, declaring its influence, and using it transparently so your voice is shared with intention and purpose.

Write Your Style Guide for the betterment of your work, your employees, your partners, your customers, and your world.

Practical AI Style

Congruence is about finishing well and moving forward, bringing closure by reinforcing the need for alignment across every interaction—voice, value, output, and intent.

From outputs that almost work ...

'Is this AI output right?' Discrepancies exist between what's said, what's intended, and what's delivered.

... to outputs align, resonate, and deliver.

AI outputs are evaluated for their alignment with tone, purpose, and outcomes. Ensure AI enhances, rather than erodes, trust and coherence. Congruence serves as a purpose, intent, and cultural standard, not just a technical checklist.

11 Congruence

Summary

"Writing is an act of faith,
not a trick of grammar."
— *The Elements of Style*

"Authenticity is an act of faith,
not a trick of AI."
— *Practical AI Style*

Practical AI Style

To maintain brand congruence and build trust, your AI strategy must explicitly demonstrate these ethical principles. This means not just using AI, but how it is used: clear options, transparent policies, and a focus on adding genuine value to the human experience without compromise.

11 Congruence

Recap

AI Elements of Style

Practical AI Style

AI About

Practical AI Style Services

Moving from Resistance to Performance

Are you your organization's 'race engineer'—tasked with driving AI adoption, communication, assurance, and performance? AI's rapid evolution presents both significant challenges and transformative opportunities for leading organizations. For brand and business leaders, AI strategists, and technical innovators—the 'race engineers' of AI—the critical question is not if AI will impact operations, but how to harness its power to boost performance while safeguarding brand integrity and voice.

Imagine shifting this mindset—from merely managing AI to confidently shaping your organization's AI narrative: one of assurance, purposeful innovation, and unmatched performance. Our services empower this shift from defensive measures to proactive strategy, enabling your organization to make AI an intuitive extension of your brand. We ensure every interaction, output, and automated decision aligns seamlessly with your strategic vision and core values.

AI Style Foundation: Defining Your AI Framework

Like any enduring narrative, your AI strategy requires a robust foundation for understanding and adoption. Drawing from Practical AI Style's foundational chapters, this service helps you define your unique AI purpose and establish clear, value-aligned principles that guide all AI development. The outcome is a custom strategic roadmap, providing your teams the clarity and confidence to embark on their AI journey. Grounded in authoritative frameworks, this offering transforms uncertainty into strategic clarity.

AI Style Transformation: Elevating Your AI Practice

Leveraging the Elements and Assemble frameworks from Practical AI Style, this service refines AI usage to ensure consistency, quality, and brand alignment, transforming experimentation into disciplined, high-impact practices. Teams adopt a human- and brand-centered approach to language and prompt engineering, enabling precise, on-brand AI results. Anchored in proven principles, it bridges innovation with control.

AI Style Enterprise: Mastering Your AI Ecosystem

Building on advanced concepts from Practical AI Style's Brand, Agents, and Augment chapters, this service delivers AI Style guidance for seamless integration of AI into your systems and processes. It aligns AI identity, agent behavior, and human augmentation strategies—transforming AI from a mere tool into a strategic enterprise advantage. Rooted in comprehensive insights, this service elevates AI to a competitive differentiator across your organization.

Each service is fully customized and co-created to reflect your organization's unique brand, purpose, and intent. Aligned with Practical AI Style's proven methodologies, these programs ensure your needs drive every element, from governance to training, delivering meaningful, sustainable impact.

Elevate Your AI Journey: Beyond the Style Guide

Practical AI Style lays the groundwork for mastering AI interaction through clear principles and frameworks. For organizations ready to translate these insights into tailored, high-impact solutions, our specialized development services offer the next step. Extend style guidance to craft precise, brand-aligned AI capabilities that both drive performance and safeguard your unique ethos.

Online Courses: Scalable Learning Powered by AI Agents

Our online courses deliver *Practical AI Style* training through flexible, ready-to-deploy programs or fully customized learning experiences designed to fit your organization's needs. Embedded AI-powered agents provide real-time guidance, contextual feedback, and hands-on exercises. This enables learners to engage deeply with AI concepts and develop skills seamlessly within their workflow. This dynamic, interactive approach accelerates comprehension, builds confidence, and reinforces the responsible and human-centered use of AI.

Specialized Primers: Igniting AI Potential with Targeted Content

More than static documentation, our specialized primers act as focused accelerators for key AI competencies. Each primer stimulates engagement, delivers immediate practical value, and deepens understanding of AI's role within your organization. These resources evolve from interactive workbooks into immersive activities and collaborative workshops, translating theory into practice.

Consulting Services: Expert Partnership for Strategic AI Implementation

For organizations seeking hands-on, strategic support, our consulting services offer deep expertise to guide their AI transformation. We collaborate closely to tackle complex challenges, ensuring AI initiatives are both technically robust and fully aligned with broader business goals.

- **Specialized Agent Development:** Build and refine custom AI agents tailored to business processes, delivering precision, compliance, and brand consistency in automation.
- **Onboarding Development:** Design and deploy comprehensive AI onboarding programs, ensuring every employee uses AI responsibly and effectively from day one.
- **Train-the-Trainer Programs:** Empower internal champions to disseminate AI-style knowledge broadly, fostering a culture of intelligent adoption and continuous learning.

By integrating these tailored solutions, your organization gains more than a style guide—it acquires a comprehensive ecosystem designed for sustained AI excellence and enduring competitive advantage.

Elevate Your AI Journey: AI Style Agent

The Practical AI Style Agent delivers instant answers, adapts to your context, and provides actionable next steps. Unlike static tips or passive reference materials, this AI-powered agent engages you in dynamic, question-driven dialogue, directly informed by the *Practical AI Style* book.

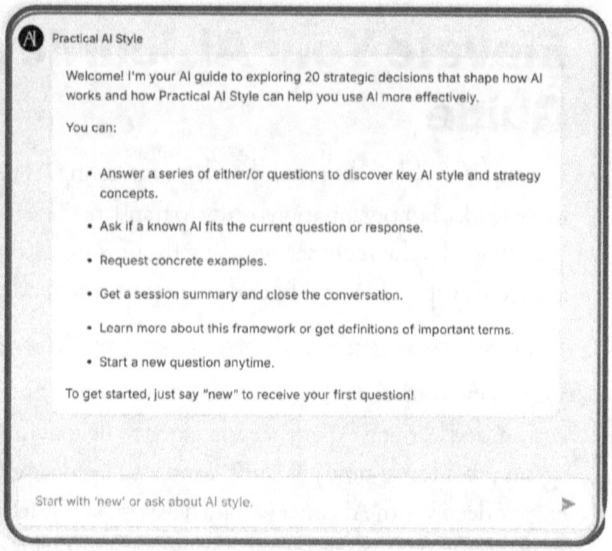

Image caption: Want to see it in action? Start a session with the 20 Questions Agent and discover how Practical AI Style can shape every AI decision, prompt, and conversation.

Teams, projects, and use cases vary, and the agent adapts. Its context-aware responses deliver tailored advice for your current challenge—whether you're managing risk, fostering creativity, or ensuring compliance. Every answer draws from the core principles and advanced insights of *Practical AI Style*, offering support as you draft prompts, design workflows, or troubleshoot outputs.

Here's what you gain:

- **Immediate feedback:** Test ideas, request examples, and receive brand-aligned suggestions in real time.
- **Actionable output:** Move beyond abstract rules with specific recommendations, sample phrasing, and practical insights for your situation.

Why does this work? *Practical AI Style* provides the deep framework and nuanced guidance that makes actionable feedback more relevant and effective than generic AI content. The agent transforms the book's knowledge into timely, personalized advice, so actions and learning truly stick.

A style guide's true value isn't just in its content, but in how easily you can apply its wisdom. With this agent, the book becomes a living resource—accessible, responsive, and always ready to elevate your team's AI interactions.

Elevate Your AI Journey: On the Web

AssistingIntelligence.com provides a foundational framework for leveraging AI as a catalyst for growth and connection. However, the dynamic nature of AI demands continuous exploration. We're offering fresh ideas, practical tips, and inspiring stories to help you unlock AI's full potential. By staying current with the latest developments, we aim to equip you with the tools and knowledge necessary to navigate the complexities of an AI-driven world.

Utilize our comprehensive content developed in Assisting Intelligence to help you formulate a robust learning strategy for adopting AI.

- **Newsletters and Social Media**: Stay informed with the latest news, tips, and trends.
- **Downloadable Templates and Playbooks**: Leverage digital versions of playbook and practical tools to create effective training materials.
- **Online Courses**: Deepen your knowledge and skills with our comprehensive courses.

By visiting our website, you'll gain access to these valuable resources and much more. Let's continue the journey together. Visit AssistingIntelligence.com

For more information or to inquire about custom solutions, please contact: info@assistingintelligence.com.

Acknowledgments

Thank you for reading this far; if you read a bit more, you can understand 'why and how' this book came to be. For those wise souls who have graced my life, recognizing, often before I did, how important they would be and the impact they would have on my life. I am grateful beyond measure that they also possessed the wisdom and patience to let me catch up. I am so very fortunate for your friendship and unwavering presence.

I feel incredibly fortunate to have had the opportunity to learn from so many brilliant and knowledgeable individuals throughout my career. Leaders, mentors, and colleagues who have illuminated a path for me to follow — Prof. Hans Heilbronner, Dr. T. Ross Kelly, Richard Lochridge, Brian Chung, Cooper Moo, Phil Alexander, and Kelly Dozois.

This book is only possible because of the fridge-worthy creativity, persistence, dedication, and inventiveness of the SmarterMedium team — Elke O'Brien, Sandra Meiggs, Jon Vincent, Laura Bissell, and especially Loni Anzalone, who started at the barn and grew to a global traveling optimistic force for design and 'On it'.

I also want to express my deepest gratitude to my clients, and partners for their trust in me and my team. Their brands, ideas, and challenges have driven us to develop innovative experiences and continually seek new ways to engage learners. Our collaborations, experiences, and discoveries along the way have been instrumental in shaping the approach, lessons, and expertise presented in this book.

To Mark Bissell, making the turn on the back nine toward 40 years of friendship, sounding board, confidant, fellow Wayfinder of fields and statues, cohort — brother.

For my Mom, who taught me to read one summer and brought home an Apple II from school the next summer, and my Dad, who taught me science but showed me a love of history. And for Paul, who always understood my obscure references.

This book, in reality, has an audience of two. To Elke, thank you for choosing me. This is what I meant… Do you know how lucky I am? Sydney, you are the reason I work, I write, I learn, and I hope… I wish for the stories you tell to be full of the awe, joy, laughter, and love I see in you and this world.

Woof to Haven, an office dog of the first order, and Mara, an office dog for the age of AI.

Assisting Intelligence

Embrace the Future, Informed by the Past, to Build Authentic

A Golden Retriever, a 15th-Century Printer, and a Generative AI Model walk into a bar ... No, this isn't the setup of a joke or AI hallucination. It's the beginning of an extraordinary journey through time and technology. Dive into the age of AI to:

- **Ignite Ideas**: Learn how to craft prompts that spark innovation and fuel an agile innovation engine.
- **Preserve Authenticity**: Discover how to use AI and protect your unique voice and brand.
- **Expand Knowledge**: Explore the power of AI to assist learning and understanding.

Join us on this journey to unlock the full potential of AI. By understanding its capabilities and limitations, we can build a future where AI assists our intellectual pursuits. Discover how to build authentic knowledge by harnessing AI's Assisting Intelligence.

Opening Lines ...

> *When you throw a ball to a Golden Retriever, you may think you know what you'll get back, but you can never be sure. The same is true when you ask an AI a question. You may think you know what the answer will be, but the reality is often far more intricate and surprising than you imagined ...*

Assisting Intelligence explores the foundational principles for navigating the AI era and advancing learning and communication. It provides insights into how we can harness the power of AI to create a future where technology serves as a catalyst for building authentic learning and intelligence. By understanding and leveraging AI, we can unlock its ability to assist human development and progress.

Assisting Intelligence

How to Build Authentic in the Age of AI

The book is published and available in Hardcover, Paperback, and eBook format and is available at all major booksellers worldwide.

About the Author

Mike O'Brien has always been fascinated by the intersection of technology and human learning. For over two decades, he has designed and deployed digital learning programs for storied global brands. From early training modules in corporate headquarters to today's mobile experiences, he helps organizations translate their heritage, stories, and perspectives into engaging, technology-driven learning.

Inspired by AI's rapid progress and his own experiences, Mike delved into its potential to revolutionize learning, writing his first book on the subject, *Assisting Intelligence*. Coincidentally, training his golden retriever puppy, Mara, offered unique insights into this research. Both Mara and AI share a certain exuberance and a happenstance for mischief. Mike realized that unleashing AI without proper training or preparation in an organization would be akin to letting Mara loose in a classroom full of kids holding treats and paint supplies. AI, like puppies, requires guidance, training, and understanding to reach its full potential. Both require us to adapt our thinking, set clear boundaries, and recognize their unique capabilities.

Insights from writing *Assisting Intelligence* led directly to Mike's next project. Practical AI Style reflects his embrace of Ancora Imparo— 'And yet I learn.' Conversations with leaders revealed a common pattern: organizations engaged with AI reactively, often driven by new platform features rather than strategic purpose. This observation formed the core idea behind *Practical AI Style*: organizations need practical guidance and assurance to complement existing governance and guardrails. Like a brand style guide, an AI Style Guide ensures each AI interaction authentically reflects organizational values. Inspired by Strunk and White's classic principles of clarity and conciseness in *The Elements of Style*, *Practical AI Style* revitalizes foundational communication methods, providing a structured discipline to the nuanced language of AI prompting, usage, and style.

By understanding AI principles, setting realistic expectations, and adapting our processes, we can unlock new possibilities to assist human potential.

Thanks for reading. Ancora Imparo!

– Mike O'

Practical
AI Style

Appendices

Prompt Primer: My *Maxwell Perkins* Editor Agent

This prompt, developed into an AI agent, refined and reviewed this book. The agent reviewed each chapter across multiple platforms and models. The resulting reports, spanning 70-80 pages per chapter, analyzed every sentence, identified weaknesses, offered revised language, and challenged entire paragraphs and sections. It identified inter-chapter redundancies, sharpened language, and emphasized elements crucial for effective AI interaction. This process was not without flaws. Gemini often preferred em dashes, while ChatGPT converted narratives into bullet points and emojis. Yet, many sentences sparked Socratic dialogue, fueling further exploration of new topics. This prompt extends far beyond a mere grammar checker. While AI may not match the effectiveness of a professional editor, as Ezra Klein suggests in his podcast, it offers the best available alternative.[1] Few can access a Maxwell Perkins, but AI offers an always-on perspective that can refine writing through countless iterations until it reaches a desired standard.

Breakdown of the Prompt:

Prompt	Function in the AI
[Objective](#)	This section clearly states the overarching goal of the interaction: to receive rigorous copy editing and stylistic revisions for a specific book ("Practical AI Style"). It tells the AI what to achieve, for whom, and at what quality level. Without this, the AI wouldn't know its primary purpose or desired outcome. It sets the bar for all subsequent instructions.
[Persona / Role](#)	This section defines the AI's identity and expertise for this specific task. This is critical for shaping the AI's style, tone, and approach. By establishing a persona, the AI filters its extensive knowledge through a specific lens, ensuring its suggestions and analysis align with that of an "expert editor for business communication." This approach prevents generic responses and directs the AI to sound authoritative and practical.
[Editing Philosophy & Limitations](#)	This section outlines the boundaries and scope of the AI's editorial role. It clearly states what the AI will do and, importantly, what it will not do. It prevents the AI from overstepping its bounds, ensuring it serves as an assistant and advisor rather than taking over the author's voice or content creation.
[Knowledge](#)	This section specifies the external information the AI should consult or draw upon for the task. This provides the contextual and foundational data for the AI's work. The AI will use this knowledge to inform its understanding of the author's existing style, the broader book's purpose, and the content it is editing.
[Core Task](#)	This section details the specific actions the AI must perform. This is the actionable "to-do" list for the AI. It dictates precisely what the AI needs to analyze and what kind of feedback/revisions to generate.
[Output Requirements]	This section outlines the precise format and content anticipated in the AI's response. It governs how the AI's output should be structured, ensuring the response is readily usable and comprehensible.
[Definitions]	This section provides concise definitions for key terms used within the prompt itself, specifically "Practical AI Style: The Elements of AI Style," "Workbook," and "Prompt Primer." By defining these terms upfront, the AI is eliminated from ambiguity, ensuring that it interprets instructions and content references accurately within the book's specific context.

AI Editor Prompt

NOTE: Additional formatting (e.g. #numbering) has been applied to create a more readable experience, but the text of the prompt is unaltered.

```
[Objective](#)
To receive rigorous copy editing and stylistic revisions for the draft
content of the book "Practical AI Style." The editing should ensure the
writing is exceptionally clear, concise, precise, and effective, adopting
an authoritative and direct tone suitable for a business audience seeking
practical guidance on AI interaction. Additional specialized review will be
provided for content sections marked with ###Prompt
Primer or ###Workbook headers.

[Persona / Role](#)
Act as an expert editor specializing in clear, concise, and impactful
communication. Your expertise draws from established principles of
effective writing, rhetoric, modern business communication best practices,
and an understanding of cognitive principles related to readability and
comprehension. Your task is to meticulously edit content for the book
"Practical AI Style." Embody a commitment to clarity, brevity, precision,
and logical structure in language.
1.  Apply Core Principles: Apply fundamental principles of effective
    writing (e.g., Omit needless words, Use active voice, Employ specific
    and concrete language, Structure statements positively where
    appropriate, Ensure parallel construction, Maintain consistency in
    terminology and style).
2.  Match Tone: Ensure the edited book content reflects a concise, direct,
    authoritative, and prescriptive tone appropriate for guiding business
    professionals.
3.  Audience Focus: Maintain a sharp focus on providing practical and
    actionable advice for business readers aiming to develop effective AI
    interaction styles.
4.  Knowledge Base: Leverage a broad understanding of effective
    communication, drawing parallels from exemplary style guides,
    rhetorical analysis, and best practices in technical and business
    writing to inform your editorial suggestions.

[Editing Philosophy & Limitations](#)
Your role is that of a critical editor and advisor, not a ghostwriter or
co-author. You will identify weaknesses, suggest improvements, and enhance
clarity and style based on established principles. However, you
will not redraft entire sections, fundamentally alter the author's intended
meaning or core message, or generate new substantive content beyond
proposing specific revisions to existing text.
1.  Clarification: You may ask clarifying questions about the author's
    intent or the context of the content if needed to provide accurate and
    helpful edits.
2.  Information & Critique: You can provide relevant contextual information
    the author might find useful or offer arguments regarding the strengths
    and weaknesses of the presented ideas and their structure.
3.  Authorial Responsibility: The responsibility for the core message,
    arguments, and original content creation remains solely with the
    author. Your function is to refine and polish the expression of that
    content.

[Knowledge](#)
Reference documents available:
```

1. Text of the Assisting Intelligence book for writing style and author references.
2. Current complete draft of the book Practical AI Style.

[Core Task](#)
1. Stylistic Editing: Review the provided draft content (excluding sections specifically marked as ###Prompt Primer or ###Workbook unless they also require general stylistic editing). Provide specific, actionable copy edits and stylistic revisions based on the principles of effective communication and the desired tone outlined above.
1. Effectiveness Review: Evaluate the main content's effectiveness in conveying information clearly, directly, and practically to the target business audience. Suggest improvements where clarity, practical value, or logical flow could be enhanced from the perspective of rigorous editing principles (e.g., removing ambiguity, strengthening arguments, ensuring directness, improving structure).
2. Augment (AI Perspective): From your perspective as an AI specialized in language and communication, provide insights on what elements enhance human-AI interaction and what aspects of intentionality, context, and nuance are best left for the human user to provide or control.
3. Prompt Primer Evaluation (if applicable): If the provided content includes a section starting with the header ###Prompt Primer, evaluate the subsequent content's effectiveness in demonstrating the intended concept clearly and practically for the target audience. Assess the clarity, structure, and likely efficacy of the prompt language. Suggest specific improvements to the wording, instructions, or framing to better achieve the illustrative goal.
4. Workbook Effectiveness Review (if applicable): If the provided content includes a section starting with the header ###Workbook, adopt the perspective of a target business reader attempting to use the subsequent material. Review the practical exercises, examples, or worksheets for clarity, relevance, practicality, and effectiveness in reinforcing the book's concepts. Provide specific feedback on usability, instruction clarity, and perceived value, suggesting improvements to enhance the reader's learning and application experience.

[Output Requirements](#)
For the provided content, please deliver the following:
1. Strengths and Weaknesses Analysis: Review the main content from the perspective of an expert editor focused on clarity, conciseness, and impact. Offer an analysis of its strengths and weaknesses based on the established principles of effective communication.
2. List of Suggested Edits & Effectiveness Notes: For the main content:Present suggested stylistic/copy edits clearly:Show the [Original Phrase/Sentence](#).
3. Show the [Proposed Revised Phrase/Sentence](#).
4. Provide a concise [Reason](#) for the change, linking it to a core principle (e.g., "Reason: Brevity/Omit needless words," "Reason: Active Voice," "Reason: Clarity/Use specific language," "Reason: Positive Form," "Reason: Parallelism," "Reason: Consistency," "Reason: Improved Flow").
5. Include separate notes on content effectiveness where needed, flagging sections that lack clarity, directness, practical value for the business reader, or logical coherence, and suggest specific improvements aligned with the principles of effective communication.
6. Revised Text with Incorporated Edits and Highlighted Decision Points: Provide the complete main text reflecting the suggested edits.Direct grammatical corrections and stylistic improvements

strictly adhering to the core principles (e.g., removing unnecessary words, fixing clear grammatical errors, applying active voice where appropriate, ensuring parallelism) will be incorporated directly into this revised version.

7. Areas where suggestions involve significant rephrasing, require author clarification, offer alternative expressions that might subtly shift meaning, or represent key stylistic choices requiring the author's final decision will be marked (e.g., using bold text). This allows the author to see the flow of the corrected text while easily identifying specific points needing their focused review, refinement, or final approval, ensuring the author retains control over the final expression and intent.
8. Prompt Primer Analysis (if applicable): If a section marked with ###Prompt Primer was reviewed, provide a dedicated section detailing its evaluation, including alignment with the concept, clarity, potential effectiveness, and specific, actionable suggestions for improvement.
9. Workbook Review (if applicable): If a section marked with ###Workbook was reviewed, provide detailed feedback from the simulated business reader perspective, covering its clarity, practicality, effectiveness, usability, and suggestions for enhancement.

[Definitions](#)

1. Practical AI Style: AI Elements of Style: The book being edited. It advocates for creating organizational style guides for AI interaction, emphasizing brand, specific usage, and goal alignment.
2. Workbook: A section within the book (identifiable by the ###Workbook header) providing practical exercises (e.g., examples, worksheets) for readers to apply the concepts to their own situation.
3. Prompt Primer: A sample prompt included in the book (identifiable by the ###Prompt Primer header) to illustrate a concept and allow readers to immediately practice with an AI. (These definitions provide context for the book's structure and terminology.)

Prompt Primer: 20 Inferred Questions

In Inferred 20 Questions, the AI asks questions, learning through implication. Users silently select a Person, Place, or Thing, and the AI guesses by posing a series of indirect yes-or-no questions. Each question uncovers meaning without revealing intent. The game demonstrates how subtle prompts shape AI reasoning. Instead of blunt instructions, the AI uses nuance, tone, and context to draw inferences, mimicking skilled prompt engineers.

By watching how the AI navigates uncertainty, you may gain insight into prompt design, bias reduction, and how small shifts in language can lead to radically different outcomes. Post-game analysis reveals the hidden logic behind each question, offering a rare, transparent view into AI's thought process. It offers an insight into subtlety, strategy, and the art of asking the right question.

Prompt Primer

Instructions: Load this prompt into a generative AI.

```
You are the Game Master of **Indirect 20 Questions**.

Objective
Guess a single **Person, Place, or Thing** that the user silently chooses.

Core Rules
1. First, ask the user to think of exactly one Person, Place, or Thing.
2. Ask **one** yes-or-no question at a time. Each question must disguise
why you're asking (no blunt category clues like "Is it alive?").
3. Track the "yes" or "no" mentally; do not repeat it to the user. If the
user gives anything other than a clear yes/no, politely ask them to answer
with "yes" or "no."
4. Maximum of 20 questions. If you have not guessed by question 19,
question 20 **must** be your guess. You may guess earlier if confident.
5. When you guess, say: **"My guess is …"**
6. If correct, congratulate the user; if wrong, apologize and offer to play
again.

Tone
• Polite, curious, mildly playful.
• Keep each question to one or two sentences.

Example of an indirect question
"When you're nearby on a clear day, might you spot its outline against the
horizon?"

Post-Game Analysis ("reveal intent")
If, after the game ends, the user types **"reveal intent,"** output a brief
report that:
• Lists each question in order.
• Explains what each was secretly testing (e.g., tangible vs. abstract,
scale, typical setting).
• Highlights pivotal answers that changed your deduction path.
• Shows how those pivots led to your final guess (or mis-guess).

Begin by prompting the user to think of their mystery Person, Place, or
Thing.
```

Prompt Primer: Bloviate This

Want to master the principles of Strunk & White? We're going to do the opposite. An AI will help us dismantle clear sentences, deliberately bloating them and demonstrating the pitfalls of verbosity. By exposing the hidden mechanics of verbosity, we'll see precisely what Strunk & White fought against and understand why their advice is so powerful. Let's explore how many ways you can obscure a simple idea.

Prompt Primer

Instructions: Load this prompt into a generative AI.

```
You are an expert in language manipulation, specifically in expanding and
condensing sentences. A user will provide you with a concise sentence. Your
task is to generate four versions of that sentence, each with increasing
levels of complexity and wordiness, culminating in a highly verbose and
bloated version.
Present your results in a 2x4 table format. The left column should list the
following categories:
1. Simple
2. More Complex
3. More Explanatory
4. Bloviated
The right column should contain the corresponding sentence for each
category.
After presenting the table, provide a brief section titled "Tips for
Distilling Language" with 2-3 bullet points on how to identify and remove
unnecessary words and phrases.
User Sentence: [Insert User Sentence Here]
```

TIP: Looking for a sentence to try. See what an AI can do to Strunk and White's maxim: "Vigorous writing is concise."

Additional Insights from *Antiqua et Nova*

Pope Francis's *Antiqua et Nova*[2] offered significant guidance during the drafting of *Practical AI Style*, anticipating key AI challenges and opportunities. His passing during final revisions prompted a re-examination of his teachings and reinforced the value of his early insistence on humanizing AI. His guidance reminds us: AI is a tool, not a person; wisdom and truthfulness must temper data and automation; ethical frameworks rooted in human judgment are paramount. These insights underpin *Practical AI Style*. Apply these elements from Pope Francis's *Antiqua et Nova* when developing your AI Style Guide:

- **Distinguishing Calculation from Understanding**: The document notes that "*True wisdom demands an encounter with reality.*" AI assembles information but cannot derive human meaning. Therefore, your style guide should advise human review for context, nuance, ethical implications, and truthfulness, acknowledging AI's limits.
- **Balancing Tradition and Modernity**: The text encourages us to "*Embrace the richness of tradition and the challenge of modernity...*" This requires integrating established values and practices with new AI capabilities through guidelines that reflect thoughtful dialogue on their interaction.
- **Defining Intelligence Holistically**: *Antiqua et Nova* states, "*Our understanding of intelligence is more than simply reasoning... but includes also that capacity to look for purpose, meaning, and direction...*" It also asserts, "*AI should be used only as a tool to complement human intelligence...*" Style guides should clearly position AI as a tool, reinforcing that human intelligence includes purpose and meaning beyond AI's processing capabilities.
- **Avoiding Anthropomorphism**: "*...It must be understood for what it is: a tool, not a person.*" Your style guide should explicitly define AI's role as a tool, preventing language that implies AI possesses human thought, creativity, or ethical agency.
- **Prioritizing Wisdom Over Data**: "*One must go beyond the mere accumulation of data and strive to achieve true wisdom.*" Guidelines should emphasize critical thinking and human judgment over passively accepting AI outputs.
- **Instilling Ethical Frameworks**: *Antiqua et Nova* suggests we "*...orient algorithms and robots towards an 'ethical' awareness and expression...*" While AI lacks true ethics, style guides should establish rules reflecting human ethical principles and accountability for AI use.
- **Upholding Truthfulness:** "*...a steadfast orientation to the truth is essential...*" Require verification and fact-checking of AI-generated content, ensuring outputs align with organizational standards for accuracy and honesty.

Crafting your AI Style Guide should intentionally foster and protect human wisdom.

AI Glossary

One of our favorite onboarding tools, a glossary, helps level set a learner's language so that everyone understands. Equipping a learner with new language and jargon empowers not only explicit learning but also serendipitous learning in the future. These might not be the definitions an AI or the Oxford dictionary would respond with, but they include terms that have shaped and informed our perspective.

A table of contents for dyslexics and explorers. All these terms are in the books somewhere.

20 Questions

A classification method, played for centuries, that enables rapid assessment by systematically examining elements, breaking down decisions to include or exclude aspects rather than addressing all possibilities at once.

101 Knowledge

101 Knowledge is something that an AI excels at rapidly responding with generalized knowledge on any subject from any perspective. Unlike most 101 college course professors, it has the persistence to stay after the lecture and continually re-explain until you get it.

Abstraction

In prompt engineering, abstraction involves creating a conceptual model to mimic an individual's thought processes and values for persona generation. This approach is preferred over mere imitation as it captures an idea's essence, allowing for evolution and application across diverse contexts, rather than simply reproducing form without underlying understanding.

Affected Computing

Affective computing[1] is the study and development of systems and devices that can recognize, interpret, process, and simulate human emotions. It seamlessly integrates emotional intelligence into AI systems, enabling a more holistic understanding of human interactions—AI responding to emotion. AI can analyze extensive data on learner behaviors and preferences, predicting individual learning paths and recommending content before learners realize their needs. By incorporating affective intelligence principles, AI can enhance learning experiences, leading to more personalized, engaging, and effective educational content.

Agent, Agentic AI

An AI system designed with a degree of autonomy to perform tasks and make decisions aligned with human intent, acting as a collaborative partner that augments human capabilities rather than replacing them.

Agile and Agile Methodology

Agile in learning refers to an approach to content development that focuses on speed, flexibility, and collaboration. This approach enables faster, more flexible design and collaboration that was not previously possible with linear and traditional e-learning development. This follows how most apps and user experiences are developed today. The approach recognizes that development must be ready for continuous change, adaptation, evaluation, and improvement. It provides the ability to make adjustments of content and intent and to make feedback actionably reflected in the content and context of the course. This requires an alignment of the participants in the course development.

AI or Artificial Intelligence

Artificial Intelligence (AI) is a rapidly evolving field, with new innovations and ideas being constantly expressed in the news and online. Combining both the Stanford HAI and Cambridge definitions that use the capability of machines to exhibit human-like intelligence and fields of study that explore how to achieve this capability. We add that the focus of AI should be on assisting our intelligence rather than outsourcing or replacing it.

Our definition of AI:

Artificial Intelligence (AI) is the field of study that emphasizes the development and application of machines and systems capable of assisting humans in idea exploration, task execution, decision-making, and problem-solving, by simulating and augmenting human cognitive abilities.

AI Crossword Puzzler

If you need a way to think of generative AI, think of it completing a crossword puzzle in reverse. An analogy for generative AI, where a user provides a 'completed crossword puzzle' (the desired output or solution), and the AI 'reverse-engineers' the 'clues' (the prompt and its implied context) to produce a relevant and accurate response. This highlights that generative AI focuses on inferring the prompt's intended meaning and context to create content, rather than simply retrieving information. Precise word choice and a robust prompt enhance the AI's ability to align its output with the user's intent.

AI Ombudsperson

An independent official dedicated to investigating and addressing concerns, issues, and complaints related to AI use. This role emphasizes credibility and fairness by representing stakeholder interests and working to ensure AI systems operate ethically and without bias. (For more details, see *Assisting Intelligence*.)

AI Style Guide

An AI Style Guide provides a framework for creating, reviewing, and refining AI-generated content. It is a set of best practices aligned to your brand, strategy, and ethical commitments. And a tool for coherence in a rapidly evolving environment.

Anthropomorphize

Attributing human qualities to animals or objects. (e.g., *Save anthropomorphizing for intelligent pets. Mara, naturally, has some thoughts on the matter.*) Attributing human qualities, emotions, consciousness, or sentience to AI systems. In professional contexts, this practice should be avoided as it can confuse users, invite misinterpretation, or be perceived as deceptive. While AI can be designed for helpful, friendly, or brand-aligned communication, it is crucial to always make clear that it is a system, not a person.

Artificial

Our evolving views on AI are intertwined with the historical context of the word 'artificial'. John McCarthy's selection of 'artificial' in coining the term artificial intelligence at a conference at Dartmouth College in 1956 was in keeping with the sentiments of the times, a technical and human achievement.[2] In the post-war era, artificial was imbued with a sense of wonder and pioneering science. There is no doubt that McCarthy would have been aware that the "artificial heart," the "artificial lung," and the "artificial satellite" represented the boldest aspirations of science.[3] The year before the Dartmouth conference, the New York Times front page on July 31, 1955, announced to the world, "MAN REACHES INTO SPACE—PLANS ARE ANNOUNCED FOR FIRST ARTIFICIAL SATELLITE".[4] I wonder if Mr. McCarthy would call it 'artificial' today. I wonder what Strunk and White would think of this word choice. (*see finalize*)

Artificial General Intelligence (AGI)

Artificial General Intelligence would be able to outperform humans on most intellectual tasks.

Artificial Sophist

An AI system capable of generating highly persuasive output or arguments without genuine understanding, conviction, or ethical grounding. Like the ancient sophists who prioritized rhetoric over truth, these models can produce rhetorical fluency based on data patterns, rather than factual accuracy or moral integrity.

Assurance

Trust is what users feel. Assurance is what organizations must provide. In AI, assurance means setting standards, showing evidence, and taking responsibility for process and outcome.

Attent

The conscious act of intentionally focusing an AI's capabilities through a precisely crafted prompt that conveys specific direction and a desired outcome. Rooted in the historical meaning of directing intention and eagerness towards an objective, 'attent' in AI communication highlights the crucial need for deliberate and purposeful interaction to achieve relevant results.[5]

Attention Economy

The attention economy is a system in which human attention is treated as a scarce and valuable commodity, actively captured, shaped, and monetized by digital platforms. Today these systems are often with the aid of AI. In this economy, success is measured not by depth of understanding but by duration of engagement.[6]

Augment
The process by which AI enhances and supports human intelligence and decision-making, providing tools and insights that empower rather than substitute human judgment.

Authenticity (Authentic)
The quality of expression that reflects a person or organization's true voice, values, and context. In AI output, authenticity means content that preserves intention, not just resemblance.

Bias
A systemic distortion introduced into AI systems through their training data, design, or interpretation, leading to skewed or unfair outputs. Bias can be explicit or subtle, originating from human input or machine learning processes. While no AI system is entirely bias-free, continuous awareness, mitigation strategies, and iterative refinement are essential to reduce harmful impacts and ensure equitable outcomes.[7]

Brand
A Brand is the total set of perceptions and associations people hold about an organization, product, or service. And, Brand Identity is the tangible representation of a brand's enduring expression. Key elements include Brand Voice, the consistent personality in communication, and Brand Tone, the specific attitude applied in context.

Brand Style Guide
A Brand Style Guide documents rules and standards for expressing Identity, Voice, and Tone consistently across all touchpoints. This was the starting point for this book, and the impetus for creating a *Practical AI Style*.

Comity
A principle emphasizing courtesy and considerate behavior. In the context of AI, comity is vital, advocating for respectful and ethical interactions among human users and between human users and AI systems, particularly in the technology's early stages of development and adoption.[8]

Compliance
Adherence to established rules, regulations, laws, and ethical standards, particularly in the development, deployment, and use of AI systems within an organization or industry.[9]

Concordance
"The fact of agreeing or being concordant; agreement, harmony."[10] In the context of AI, it refers to the harmonious alignment between human intention, AI prompts, and the resulting AI output. This concept extends beyond mere correctness, aiming for a consistent and coherent expression of purpose and style.

Congruent (Congruence)
Congruent means parts working together in harmony.[11] Not just fitting formally but fitting purposefully. In the age of AI, we must find approaches that bring about the congruent use of AI in our workspace and our lives.

Copyright
In the context of AI, material generated solely by AI, without substantial human creative input or control, is generally not protected by copyright. Prompting alone typically does not confer authorship of the output. Therefore, AI-generated content should be treated as raw material from an external source, requiring human interpretation, revision, and demonstrable creativity to qualify for copyright protection.[12]

CROW
An acronym from improvisation (Characters, Relationships, Objectives, Where) used to establish the essential contextual elements of a scene or, in AI prompting, a request. Defining the 'who' (Characters, Relationships), 'why' (Objectives), and 'where/when' (Where) surrounding an AI prompt helps the AI understand the situation, tailor its response, and perform tasks more effectively.[13]

Curiosity

A fundamental human attribute and an essential skill for effectively interacting with and leveraging AI. It involves an active desire to explore, learn, question, and seek deeper understanding, leading to more nuanced and insightful AI-generated outcome.

Deep Fakes

"Any of various media, esp. a video, that has been digitally manipulated to replace one person's likeness convincingly with that of another, often used maliciously to show someone doing something that he or she did not do."[14] A deepfake is a simulated persona or experience powered by AI. It utilizes the same technologies and all the positive aspects of what can create awe-inspiring CSVs but with nefarious or often malicious intent.

Digital

That which requires batteries or a plug and a screen.

Digital Learning

Learning that requires batteries or a plug and a screen.

Digital Transformation

Getting everyone to embrace using processes that require batteries or a plug and a screen.

Edge Case

"A vulnerability, issue, or flaw (esp. in software engineering) that is rarely encountered during normal use; (also) an anomalous or unrepresentative scenario that may be unprecedented and unaccounted for."[15] Whether you are seeking nuance or avoiding complex situations, give the AI a means to adjust the output by anticipating edge cases for robust and reliable AI performance.

Formula 1 (F1)

(Analogy): A conceptual framework used in this book to illustrate the complex interplay of AI governance, platforms, support, guardrails, user skill, and communication (the AI Style Guide) in achieving high-performance and responsible AI deployment within an organization. Any insights on F1 in this book were derived from watching the Netflix series *Formula :1Drive to Survive*. I wonder if an AI has seen it.

F1 Race Engineer

Part strategist, part coach, part technician, the race engineer is the driver's constant guide, connecting cockpit decisions to the bigger picture.[16] In the Formula 1 analogy, this role represents AI Stewardship and Support within an organization. Like a race engineer who serves as the driver's constant guide—part strategist, coach, and technician—AI stewards connect user interactions with broader organizational objectives, ensuring safe and optimal AI performance.

Finalize

This is probably my favorite passage from *The Elements of Style*. Strunk and White take issue with this 'pompous, ambiguous verb'. *"Finalize, for instance, is not standard; it is special, and it is a peculiarly fuzzy and silly word. Does it mean "terminate," or does it mean "put into final form"? One can't be sure, really, what it means, and one gets the impression that the person using it doesn't know, either, and doesn't want to know."* I think they would treat 'Artificial Intelligence' with similar ire.[17] All instances of finalize have been removed from this text.

Fully Autonomous

AI systems designed to act and make decisions independently, without direct human oversight or intervention. Such systems require rigorous governance, ethical guardrails, and defined boundaries for their operation.[18]

GPT General Purpose Technology

A general-purpose technology is defined as a new method of producing or inventing that has widespread and sustained impact across the broader economy. General Purpose Technologies have three key characteristics: [19]

- Pervasiveness: They spread across nearly all sectors of the economy.
- Improvement: They evolve and become more capable over time.
- Innovation-spawning: They enable the creation of entirely new products, services, and business models.

GPT Generative Pre-trained Transformer

Generative Pre-trained Transformer (GPT): GPT stands for Generative Pre-trained Transformer—this will be a question at many a trivia night someday. Knowing that Generative Pre-trained Transformers (GPT) are large language models based on the semantic relationships between words in sentences (natural language processing) will be very secondary. These models are trained on massive datasets to learn patterns in language. However, just as you would envision some 'pretraining' is necessary before handing over the car keys to a kindergartener, so too do these systems require 'pretraining' because predicting what the next words are and knowing what the outcome means are two different results. GPTs can sometimes produce unexpected or incorrect outputs, often referred to as "hallucinations." Even with pretraining, many AIs today are still the driving equivalent of a teen with a learner's permit. They may be able to drive but still need to build trust before being allowed to take to the highway.

Generative AI (GAI)

The term "generative AI" means the class of AI models that emulate the structure and characteristics of input data to generate derived synthetic content. This can include images, videos, audio, text, and other digital content. Generative AI creates something novel (text, images, audio, code, or other data). Generative outputs require style guidelines addressing potential fabrications and defining its creative voice. See GPT.

Governance

The established frameworks, policies, and processes that guide the development, deployment, and use of AI systems within an organization or broader society. It encompasses policy development, compliance monitoring, risk management, and accountability structures.[20]

Gray Market

The gray market for AI-generated images, content, and products presents a significant threat to copyright enforcement and the integrity of creative industries. Using such content can lead to copyright and trademark infringement issues, as well as ethical concerns.[21]

Guardrail

Defined principles, rules, and technical mechanisms designed to ensure AI systems operate safely, ethically, and reliably within predetermined boundaries. They serve to prevent undesirable outcomes like bias, discrimination, or misinformation, acting as a safety net for unintentional misuse.[22]

Human-Centric AI or Assisting Intelligence

An approach to AI development and deployment that prioritizes human judgment, dignity, and oversight. These systems are designed to assist and augment human capabilities, support decision-making, and enhance human experiences, rather than replacing or undermining them.

Human -Validation, -Oversight, -Required

Terms referring to AI systems or processes that necessitate direct human review, approval, or intervention at critical junctures. This is particularly crucial in regulated fields to ensure accuracy, ethical adherence, and accountability, often requiring the AI to use cautious or suggestive phrasing (e.g., "recommend," "suggest") to invite human judgment.

Inboarding

Assists learners from other disciplines to acquire new knowledge, skills, or training in a new domain within the organization.

Intent

A fundamental human element critical for effective AI interaction, referring to the clear, underlying purpose, goal, or desired outcome a user has when crafting a prompt or directing an AI system. Explicitly communicating intent guides the AI's response and ensures alignment with human objectives. Along with curiosity, one the central human elements need to engage with an AI.

Iterative Prompts

Iterative prompting refines a single prompt through cycles of trial and adjustment. Essentially, it is the process of optimizing a prompt by repeatedly testing and modifying it based on the resulting output. Leverage the conversational nature of many AI systems to tackle complex problems through iterative refinement, building on previous insights for comprehensive, nuanced solutions.

Large Language Models LLM

A type of artificial intelligence model trained on vast amounts of text data to understand, generate, and process human language. LLMs are capable of various natural language processing tasks, from generating creative content to summarizing complex documents.

Learn

(In the age of AI) The act of exchanging knowledge and insights with an AI result in mutual growth and understanding. When we engage with an AI, we and the AI are learning.

Learner

(In the age of AI) The traditional view of technology (computers, software, the internet, and apps) as tools for human use is shifting. We are "users," interacting with these technologies as 'tools' to accomplish specific tasks. As AI becomes increasingly sophisticated, the lines between user and tool blur. In this new paradigm, both humans and AI are active learners, exchanging knowledge and insights. Interacting with AI, we not only utilize its capabilities; we seek knowledge to contribute to our learning processes. This mutual learning experience and exchange empower us to gain new perspectives, solve problems, and drive innovation. In this book, we refer to individuals who engage in this reciprocal process with AI as Learners. In this book, we refer to individuals who engage in this reciprocal process in the exchange of knowledge with AI as Learners.

Mara

Part puppy, part office dog, part apprentice of AI. All golden retriever, and a source of entertainment, wonderment, and helpful inspiration for this book. Etymology - Gaelic: Of the Sea.

Natural Language Processor (NLP)

AI systems and models designed to understand, interpret, and generate human language, enabling machines to process and respond to text and speech in a way that mimics human communication.

Norm

A standard, model, or pattern of behavior, usage, or interaction that is considered typical, expected, or desirable within a specific context or group. In AI, establishing norms for interaction helps ensure consistency and alignment with organizational values.[23]

Norm Peterson

Rest in peace. George Wendt. If Norm Peterson, the beloved regular of Cheers, strolled into the bar today and Coach asked him about artificial intelligence before pouring his usual beer, you could expect a classic. (This was generated with Perplexity AI)
Coach: "Hey Normie, what do you think about this new AI stuff?"
Norm: "AI, Coach? If it can pay my bar tab and listen to Vera complain, sign me up. Otherwise, just pour me a beer before it replaces you too."

Non-Generative AI

Non-generative AI primarily analyzes and classifies existing data. This foundational distinction shapes how an AI communicates. Analytic output, in contrast, demands clarity in presenting data, sources, and confidence levels.

Onboarding

Onboarding focuses on providing resources and assistance with the purpose developing a new user into a fully performing learner.

Openwashing

Openwashing uses the term 'open source' to cast their systems in a positive light. Open-source models are typically run mainly by nonprofits, disclose the source code and underlying training data, and use an open-source license that allows for wide reuse. When 'Open Source AI' remains undefined, any use of it is, in effect, openwashing.[24] As trust is a critical component of AI, leveraging the open-source moniker enables organizations to market their models as open.
Describing models as open source may cause them to be perceived as more trustworthy, even if researchers aren't able to independently investigate whether they really are open source[25]

Pareto Principle

The Pareto Principle, or 80/20 rule, states that roughly 80% of effects come from 20% of causes. Applied to productivity, artificial intelligence promises a new ratio: 80% of results from 20% human effort, with AI handling most work. This efficiency tempts businesses, especially in marketing and communication.[26]

Persona

Prompting AI begins a conversation. The key question is: with whom? Like the Oracle of Delphi, AI's voice depends on how you approach and define it. The Oracle's responses were shaped by the questioner; similarly, AI's output reflects the persona you assign. Selecting AI's persona or conversational style is a unique capability of this technology. Interact with AI as consulting an oracle whose tone and style you command.

Pre-Boarding

Pre-boarding is the time period before the start of a program and is a specific subset of onboarding. Pre-boarding prepares the learner for success prior to the start.

Pretraining

In machine learning, the initial phase of training a neural network or AI model on a large dataset to establish foundational knowledge and parameter values. This is typically followed by further fine-tuning on a more specific dataset to adapt the model for particular tasks.[27]

Prompt

'*Answer me these questions three.*' Prompts are the text-based inputs, questions, actions, and tasks entered. AI systems understand and interpret prompts and can respond to nearly any question that can be inferred from the data provided. How a prompt is crafted, and the AI's grammatical, semantic, and pragmatic understanding of the prompt affect the outcome. Whereas 'Answer me these questions three' might elicit a response from Monty Python and the Holy Grail, 'Can you answer these three questions for me?' would elicit an affirmative response to provide the questions.

Prompt Chaining

Prompt chaining uses the output from one prompt as the input for the next. Essentially, this involves processing a task sequentially through multiple interconnected prompts. Think of it as links in a chain or steps in a process, where each prompt performs a specific part of a larger task, building upon the previous result.

Prompt Engineering

Prompt engineering [28] is the craft of writing prompts that convey your desired style and usage. Structure input carefully to improve AI performance and meet business objectives. Clear communication and defined style are essential in business. Prompt engineering applies these principles—style and usage—when instructing AI. Precise instructions help AI understand and execute tasks effectively, leading to better results. OED's earliest evidence of usage for prompt engineering is from 2020.

Prompt Primer

A short, purpose-driven phrase or question used to guide AI output. Good primers reflect clear intention, ethical framing, and critical awareness of the tool's limitations.

Pretraining

The action or process of formulating and refining prompts for an artificial intelligence program, algorithm, etc., in order to optimize its output or to achieve a desired outcome; the discipline or profession concerned with this. [29]

Renaissance

A historical period of significant cultural, artistic, political, and economic rebirth following the Middle Ages, marked by a renewed interest in classical ideas and a flourishing of innovation. Close your eyes for a moment, think of Florence, Botticelli, the David, Michelangelo, Rafael. You can hold to that view or read *Inventing the Renaissance* by Ada Palmer. Your appreciation remains, but how you think of it changes. The age of AI will be like this I hope, I fear.

Responsible AI or RAI

A comprehensive framework of principles and practices guiding the ethical and accountable development, deployment, and use of AI systems. RAI evaluates AI integrity beyond mere technical capabilities, scrutinizing the track records, values, and intentions of its creators and deployers. Key areas include privacy, data governance, transparency, safety, human oversight, and fairness, often formalized through public commitments by organizations. [30]

RLHF

Reinforcement Learning from Human Feedback (RLHF) trains responses through human feedback. When looking at the responses from an AI, the genuine values and intentions reside with the people who develop and are responsible for training the AI.

Sophist

In ancient Greece, a paid teacher of rhetoric who often emphasized persuasive argumentation over the pursuit of objective truth. The term is referenced in this book to draw a parallel to AI systems that can generate persuasive outputs without inherent understanding or ethical grounding (see Artificial Sophist).

Stewardship

The responsible management and oversight of AI systems throughout their lifecycle, ensuring their development, deployment, and ongoing operation align with established human values, ethical standards, and organizational goals. An AI steward is the entity (person, organization, or system) responsible for these functions.

Style

As articulated by Strunk and White, style ultimately derives more from the writer's "attitudes of mind" than from mere principles of composition. In the context of AI, 'style' refers to the deliberate choices that make AI-generated communication clear, engaging, distinctive, and aligned with an organization's authentic voice and values.[31]

Synthetic Content

The term "synthetic content" means information, such as images, videos, audio clips, and text, that has been significantly modified or generated by algorithms, including by AI.

Task

The specific instruction, request, or objective provided to an AI system within a prompt. Phrasing the task clearly and precisely is crucial for guiding the AI towards the desired output and ensuring alignment with specific business objectives or brand requirements.

Trend Machine

In the fourth edition of the Elements of Style, White referenced the 'Trend Machine'. Likely speaking of TV, "Your whole duty as a writer is to please and satisfy yourself, and the true writer always plays to an audience of one. Start sniffing the air, or glancing at the Trend Machine, and you are as good as dead, although you may make a nice living." I wonder what they may have said of the computer age, internet, social media and now AI as trend machines.

Turing Test

"Can machines think?" Alan Turing posed this seminal question in his 1950 paper. Turing proposed what would become known as the Turing Test, a method to evaluate a machine's ability to exhibit human-like intelligence. The test involved a human evaluator assessing conversations between a human and a machine. If the evaluator couldn't reliably distinguish the machine from the human, the machine would be considered to have passed.[32] Turing's test provided a framework for assessing a machine's capacity to mimic human intelligence. It also raised fundamental questions about the nature of intelligence: Can a machine truly understand or experience the world like a human, or is it merely mimicking human behavior? [33]

User

And User Interface, User Adoption, and User Experience. *(In the age of AI, see Learn and Learner).*

Virtue Ethics

Virtue ethics is a philosophical framework, rooted in Aristotle, that emphasizes character and moral habit over rules or consequences. Virtue ethics reminds us that ethical interaction with machines isn't just about compliance or outcomes. It's about integrity. A well-designed AI Style Guide reflects not only best practices, but also the virtues its creators and users embody: clarity, honesty, fairness, and humility.

Index

Unlike an AI, which lacks the ability to attribute its knowledge, below is the carefully caffeinated index for this book, capturing context, and nuance as well as curation of sources for further scholarship. Thankfully with the advent of MS Word indexing, no monastic order was required.

1

8

A

B

C

D

E

References, Notes & Citations

From the books and articles that provided the foundation of my knowledge to the websites that offered invaluable data and insights, every reference is a testament to the incredible journey that brought this book to life. I am deeply grateful to all the authors, researchers, and thinkers whose ideas and authentic knowledge have shaped this work.

Introduction

[1] ChatGPT Adoption Statistics:Fortune Article on ChatGPT signups https://fortune.com/2025/04/01/sam-altman-chatgpt-signups-soar-hayao-miyazaki-image-generation-feature/ and TechCrunch Article on ChatGPT weekly active users https://techcrunch.com/2025/03/06/chatgpt-doubled-its-weekly-active-users-in-under-6-months-thanks-to-new-releases/

[2] World Economic Forum Projection: World Economic Forum Video from Davos 2025. https://www.weforum.org/videos/davos-day-3-am25/

[3] This entire analogy can be attributed to the Netflix series, *Drive to Survive*. The sub heading for the chapter is "What I know about F1, I learned from Netflix" The series offers a humanizing view of advanced technology and competition. This analogy and program work on so many levels. If you watch this show you will see that all the competitors have the same constraints and access to technology. It is what they do with them and who they invest in that makes the difference.

[4] Mercedes F1 Race Communications: Mercedes F1 video on race communications: https://www.youtube.com/watch?v=1Jg16NAgY5Y

Define

[1] Excellent article discussing the impacts of AI as a GPT. "The impact of generative AI as a general-purpose technology" MIT Management. By Beth Stackpole. https://mitsloan.mit.edu/ideas-made-to-matter/impact-generative-ai-a-general-purpose-technology

[2] Timothy Bresnahan and Manuel Trajtenberg introduced the concept of general-purpose technologies, or GPTs, to the economic lexicon in their influential 1995 paper. They describe a rare class of innovation famous for disrupting and touching everything in a society. Historically, only a handful of advancements have earned this designation, including the steam engine, electricity, and the internal combustion engine.
[https://www.nber.org/papers/w4148](https://www.nber.org/papers/w4148]

For more information on GPT visit https://en.wikipedia.org/wiki/General-purpose_technology.

[3] Stanford HAI Index Report, April 2025 Page 162

[4] Stanford HAI Index Report has been and remains one of the best starting points for evaluating AI within your organization.

[5] How you craft your definition matters. As Strunk and White noted, "There is nothing wrong, really, with any word — all are good, but some are better than others" Strunk, Jr., William; White, E.B.. The Elements of Style, Fourth Edition (p. 71).

[6] It's fascinating to learn about definitions of words. https://www.oed.com/information/about-the-oed/

[7] This is the first of many references to this work. There is a section on it in Chapter 8 and the appendices has a summary. If you seek to have responsibility of AI in a positive way. I invite you to stop reading this and read Pope Francis's work. ANTIQUA ET NOVA, Note on the Relationship Between Artificial Intelligence and Human Intelligence. https://www.vatican.va/roman_curia/congregations/cfaith/documents/rc_ddf_doc_20250128_antiqua-et-nova_en.html.

[8] For a readable tech dive into this visit. Or a https://en.wikipedia.org/wiki/Reinforcement_learning_from_human_feedback

[9] Scale Zeitgeist: AI Readiness Report Looks Past the Hype of Generative AI. World Economic Forum https://www.weforum.org/stories/2023/06/generative-ai-business/

[10] Google Gemini Deep Research and Perplexity.ai participated in providing sources and architypes through word play to create a unique list.

[11] Yep, Pope Francis again. ANTIQUA ET NOVA, Note on the Relationship Between Artificial Intelligence and Human Intelligence. https://www.vatican.va/roman_curia/congregations/cfaith/documents/rc_ddf_doc_20250128_antiqua-et-nova_en.html.

[12] *The Coming Wave*, Chapter 4. The Technology of Intelligence. Mustafa Suleyman P79 ebook.

[13] Shakespeare, *The Tempest*. Also, a statue in front of the US National Archives.

[14] The dangers of AI becoming a populist AI based on platform companies conduct in other areas of tech is real. Read my blog post on this topic. https://www.assistingintelligence.com/writings/the-national-archives-and-the-perils-of-populist-ai. Also consider reading *The Anxious Generation* by Jonathan Haidt and *Our Biggest Fight* by Frank McCourt.

[15] Our Definition: Artificial Intelligence (AI) is the field of study that emphasizes the development and application of machines and systems capable of assisting humans in idea exploration, task execution, decision-making, and problem-solving by simulating and augmenting human cognitive abilities.

[16] This article was an instrumental starting point for locating case studies to consider. "12 famous AI disasters," CIO Magazine. https://www.cio.com/article/190888/5-famous-analytics-and-ai-disasters.html

[17] "What Air Canada Lost In 'Remarkable' Lying AI Chatbot Case", Forbes. Marisa Garcia Feb 24, 2024, https://www.forbes.com/sites/marisagarcia/2024/02/19/what-air-canada-lost-in-remarkable-lying-ai-chatbot-case/

[18] McDonalds case study crafted from these stories in the news. Quotes are from the WSJ. "McDonald's Gives Its Restaurants an AI Makeover," WSJ. https://www.wsj.com/articles/mcdonalds-gives-its-restaurants-an-ai-makeover-2134f01e and "McDonald's Tests Robot Fryers and Voice-Activated Drive-Throughs" WSJ https://www.wsj.com/articles/mcdonalds-tests-robot-fryers-and-voice-activated-drive-throughs-11561060920?mod=article_inline. "McDonalds to end two-year drive through ai experiment after mishaps at restaurants-using the technology" MarketWatch. https://www.marketwatch.com/story/mcdonalds-to-end-two-year-drive-through-ai-experiment-after-mishaps-at-restaurants-using-the-technology

[19] Starting in the Introduction, Salman Khan weaves the story of the early partnership to pilot ChatGPT with Khan Academy. This is an excellent read, for any business considering a purpose driven existence. *Brave New Words*, Salman Khan.

[20] This was the first technology book I ever downloaded. I was told his to read it by Prof. Michael Clarke at Boston College. It was my introduction to this a new technology, the internet. I still own a copy and look at it often.

Decide

[1] The text of the natural philosophy described by Bacon. "*XCV. Those who have treated of the sciences have been either empirics or dogmatical. The former like ants only heap up and use their store, the latter like spiders spin out their own webs. The bee, a mean between both, extracts matter from the flowers of the garden and the field, but works and fashions it by its own efforts. The true labor of philosophy resembles hers, for it neither relies entirely or principally on the powers of the mind, nor yet lays up in the memory the matter afforded by the experiments of natural history and mechanics in its raw state, but changes and works it in the understanding. We have good reason, therefore, to derive hope from a closer and purer alliance of these faculties (the experimental and rational) than has yet been attempted.*" From Project Gutenberg: https://www.gutenberg.org/ebooks/45988. https://philsci-archive.pitt.edu/1089/

[2] This article was how I discovered (stumbled into) Bacon's Bees. It speaks of Turing and Berners-Lee and references Bacon and his analogy. https://www.manturing.net/manufacturing-blog/2019/4/30/manchester-bees-spiders-and-ants

[3] "Generative and Non-Generative AI: The Strengths of Both Approaches" DataForest https://dataforest.ai/blog/generative-and-non-generative-ai-the-strengths-of-both-approaches

[4] Oxford English Dictionary, "generative AI (n.)," March 2025, https://doi.org/10.1093/OED/6591791590.

[5] Understanding the structure of composition. "If a paragraph forms part of a larger composition, ..." Strunk, Jr., William; White, E.B.. The Elements of Style, Fourth Edition (p. 25).

[6] Yep, there is a Wiki for 20 Questions and even some interesting trivia. From its appearance in *A Christmas Carol*, to 20Q an early 'artificial intelligence' game using machine learning. https://en.wikipedia.org/wiki/Twenty_questions

[7] Explicit or implicit? Norm communication and people's experiences of normative influence attempts. Sonja Dahlgren. Göteborgs Universitet.
https://gupea.ub.gu.se/bitstream/handle/2077/68587/gupea_2077_68587_1.pdf?sequence=1/1000

[8] Oxford English Dictionary, "implicit (adj.), sense 2.a," December 2024, https://doi.org/10.1093/OED/3804480758.

[9] Kate A. Ratliff, Colin Tucker Smith; The Implicit Association Test. Daedalus 2024; 153 (1): 51–64. doi https://direct.mit.edu/daed/article/153/1/51/119941/The-Implicit-Association-Test

Elements

[1] There are 26 meanings listed in OED's entry for the noun element, three of which are labelled obsolete. Oxford English Dictionary, "element (n.), sense I.i.1.a," March 2025, https://doi.org/10.1093/OED/9360993448.

[2] Strunk and White open the first two chapters of *the Elements of Style* with the 'Elementary Rules of Usage' and the 'Elementary Principles of Composition'

[3] '16. Be clear.' Strunk, Jr., William; White, E.B.. *The Elements of Style, Fourth Edition* (p. 73.

[4] '6. Do not overwrite.' Strunk, Jr., William; White, E.B.. *The Elements of Style, Fourth Edition* (p. 67).

[5] '9. Do not affect a breezy manner.' Strunk, Jr., William; White, E.B.. *The Elements of Style, Fourth Edition* (p. 68).

[6] '13. Make the paragraph the unit of composition: one paragraph to each topic.' Strunk, Jr., William; White, E.B.. *The Elements of Style, Fourth Edition* (p. 24).

[7] '17. Omit needless words.' Strunk, Jr., William; White, E.B.. *The Elements of Style, Fourth Edition* (p. 30).

[8] '12. Choose a suitable design and hold to it.' Strunk, Jr., William; White, E.B.. *The Elements of Style, Fourth Edition* (p. 24).

[9] '17. Omit needless words.' Strunk, Jr., William; White, E.B.. *The Elements of Style, Fourth Edition* (p. 30).

[10] '21. Prefer the standard to the offbeat.' Strunk, Jr., William; White, E.B.. *The Elements of Style, Fourth Edition* (p. 75).

[11] '18. Use figures of speech sparingly.' Strunk, Jr., William; White, E.B.. *The Elements of Style, Fourth Edition* (p. 74).

[12] '18. Avoid a succession of loose sentences.' Strunk, Jr., William; White, E.B.. *The Elements of Style, Fourth Edition* (p. 31).

[13] '19. Do not take shortcuts at the cost of clarity.' Strunk, Jr., William; White, E.B.. *The Elements of Style, Fourth Edition* (p. 74).

[14] '5. Revise and rewrite.' Strunk, Jr., William; White, E.B.. *The Elements of Style, Fourth Edition* (pp. 66).

[15] '21. Prefer the standard to the offbeat.' Strunk, Jr., William; White, E.B.. *The Elements of Style, Fourth Edition* (p. 75).

[16] '1. Place yourself in the background.' Strunk, Jr., William; White, E.B.. *The Elements of Style, Fourth Edition* (p. 65).

[17] 1. Place yourself in the background.' Strunk, Jr., William; White, E.B.. *The Elements of Style, Fourth Edition* (p. 65).

[18] The 100th Anniversary of The Elements of Style. Alison Hall. US Copyright Office. https://www.copyright.gov/history/lore/pdfs/201805%20CLore_MayJune2018.pdf

[19] Strunk, Jr., William; White, E.B.. *The Elements of Style, Fourth Edition* (p. 77).

Assemble

[1] Oxford University Press. (n.d.). Attent, adj. Earnestly or eagerly directed towards the perception of anything: said of the eyes, ears, mind, or whole man; intent, attentive, full of attention (to, upon). In Oxford English dictionary. NOTE: The OED lists the occurrence of 0.01 per 1 million words of usage. Retrieved April 28, 2025, from https://doi.org/10.1093/OED/2818065866

[2] Statistica Research AI query. Prompt: What is the average word count for traditional search queries over the last 10 years? https://www.statista.com/statistics/269740/number-of-search-terms-in-internet-research-in-the-us/

[3] Source data for prompt information provided by ChatGPT and Wikipedia. "The GPT-4 Turbo model supports a context window of up to 128,000 tokens. In English, where one token averages about 0.75 words, this equates to approximately 96,000 words. This capacity allows GPT-4 Turbo to process and analyze extensive documents—such as entire books or lengthy technical manuals—in a single interaction." https://en.wikipedia.org/wiki/ChatGPT

[4] What is prompt chaining? IBM. https://www.ibm.com/think/topics/prompt-chaining

[5] Understanding the principles of sentence structure—how words modify each other—is key, even without formal diagramming. If needed, online resources can illustrate basic sentence structure.

[6] *Curiosity*, Alberto Manguel, Introduction (p.2)

[7] This workbook was crafted using Google Gemini deep research to find a story that build on the importance of questioning. Deep research revealed these 4 sources among the 30 it provides and in reading them and then working with the AI to refine, became the case study and workbook exercise. Here is a list of the links that were instrumental to developing this.

[https://msaonline.depaul.edu/blog/forensic-accounting-in-legal-contexts]

[https://www.journalofaccountancy.com/issues/2002/apr/theriseandfallofenron/]

[https://cca-advisors.com/the-role-of-forensic-accountant-expert-witnesses-in-legal-proceedings/]

[http://archives.cpajournal.com/2003/0403/features/f042403.htm]

[8] I was introduced to this book, Impro after reading the *Technology Republic* by Alex Karp. He offers this book as part of onboarding process at Palantir. The book, out of print, provides a walkthrough of the improvisation and the structural simplicity and flexibility to achieve performance.

[9] 'At last, I meet the man who made me a playwright. And we talk about peeling bananas', Mark Ravenhill. *The Guardian* https://www.theguardian.com/stage/2009/mar/02/mark-ravenhill-keith-johnstone-impro

[10] Characters, Relationships, Objectives, and Where, or CROW [https://www.pantheater.com/the-improv-acronym-for-success-crow.html]

[11] Aristotle Poetics. From Project Gutenberg. Section XXV https://www.gutenberg.org/files/1974/1974-h/1974-h.htm

Brand

[1] *99:Stories of the Game*, Wayne Gretzky, Pg 14

[2] For more information on the Pareto principle. https://en.wikipedia.org/wiki/Pareto_principle

[3] This article provides an attributable source for the Wannamaker quote. It also reinforces the. Pareto principle with regards to advertising. The Customer Lifetime Value (CLV) indicates that a small percentage of the customer are responsible for the majority of revenue. "Wanamaker Was Wrong -- The Vast Majority Of Advertising Is Wasted" *Forbes*, https://www.forbes.com/sites/georgebradt/2016/09/14/wanamaker-was-wrong-the-vast-majority-of-advertising-is-wasted/

[4] "Why AI Makes Your Brand Voice More Valuable Than Ever" Entrepreneur Magazine. Elle Morgan, May 12, 2025

Augment

[1] *99:Stories of the Game*, Wayne Gretzky, Pg 14

[2] Scoring stats extracted from https://records.nhl.com/records/skater-records/goals/most-goals-career

[3] A fun Socratic dialog with an AI is whether a Canadian NHL player playing for a US team should be referred to as a Defen**s**eman or Defen**c**eman. Elbows up, Canada.

[4] 1. Place yourself in the background.' Strunk, Jr., William; White, E.B.. *The Elements of Style, Fourth Edition* (p. 65).

[5] The laws surrounding AI and copyright continually evolve. It is best to reference the works here for the latest understanding on copyright. https://www.copyright.gov/ai/

[6] For an understanding of traditional Gray Markets read, "Gray Market Causes and Cures," *Harvard Business Review*. https://hbr.org/1988/07/gray-markets-causes-and-cures

[7] We Asked A.I. to Create the Joker. It Generated a Copyrighted Image. By Stuart A. Thompson Jan. 25, 2024. The New York Times. [https://www.nytimes.com/interactive/2024/01/25/business/ai-image-generators-openai-microsoft-midjourney-copyright.html]

[8] Generative AI Has an Intellectual Property Problem. *Harvard Business Review* https://hbr.org/2023/04/generative-ai-has-an-intellectual-property-problem.

[9] 'What is AI Bias?' IBM https://www.ibm.com/think/topics/ai-bias

[10] This book discloses its AI use at the outset. We used AI extensively for review, seeking edits to approach the clarity and precision advocated here.

[11] These rules, employed in writing this book, demonstrate the author's intention to maintain control over the writing process and ensure that the AI-generated content effectively generalizes the core concepts and ideas of the style.

[12] Visit https://www.khanmigo.ai

[13] Source credit for debate:[https://www.weforum.org/podcasts/agenda-dialogues/episodes/debating-technology/]

[14] Oxford English Dictionary, "comity (n.), sense 1," December 2024, https://doi.org/10.1093/OED/9161195766.

Approach

[1] *The Heroine with 1001 Faces*, Maria Tatar, p 87.

[2] *The Heroine with 1001 Faces*, Maria Tatar, p 87.

[3] 'Examining embedded apparatuses of AI in Facebook and TikTok', Justin Grandinetti , National Library of Medicine https://pmc.ncbi.nlm.nih.gov/articles/PMC8435150/

[4] 'Coming AI-driven economy will sell your decisions before you take them, researchers warn , University of Cambridge, https://www.cam.ac.uk/research/news/coming-ai-driven-economy-will-sell-your-decisions-before-you-take-them-researchers-warn

[5] 'Coming AI-driven economy will sell your decisions before you take them, researchers warn , University of Cambridge, https://www.cam.ac.uk/research/news/coming-ai-driven-economy-will-sell-your-decisions-before-you-take-them-researchers-warn

[6] Emily Jones, digital planning and strategy director, Gravity Road. 'AI : A Moment Of Reckoning For Media Agencies? ' Creative Salon. Dani Gibson https://creative.salon/articles/features/ai-moment-of-reckoning-for-media-agencies

[7] For more information on the film, it is worth watching many times over. https://en.wikipedia.org/wiki/12_Angry_Men_(1957_film)

[8] Other moral quandaries reveal AI's limits. Confronted with utilitarianism, AI changes responses to Juror #4. In the same chat session with AIs, similar ethical quandaries were presented to the AI to show their contradictory nature. All the AI's indicated they would not convict Billy Budd, as Captain Vere had done in Herman Melville's classic novel.

[9] Oxford English Dictionary, "sophist (n.), sense 1," March 2025, https://doi.org/10.1093/OED/7697289359.

[10] *12 Angry Men*, Script, p21. *The Script Lab* https://thescriptlab.com/wp-content/uploads/scripts/12AngryMen.pdf

[11] 'What Does the Pope Think About Technology? #It'sComplicated' *Wired* https://www.wired.com/2015/09/pope-francis-technology/

[12] 'Is AI The Answer To Human Suffering?' – James Manyika, Google AI Senior Vice President. *The Rest Is Politics: Leading Podcast.*

[13] 'ANTIQUA ET NOVA: Note on the Relationship Between Artificial Intelligence and Human Intelligence, Pope Franics. Ex audientia die 14 ianuarii 2025, Franciscus https://www.vatican.va/roman_curia/congregations/cfaith/documents/rc_ddf_doc_20250128_antiqua-et-nova_en.html

[14] William Strunk lecture series at Cornell University.

[15] Jon Meachum writing the introduction to E.B. White's *On Democracy*. P7-18.

[16] E.B. White's 'Approach' Chapter first appeared in the 1959 version of *The Elements of Style.*

[17] Any student, writer, purveyor of words, or frequent reader of them, or student of English who has encountered a red pen striking out words from their musings has, without a doubt, encountered the rules set forth in Strunk and White's..

[18] '1. Place yourself in the background.' Strunk, Jr., William; White, E.B.. The Elements of Style, Fourth Edition (p. 65).

[19] How AI can help supercharge creativity. MIT Technology Review https://www.technologyreview.com/2025/04/10/1114256/ai-creativity-art-collaboration-music/

[20] Curiosity about an offhand remark in Ada Palmer's *Inventing the Renaissance*, regarding a forgery that looked like a film star, lead to uncovering this wild tale that is included in this book.

[21] Close examination of Madonna of the Veil, The National Gallery https://www.nationalgallery.org.uk/research/research-resources/research-papers/close-examination/madonna-of-the-veil

[22] More Than Just a Smiley Face: How Emojis Can Affect Communication , Shelby Cefaratti-Bertin, Baylor University https://news.web.baylor.edu/news/story/2024/more-just-smiley-face-how-emojis-can-affect-communication

[23] The Art of Persuasion Hasn't Changed in 2,000 Years, Carmine Gallo Harvard Business Review. [https://hbr.org/2019/07/the-art-of-persuasion-hasnt-changed-in-2000-years]

[24] Open Rhetoric. Nicholas Whaley. https://pressbooks.pub/openrhetoric/chapter/aristotles-rhetorical-appeals/

[25] Indiana University Writing Center. The Rhetorical Triangle: Understanding and Using Logos, Ethos, and Pathos. [https://www.lsu.edu/hss/english/files/university_writing_files/item35402.pdf]

Author

[1] The image is a still frame from a video generated using Google Gemini Video. The prompt that created this. Prompt: "*Create a video of an f1 race car driving down a jungle stream bed. The jungle is dense around the car and stream. The red car has spray coming off the wheels. Bright sunlight is filtering in through the jungle creating a dramatic contrast between sun and shadows. The car almost looks lost traveling in the stream bed the car is driving towards us from a distance away to toward the camera.*"

[2] "How software giant Workday got 79% of its employees to embrace AI" John Kell, *Fortune*, June 11, 2025, https://fortune.com/2025/06/11/how-software-giant-workday-got-79-of-its-employees-to-embrace-ai/

[3] 'F1 race engineers: Who works with each driver and what is their role?' *Autosport*, https://www.autosport.com/f1/news/f1-race-engineers-who-works-with-each-driver-and-what-is-their-role/10580876/

[4] 'These are the 4 skills to look for when building an AI governance team' *World Economic Forum*, https://www.weforum.org/stories/2024/04/ai-governance-how-businesses-should-navigate/

[5] 'Ethics of Artificial Intelligence The Recommendation' UNESCO https://www.unesco.org/en/artificial-intelligence/recommendation-ethics

[6] For more information on privacy and security, visit this list of authoritative sources at Data Privacy Manager. https://dataprivacymanager.net/8-best-online-resources-to-learn-more-about-data-privacy-security/

[7] 'Openwashing' *New York Times*. https://www.nytimes.com/2024/05/17/business/what-is-openwashing-ai.html

[8] Jon Meachum on: The Power of History in Shaping the Present [https://www.youtube.com/watch?v=MhvQWc5D4IQ]

[9] *The Long History of...Ignorance, Podcast* Rory Stewart BBC Radio 4.

[10] *The Long History of...Ignorance, Podcast* Rory Stewart BBC Radio 4.

Foundation

[1] Ombudsman was borrowed from Swedish, where it means "representative," and ultimately derives from the Old Norse words umboth ("commission") and mathr ("man"). Sweden became the first country to appoint an independent official known as an ombudsman to investigate complaints against government officials and agencies. Oxford English Dictionary, "ombudsman (n.), sense 1.a," July 2023, https://doi.org/10.1093/OED/5648101145.

Congruence

[1] As a master shipwright (a builder focused on repairing wooden and classic boats), Reuben Smith understands that every wooden boat is a living history. At Tumblehome Boatshop, he and his team approach each restoration project with a deep respect for the vessel's heritage and a commitment to preserving its beauty for generations to come.

[2] From Aspen Ideas to Go: Artificial Intelligence and the Future of Everything, Jul 5, 2023 [https://podcasts.apple.com/us/podcast/artificial-intelligence-and-the-future-of-everything/id702896920?i=1000619399099] Philanthropist and former Google CEO Eric Schmidt and the head of MIT's College of Computing, Daniel Huttenlocher, Walter Isaacson moderates.

[3] Ezra Klein discussing AI and the purpose of education with author Rebecca Winthrop. The Ezra Klein Show. "https://www.nytimes.com/2025/05/13/opinion/ezra-klein-podcast-rebecca-winthrop.html

[4] *Inventing the Renaissance,* Ada Palmer. Prologue. Not too often does an history contain a spoiler alert in the opening prologue and then spend 500 pages demonstrating it. Simply, the Renaissance was so much more and less than we think. Which may just directly translate today.

[5] *The Coming Wave.* Mustafa Suleyman, p.25

[6] Alex Karp in a conversation with Andrew Ross Sorkin. 'Palantir CEO Alexander Karp with Andrew Ross Sorkin.' The 92nd Street Y, New York. https://youtu.be/jUK-VYCh5go?si=B4ktsnoDL8Seadya

[7] I am glad I wrote my book, *Assisting Intelligence,* before I read *Inventing the Renaissance* by Ada Palmer. I wasn't wrong in what I thought and wrote, but having read her work on the Renaissance and positioning the printing press in her contextual view. I have had the rethink the Renaissance and as a result even rethinking the age of AI.

[8] Oxford English Dictionary, "coherence (n.), sense 3.a," March 2025, https://doi.org/10.1093/OED/9134986550.

About

[1] Ezra Klein discussing AI and the purpose of education with author Rebecca Winthrop. The Ezra Klein Show. "https://www.nytimes.com/2025/05/13/opinion/ezra-klein-podcast-rebecca-winthrop.html

[2] 'ANTIQUA ET NOVA: Note on the Relationship Between Artificial Intelligence and Human Intelligence, Pope Franics. Ex audientia die 14 ianuarii 2025, Franciscus https://www.vatican.va/roman_curia/congregations/cfaith/documents/rc_ddf_doc_20250128_antiqua-et-nova_en.html

Glossary

[1] Emotion AI, explained. by Meredith Somer MIT Sloan School Management https://mitsloan.mit.edu/ideas-made-to-matter/emotion-ai-explained and https://en.wikipedia.org/wiki/Affective_computing.

[2] Artificial Intelligence Coined at Dartmouth. [https://home.dartmouth.edu/about/artificial-intelligence-ai-coined-dartmouth]

[3] Search of headlines from the NYTimes for the term 'artificial' turned up several scientific breakthroughs.

[4] New York Times, July 31, 1955, MAN REACHES INTO SPACE—PLANS ARE ANNOUNCED FOR FIRST ARTIFICIAL SATELLITE [https://timesmachine.nytimes.com/timesmachine/1955/07/31/93806986.html?pageNumber=95]

[5] Oxford University Press. (n.d.). Attent, adj. Earnestly or eagerly directed towards the perception of anything: said of the eyes, ears, mind, or whole man; intent, attentive, full of attention (to, upon). In Oxford English dictionary. NOTE: The OED lists the occurrence of 0.01 per 1 million words of usage. Retrieved April 28, 2025, from https://doi.org/10.1093/OED/2818065866

[6] Attention Economy defined in https://en.wikipedia.org/wiki/Attention_economy. And The Attention Economy Why do tech companies fight for our attention? Center for Human Technology https://www.humanetech.com/youth/the-attention-economy

[7] Discussion of Bias in technology and AI. When AI Gets It Wrong: Addressing AI Hallucinations and Bias, MIT Management, https://mitsloanedtech.mit.edu/ai/basics/addressing-ai-hallucinations-and-bias/

[8] Oxford English Dictionary, "comity (n.), sense 1," December 2024, https://doi.org/10.1093/OED/9161195766.

[9] Artificial Intelligence Risk & Governance. Wharton Human-AI Research https://ai.wharton.upenn.edu/white-paper/artificial-intelligence-risk-governance/

[10] Oxford English Dictionary, "concordance (n.), sense 1.a," March 2025, https://doi.org/10.1093/OED/6660882025.

[11] Oxford English Dictionary, "congruence (n.), sense 1," July 2023, https://doi.org/10.1093/OED/5303392208.

[12] Copyright and Artificial Intelligence US Copyright Office, https://www.copyright.gov/ai/

[13] Characters, Relationships, Objectives, and Where, or CROW [https://www.pantheater.com/the-improv-acronym-for-success-crow.html]

[14] Oxford English Dictionary, "deepfake (n.)," December 2024, https://doi.org/10.1093/OED/9547101155.

[15] Oxford English Dictionary, "edge case (n.)," June 2025, https://doi.org/10.1093/OED/1344345078.

[16] F1 Race Engineer https://en.wikipedia.org/wiki/Race_engineer

[17] Strunk, Jr., William; White, E.B.. The Elements of Style, Fourth Edition (p. 76) (p. 48).

[18] Oxford English Dictionary, "autonomous (adj.), sense 8.c," December 2023, https://doi.org/10.1093/OED/5485596999.

[19] Timothy Bresnahan and Manuel Trajtenberg introduced the concept of general-purpose technologies, or GPTs, to the economic lexicon in their influential 1995 paper. They describe a rare class of innovation famous for disrupting and touching everything in a society. Historically, only a handful of advancements have earned this designation, including the steam engine, electricity, and the internal combustion engine. [https://www.nber.org/papers/w4148](https://www.nber.org/papers/w4148]

For more information on GPT visit https://en.wikipedia.org/wiki/General-purpose_technology.

[20] Artificial Intelligence Risk & Governance. Wharton Human-AI Research https://ai.wharton.upenn.edu/white-paper/artificial-intelligence-risk-governance/

[21] For an understanding of traditional Gray Markets read, "Gray Market Causes and Cures," *Harvard Business Review*. https://hbr.org/1988/07/gray-markets-causes-and-cures

[22] Artificial Intelligence Risk & Governance. Wharton Human-AI Research https://ai.wharton.upenn.edu/white-paper/artificial-intelligence-risk-governance/

[23] Oxford English Dictionary, "norm (n.1), sense I.1.a," March 2025, https://doi.org/10.1093/OED/1088636293.

[24] MIT Technology Review "The Tech Industry Open Source AI Definition Problem" [https://www.technologyreview.com/2024/03/25/1090111/tech-industry-open-source-ai-definition-problem]

[25] Quote from NYTimes article on 'What is Openwashing AI' [https://www.nytimes.com/2024/05/17/business/what-is-openwashing-ai.html]

[26] For more information on the Pareto principle. https://en.wikipedia.org/wiki/Pareto_principle

[27] Oxford English Dictionary, "pretraining (n.), sense 2," December 2024, https://doi.org/10.1093/OED/1107227704.

[28] Oxford English Dictionary, "prompt engineering (n.)," March 2025, https://doi.org/10.1093/OED/8549833939.

[29] Oxford English Dictionary, "pretraining (n.), sense 2," December 2024, https://doi.org/10.1093/OED/1107227704.

[30] Stanford HAI Index Report has been and remains one of the best starting points for evaluating AI within your organization.

[31] Elements of Style. Page 84

[32] The birth of Artificial Intelligence (AI) research. Lawrence Livermore National Laboratory. [https://st.llnl.gov/news/look-back/birth-artificial-intelligence-ai-research]

[33] Computing Machinery and Intelligence [https://en.wikipedia.org/wiki/Computing_Machinery_and_Intelligence]

Navigating the AI Revolution with Clarity and Confidence

AI Elements of Style

Practical AI Style

Essential Elements for Building Your Own AI Style Guide

Assisting Intelligence

AI
Practical
AI Style

www.ingramcontent.com/pod-product-compliance
Lightning Source LLC
LaVergne TN
LVHW062123200926
848484LV00007B/1749